OUR
GAZZA

Reach Sport

www.reachsport.com

Published in Great Britain and Ireland in 2020 by Reach Sport, 5 St Paul's Square, Liverpool, L3 9SJ.

www.reachsport.com
@Reach_Sport

Reach Sport is a part of Reach PLC.
One Canada Square, Canary Wharf, London, E15 5AP.

Hardback ISBN: 978-1-911613-57-2
eBook ISBN: 978-1-911613-58-9

Photographic acknowledgements:
Reach PLC (Mirrorpix), PA Images.
With thanks to Richard Pelham, Alan Myers and Alex Smailes.

Senior Production Journalist: Harri Aston

Printed and bound by CPI Group (UK) Ltd, Croydon, CR0 4YY.

OUR GAZZA

THE UNTOLD TALES

JOHN RICHARDSON

PAUL GASCOIGNE

Born: May 27, 1967. Gateshead, England.

Club career statistics

Newcastle United (01.08.1984-18.07.1988)
Total games (subs)/goals – 97 (10)/25

Tottenham Hotspur (18.07.1988-01/06.1992)
Total games (subs)/goals – 112 (2)/33

Società Sportiva Lazio (01.06.1992-10.07.1995)
Total games (subs)/goals – 41 (0)/6

Glasgow Rangers (10.07.1995-26.03.1998)
Total games (subs)/goals – 92 (11)/39

Middlesbrough (26.03.1998-17.07.2000)
Total games (subs)/goals – 44 (4)/4

Everton (17.07.2000-17.03.2002)
Total games (subs)/goals – 22 (16)/1

Burnley (17.03.2002-01.07.2002) 3(3)/0;

Boston United (30.07.2004-05.10.2004) 3(2)/0.

England (senior) (1988-1998)
Total games/goals – 57/10

www.soccerbase.com

Contents

Introduction

By John Richardson

Would I like to interview a chubby rising star from Newcastle United's youth team? The invitation had come from Magpies youth coach Colin Suggett, someone who wasn't prone to exaggeration but who clearly thought it was time for Tyneside to learn more about the kid from Dunston.

I worked for *The Journal*, Newcastle's local morning paper, and as their football man I was the chosen one to hold court with Paul Gascoigne, who had never been interviewed before. Little did I know this was going to be a career-changing moment for someone trying to make his way in a very competitive business. Gazza would eventually take over my working life.

Approaching the young Gazza at the club's downtrodden Benwell training ground, a careful introduction and the request for a few minutes of the teenager's time was immediately met with the retort: "Aye, how much are ye going to pay me man?" Considering none of Newcastle's senior players had ever asked for any money, it appeared that this relationship with the little upstart would be over before it had even started.

Just as I was about to tell him to shove any interview up his backside, a big smile spread across his face. "Nah, I'm only joking," he replied. "Course I'll speak to yah. My mam gets *The Journal*."

So we were off and running on a journey which would change both of our lives and produce so many tales – many outrageous, many rip-roaring and some very poignant. It's a hearty melting pot of a life – his, not mine – which has often captivated those who have shared his adventure or have merely been bystanders.

Hopefully, in the ensuing chapters, you will be able to laugh out loud, smile or sometimes grimace at the life and times of the most charismatic and naturally-skilled footballer of the modern era. By speaking to some of those directly involved with Gazza and researching the annals of his amazing life, we've managed to produce a compelling insight into the often crazy and some-times sad world of this footballing maverick.

At the age of 17 he was the captain of the Newcastle youth side which would go on to win the FA Youth Cup with players like Joe Allon, Ian Bogie, Kevin Scott, Paul Stephenson and Brian Tinnion, who all enjoyed different degrees of success in their careers. There were already stories of the crazy antics of this loveable rogue doing the rounds but, luckily for him, they never made it into print because he was still mostly unknown. Jack Charlton, who was the manager at the time, told me there was a kid in the youth team who was driving some of the senior players mad with his antics and was always stuffing his face with sweets, eating all the wrong things. "Why don't you get rid of him?" I asked in all innocence. "You obviously haven't seen him play," Jack snapped back.

Anyway, I was shortly off to the *Daily Mail* to cover football in the Manchester area and on Merseyside, so why should I care? Everybody exaggerates. I'd lost count of the so-called boy wonders who were going to take the football world by storm. After just 12 months I'd left the *Daily Mail* for *The Sun*

– and suddenly Gazza was back in my life. The lure of covering football again in the North East, with the opportunity of ghost writing columns for Chris Waddle and Peter Beardsley, helped seal the deal.

Regular trips to St. James' Park also provided a close-up view of the emergence of the cheeky chappie from the banks of the Tyne. The ground, a pale shadow of the impressive stadium of today, was in a state of disrepair with the players having to change inside cabins in a corner of the ground. Luckily, members of the media were able to mingle freely with the players in the days before press officers came on the scene trying to direct traffic. Without fail, Gazza would come out of the temporary dressing room with some trick up his sleeve. A water pistol was a favourite, squirting it in our direction before laughing to himself and heading onto the pitch.

Jackie Milburn, a Newcastle legend from the 1950s, was the North East football correspondent for the *News Of The World* and he loved Gazza, both on and off the field.

"There's no way we'll be able to keep him," Wor Jackie would say. He was to be proved right. *The Sun* had also spotted his potential and decided to sign Gazza up. I was assigned to be his ghost writer. The job should have come with danger money.

At Newcastle it was quickly a case of trying to keep things out of the paper rather than putting them in. With his big mate Jimmy 'Five Bellies' Gardner, nothing was off limits. Taking pot shots at sparrows with his air rifle at the Newcastle training ground isn't what my sports editor wanted to hear about, although the news side would have filled their boots. Often, Gazza would appear with a mountain of Mars bars, crisps or ice cream when we met for his column piece. "Don't tell the gaffer," he would plead. But he was conscious of having to deliver something which was interesting, telling me he often stayed awake at night thinking what he could talk about.

As the big clubs descended it was obvious, as Jackie predicted, Newcastle would have a fight to keep him. As his ghost writer with the so-called inside knowledge and a demanding newspaper to serve, the pressure was on to provide the exclusive of where Gazza would end up. At the same time I was being told things in confidence that I couldn't write. If I did then the relationship I was building with him would be over. As decision day approached, so did the pressure. "Come on, you've got to write which club he is going to end up at," screamed my sports editor. "It hasn't been decided yet. I can only name the clubs interested in him at the moment," I replied. It wasn't what he wanted to hear. "We pay him a lot of money for this column. Make him tell you." "He doesn't know himself yet," I said. "Well the *Daily Mirror* have a back page saying he's off to Manchester United. The *Daily Mail* says it's Liverpool. Who is right?" "Neither," I announced, which left everyone on the sports desk bemused.

Thanks to my friendship with Gazza's then agent Alastair Garvie, who had been Newcastle's assistant secretary, I was being kept in touch all the way on developments. He told me Spurs were determined to take Gazza to White Hart Lane and that the manager, Terry Venables, would do everything to get him there.

"So can I write it, Ally?" I pleaded. "My job could be on the line if I don't get the exclusive."

"You can't because he could still end up at Manchester United or Liverpool."

My heart sank. I could now be in the shit because two of *The Sun's* rivals had already written that either Old Trafford or Anfield could be his final destination.

Finally, the call I had hoped for came from Ally. "It's sorted, he's going to Spurs." I couldn't wait to ring the office. "It's Spurs and I'm writing it now." "Never doubted you for a minute," came the reply. Really!!

So it was off to Spurs and the beginning of Gazza-mania and regular trips to Waltham Abbey Hotel – Gazza, Jimmy and his entourage had already been evicted from another hotel – and White Hart Lane. One of the biggest problems was getting Gazza away from the ground. He couldn't move anywhere without being mobbed. After one game which I was covering, he had a bright idea. Jimmy would drive Gazza's car, I would sit in the front passenger seat and Gazza would be hidden in the boot. So off we went into the North London evening but the traffic was gridlocked. There was no way we could let him out because the fans walking past would have spotted him. Jimmy and I were busily talking away, having by now forgotten about Gazza. Suddenly, we could hear a knocking noise from the boot area. It was getting progressively louder. "Bloody hell, Jimmy, Gazza's still in there isn't he?!" I blurted out. Imagine the looks on a number of motorists' faces when a white-faced Gazza tumbled out onto the road gasping for air after nearly being poisoned by the exhaust fumes. "Christ, man, are ye trying to kill us like?" he shouted at the pair of us.

At another Spurs match, Gazza was substituted after just around 20 minutes because he had appeared completely exhausted. He could hardly place one foot in front of the other. No one was more perplexed than Terry Venables. At half-time,

Terry came into the dressing room to find Gazza flat out on one of the benches. It transpired that he had decided to follow team-mate Gary Lineker's custom of having a hot bath before a game, aimed at helping soothe the England striker's back problem. Sadly, for Gazza, it had left him devoid of any energy. It was a practice he never repeated.

On a pre-season trip to Northern Ireland, the Spurs team based in Belfast had arranged to make the short trip to Derry by plane. Gazza, who hated flying, was having none of that. It was decided that he would be driven there and back which, because of the sectarian violence afflicting the province at the time, meant a full-scale operation involving the army had to be put in place to safeguard Gazza. I quickly discovered I was more at risk than Gazza. On the morning of the game, following yet another atrocity, my paper had decided to go with 'IRA Bastards' as its huge front-page headline. Not the best of timing for a *Sun* reporter when Derry's ground is overlooked by The Bogside, a notorious area populated by IRA sympathisers.

On arriving at the ground, I had already been warned that a number of suspicious characters had been spotted peering into the open press box looking at the names of the various newspapers covering the game. Luckily, instead of *The Sun* being printed on my seat, it had *News International* – the owners of the paper which also printed *The Times*. So for one night only I worked for *The Times* if anybody asked. There was no one from *The Sun*! When I told Gazza, he just said: "You should have borrowed my air rifle, man!"

He then asked me to travel back with him in the car and I thought there was no way that prospect was any worse than the ordeal I had just gone through.

A few drinks were taken at the team hotel back in Belfast that night and Paul Stewart, who was actually quite close to Gazza at Spurs, clearly wasn't happy with me. Like a few papers, *The Sun* gave merit marks for all the individual players. Honestly, they cause more trouble than they are worth. Anyway, Stewie came over and said sneeringly: "I suppose Gazza has got his normal eight out of 10, or even a nine, despite him being crap? What have I got? My normal five or six?" I told him because it was a friendly I hadn't had to give any marks. "What would you have given me, then?" he said. "Probably a four," I replied. "You fucking arsehole, you're up his backside," he replied as he took a swing at me. Luckily, he'd had a few too many, missed and went crashing onto the glass coffee table as I made a hasty exit for my room. About half an hour later, the internal phone goes and it's Gazza. "Bloody hell man, what have you done to Stewie?" Evidently, he had gone around telling people I'd hit him and wanted me booted out of the hotel, but not before he gave me a good hiding. It was the drink talking. Luckily, Gazza calmed him down and peace was restored. Mind, I think I gave him a five the next time I covered Spurs!

It wasn't long before Gazza's talents attracted interest from England boss Bobby Robson, a fellow Geordie. It seemed that the breakthrough was perfectly timed for Italia 90. It meant that his columns were becoming bigger and more regular, although he never failed to provide a line. He always took them seriously and was loyal to me, insisting I was the only journalist he would deal with in terms of his column.

When it was announced he was going to the Italy, the sports editor told me I hadn't been accredited because there were more senior reporters assigned to the job of covering England.

It meant that somebody else would have to help write Gazza's column during the tournament. He had decided it would be Alex Montgomery, the paper's chief football writer. I didn't have a problem with that because I respected Alex, a terrific bloke who always went out of his way to help young reporters.

I was to inform Gazza what was happening and that he would be in good hands with Alex. He seemed to be okay with the new arrangement and off they all went as I looked forward to watching the games unfold with my mates in the local pub. My peace and quiet was shattered in a phone call from my panicking sports editor. "That bloody idiot Gascoigne, your ruddy mate, has refused to do anything with Alex so we're trying to get you accredited. If we manage that then you will have to get out there as soon as possible." They somehow managed to wangle some accreditation and off I went to Sardinia, where the England squad was based.

On my arrival I discovered there was a major problem. Except for dedicated media days, the England hotel and its surrounds were on lockdown and I had missed a couple of open days for the reporters. I needed to get to Gazza fast. I managed to get a message to him that I needed a column as soon as possible. Back came the reply to stand close to the first tee on the golf course which surrounded the team's hotel and grounds. I did as requested and eventually a golf buggy containing Gazza and his big mate Chris Waddle arrived. "Get on, man," Gazza shouted. The pair then piled golf bags all over me and off we headed through the hotel gates with me well hidden from view. In a quiet area with no England management in sight, I was able to extract my dictaphone and grab the first couple of columns. I asked Gazza what had gone on with Alex. "He's Scottish," chortled Gazza. "Nah, he was alright but you wouldn't want to miss this, would you?" To be fair, the experience had been a bit stressful because the golf buggy had to be utilised on a few more occasions.

It was an incident-ridden ride into the semi-finals for England and then, of course, defeat against West Germany was followed by Gazza's tears. Suddenly, Gazza was going to be transported from the back pages – or the toy department as the editor, Kelvin MacKenzie, called them – to the front pages. Everybody on the paper wanted a slice of Gazza and he would still only talk to me. On his return to England, all my other work was put to one side – it was Gazza on this and Gazza on that.

He was also in demand from other European clubs who had heard that Spurs would sell for the right price, although it was a surprise when Lazio managed to win the scramble for his signature. That was all to come. First there was the 1991 FA Cup final – Gazza going out in a blaze of glory by helping Spurs land the trophy against Nottingham Forest. It was always going to be a demanding day but a wild challenge on Gary Charles made it even harder. He had been carted off to the Princess Grace Hospital and both news and sport wanted some words from him for Monday's paper. How the hell was I going to manage that? It was a private hospital and no one was allowed in. But Gazza being Gazza, nothing is impossible. To my great relief he somehow managed to get to a phone and rang me. "It's me and I'm on my way to the operating theatre so you'll have to be quick," he blurted. "Just tell me what's gone on since you arrived in the hospital?" I answered hurriedly. He told me about his team-mates coming around with the Cup and how stupid he had been before I could hear the phone being snatched off him.

It was a long haul back to fitness, not helped by him damaging his knee again in a Newcastle nightclub before the regular trips to Rome for pieces about Lazio, always with *Sun* photographer Dickie Pelham in tow. Gazza trusted Dickie, which made life in the Eternal City good fun. He was always up for a photo-shoot and being away from the madding crowd helped with the columns.

One day, though, things became a little heated. Dickie was asked to take some scenic pictures of Gazza and his then girl-friend, Sheryl. So we all travelled to a well-known beauty spot overlooking the city. Everything was going to plan until Dickie heard a 'click click' noise coming from the bushes near where we were stationed. It was a member of the notorious paparazzi who could sell the pictures of the pair to any rival newspaper who wanted them. It meant *The Sun* missing out on a montage of exclusive pictures. Quick as a flash, Dickie dived into the bushes and, sure enough, a paparazzi photographer was flushed out but he had a mate on a moped – the pair having obviously travelled together in search of Gazza, who was now aware of what was happening and pulled the photographer off the back of his bike. He went flying and so did his camera, allowing Dickie to rip the film out of it before handing the camera back. The situation had been rescued, only for the police to arrive a few minutes later with the chastened photographer. Luckily, Gazza's minder, a burly Italian, explained what had occurred and Gazza was let off with a warning.

Gazza also helped rescue the career of someone who would later rise to huge prominence in the Rupert Murdoch empire, Rebekah Wade. Rebekah was, at the time, a reporter for the *News Of The World* magazine and had come out to Rome hoping to interview Sheryl. Rebekah had asked me to try to set it up because she didn't know either of them. I asked Gazza to try to persuade Sheryl because Rebekah was under pressure to produce something. Yes, he said, Sheryl would meet Rebekah in their hotel. Fantastic. But the interview didn't go well and it was a tearful Rebekah who turned up at my hotel saying there was no way she could go back to London with what had been a fraught interview. Could I go back to Gazza and see whether Sheryl would commit to a second chat? At first, Gazza told me there was no way. Rebekah had one chance and had blown it. I exaggerated and told him that she could lose her job. Surely, neither of them wanted that? After much persuasion from Gazza, Sheryl relented. Rebekah secured a far better inter-view and the pair became good friends as Rebekah impressed so much at the paper that she eventually became News Of The World editor and later chief executive officer.

With Gazza injured on a number of occasions, the trips to Rome became less frequent, although one pre-season assign-ment proved quite eventful. The forgiving Lazio manager Dino Zoff, who treated Gazza almost as a naughty son, had left and the strict disciplinarian Zdeněk Zeman had taken over and didn't take kindly to Gazza's pranks – like sabotaging the kitman's shirts, shorts, socks, anything he could get his hands on, or placing a dead snake in Roberto Di Matteo's coat pocket. What he would have done when Gazza turned up under Zoff's management with a hair extension mocking Roberto Baggio's 'Divine Ponytail' is anybody's guess. Anyway, we're based in Switzerland and I'm the only journalist allowed in the team hotel, courtesy of doing Gazza's columns.

In the early hours of one night, my bedside phone goes. It was

Gazza, who as usual is finding it hard to get to sleep. I was the only one allowed a mini-bar in their room. Alcohol was banned for the Lazio players. "Have ye got any brandy?" Gazza enquired. I said I had but why was he asking? "I can't sleep, man. A couple of brandies should do the trick." I felt sorry for him because I knew from personal experience how he struggled to settle down at night. It's why you are asked to play table tennis or snooker at 3am. I agreed to let him have some brandy so I smuggled a couple of miniature bottles to his room. Mission completed, I returned to my room. An hour or so later I'm woken up by the phone going again. It's Gazza. "Has all the brandy gone?" "Yes it has," I answered. "How about the gin? Are there any bottles of that?" Yes there were and off I went, desperate not to be noticed. Having drunk the gin, Gazza still wasn't finished. It's now the dead of night and he's after anything that's left. Finally, I'm able to get to sleep with a mini-bar now ransacked.

The next morning I made my way to the breakfast room bleary-eyed after a lack of sleep. Standing in the entrance to the room is an agitated Lazio manager. In his broken English he informed me that my stay at the hotel had come to an end. "I want you to fuck off," he demanded. "Why?" I asked, knowing what the answer would be. "Because Paul Gascoigne won't be able to train this morning because he is smelling of drink and you have the only mini-bar." To be fair to Gazza, he had refused to snitch on me but the evidence was there for all to see – my mini-bar was empty and I hadn't had a single drink. That was it, I was on my way back to England.

Gazza was soon on his way to Scotland to join Rangers. I had hardly ever seen him more content with his football and, in Ally McCoist, he had an able sparring partner. He was still contracted to *The Sun* so instead of Rome it was trips to a wonderful hotel on the banks of Loch Lomond, Cameron House, where Gazza and usually Jimmy 'Five Bellies' were ensconced. One evening I arrived at the hotel for another column. I thought I was safe, as far as any of Gazza's tricks were concerned, because it was the eve of a game. So it was a surprise when Jimmy spotted me checking in and told me to join him and Gazza in the bar for a game of shots. I thought to myself there was no way Gazza could be involved because Rangers were playing the next night.

"Right," announced Gazza. "We're lining up the shots and the last man still sitting here is the winner. The first one to drop off the stool will be put to bed." "What about you, Gazza? Are you injured or something?" "Nah, I'm playing, I'll be alright," he insisted, although he knew Walter Smith, the manager, would kill him if he knew what was going on. Sad to say, I was the first faller. I woke up on my bed still fully clothed. At least I was safe and sound – or so I thought! A visit to the bathroom revealed that my eyebrows had been shaved off and there were chunks of hair missing. The next morning I staggered in for breakfast to find Jimmy in a right state. He had been sick all night. Gazza had won the game. I asked Jimmy whether Gazza was still in bed with a massive hangover. "No," said Jimmy. "He's gone off to Ibrox." Needless to say he was the man of the match that night.

Gazza, though, did have huge respect for Walter and his assistant, Archie Knox. I've never seen him look so worried one morning. "It's Walter's 50th birthday. What can I get him?" he asked me. He was beside himself – it was like he had seen a ghost. I told Gazza I'd heard that Walter was a big heavy metal music fan. I thought to myself it was time to get Gazza back. "Like who?" he asked. "Oh, stuff like Metallica and Motörhead,"

I replied. "Are you sure?" "Yes, some of the lads have heard him play it in his car," I said. So he was just about to leave the hotel in search of some CDs when I couldn't help myself. I started laughing and he knew he'd been had. "Come on, man, seriously what can I get him?" We settled in the end on some nice bottles of wine. Walter doesn't know how close he came to receiving some head-banging music instead.

My head was banging on another trip north of Hadrian's Wall. I'd flown up to Glasgow from Manchester Airport and was going back later that day. When I arrived at Ibrox for the arranged meeting with Gazza, he was nowhere to be seen. I was informed he was with Ally and Derek McInnes on a club promotion event in the city. I tracked them down. I knew Ally quite well from his Sunderland days. Gazza said that I could join the three of them on a bit of a pub crawl and he would do the column later. No problem, I said, as long as I could get a flight home later on. Anyway, we went from pub to pub in parts of Glasgow you wouldn't know existed. They were obviously doing their best to not be spotted as they sank the pints. That was a bit hard, mind, considering they were still wearing Rangers tracksuits.

As the drinking binge showed no signs of ending I was beginning to get worried whether he or I would be sober enough to work out a column between us. Gazza kept on putting it off, saying he would do it at the next pub. Every time I took my dictaphone out he would say: "Not yet, man."

We're still going strong and it's now around 8pm and I've got a plane to catch. It will now have to be the last one of the day at around 10.30pm. It was Ally who finally persuaded him to talk to me about the column. It was just a few days after Eric Cantona's infamous kung-fu kick at Selhurst Park. I asked

Gazza about his thoughts, expecting him to say how disgraceful the whole episode had been.

Obviously, now fuelled with around 10 pints of beer, he said he wished more players would do the same if they were abused during games.

"Are you sure, Gazza? This is a bit inflammatory," I warned. "Na, I mean it. If fans want to dish out stick then expect players to give them a good thumping." This was dynamite stuff.

Anyway, it was now time to go. I got a taxi to the airport but once I was in the building it was obvious I wasn't in the best of states. That was confirmed when I went hurtling over a coffee table landing flat on my back. Airport security picked me up and promptly informed me I wouldn't be flying home that night. I was booked into the airport hotel with the promise of a flight in the morning.

On the flight back to Manchester I started transcribing what Gazza had told me for his latest column. There was no way I could use it. It would have got him into serious trouble. I told the office I was still transcribing his column and would ring them back. In the meantime I managed to get hold of Gazza, who – surprise, surprise – couldn't remember saying what he had originally told me and we came up with something else.

His *Sun* columns came to a halt shortly after that but it had been a great run and an exciting ride, proof that there is never a dull moment with Gazza.

Everyone who comes into contact with him has a story to tell. Hopefully you will enjoy some of them in the following pages. Safe to say there is only one Gazza.

John Richardson, 2020

1

'We were in the communal bath in the away dressing room after the game and Elton John came in to congratulate us. Paul, completely starkers, lifted himself out of the bath and shouted: "Elton, give us a song!"'

– Joe Allon, former FA Youth Cup winner and Newcastle United team-mate

Colin Suggett

Colin Suggett, a cultured midfielder for Sunderland, West Brom, Norwich and Newcastle, was manager of the Magpies side which won the 1985 FA Youth Cup. The star of that team was Paul Gascoigne, who often had 'Suggy' pulling his hair out en route to becoming one of this country's greatest players.

I'd gone to watch another lad at a game at Houghton-le-Spring on a Saturday morning with an almighty gale blowing. And here was this little fat lad who kept running around and using the wind to his advantage. Nothing seemed to bother him.

I returned home and I rang up one of my Newcastle scouts, Brian Clark. I asked him who was this little fat lad I had just seen playing for Gateshead Boys? He told me it was Paul Gascoigne and he had already recommended him to Newcastle United but had been knocked back. He added that, in his mind, he was a good player. I told him to bring him to the club.

The weight on him was just puppy fat which I felt would eventually go, providing of course he looked after himself, which was often not the case. We got that sorted. The manager at the time, Jack Charlton, tried to make sure he ate properly. I would also often drop him off at a café near the training ground and pay for him to have a steak.

One summer, I decided to contact Stan Long, who was the coach of local running star and great Newcastle United fan Brendan Foster. I asked if he would let Gazza join some of his sessions at Gateshead to help with his weight. He agreed and told me to tell Gazza to meet him and the rest of the runners on one of the grass banks near the International Stadium at 6pm on the Tuesday. If everything went well he could join in every Tuesday and Thursday night.

On the Wednesday, I rang him up and asked whether Gazza had turned up. Oh yes, he answered, they had found him lying on the grass flat out with his hands behind his head, fast asleep. Anyway, Gazza was invited to join them. At first, the rest of the runners left him behind, but he wouldn't give up and chased and chased them. He managed to at least get around the course, even though he was well off the pace. They would now see how he did on the Thursday.

Sure enough, Gazza turned out again on the Thursday despite finding the first session difficult. He lasted the six weeks the sessions were on for and when he came back for pre-season training he looked completely different. As part of the training we would finish off by running 12 laps of a local cricket pitch. A county cross-country runner would often join us. Well, they all set off and after nine laps the two of them were almost a lap ahead of the other young players. In the end, Gazza sneaked away and this hardened runner couldn't believe it. That's when Gazza became an athlete.

When he was dedicated to something, nothing would stop him wanting to be the best. He loved playing tennis and quickly became a really good player. He would often march into the local park where they had some tennis courts and challenge people to a game. He always picked things up very quickly. You didn't have to show him anything more than, say, a couple of times for him to become proficient.

Yes, he was hard work at times, but it was worth it. I used to have this mental dog-collar on him – you had to keep yanking him back. He was always up to mischief. But if I told him off he would often start crying so I would take pity on him.

After yet another bollocking, he thought I'd gone out of the dressing room as he jumped into the bath with the rest of the lads. He then boasted to his team-mates that I fell for it every time he cried. I heard that, so I grabbed a bucket of ice cold water and waited for him to come out of the bath before throwing it all over him. "Now you can cry," I shouted. "Suggy, I'm sorry," he yelled.

He quickly developed into a standout player and was part of a really good side which won the FA Youth Cup. After a goalless draw in the first leg of the final at home to Watford, we easily won 4-1 at Vicarage Road. Big Jack, the manager, came down to watch the game. Afterwards he came into the dressing room with Elton John, who was the Watford chairman. Jack brought in two bottles of champagne for the players and said well done. All Gazza could do was sing 'Elton, Elton give us a song!' Jack told him to behave himself. Everyone was in awe of Elton except Gazza, who couldn't help himself.

He was the same when we signed the Brazilian striker Mirandinha. Mira arrived in the winter. We were coming back from a game and it was snowing. Gazza was on the back seat with Mira and I asked him what he was doing. "I'm teaching him English," he replied. 'That's good of him,' I thought. So I approached Mira and asked him what he had learned so far. "It's fucking freezing," he said. I warned Gazza about teaching him any more swear words!

I remember when he had first joined the club, the players were lined up to greet him and introduce themselves. Gazza kept moving in and out of the line, continuing to introduce himself – much to Mira's disbelief – while the rest of the players couldn't stop laughing.

As a young player I'd never seen anyone better. After being taught certain things, not only would he grasp them but he would then set an example to the other players. After training he would grab a bag of balls and implore me to join him in taking some free-kicks. He had looked up to me in that respect because during my career I hadn't done badly at set-pieces. One day he asked me again to go with him but I refused. He looked at me in astonishment. "But you always come out with me to practise them," he said. "Gazza, you don't need me now. You're better than me, so show the rest of your team-mates."

I knew from an early age he was destined for the first team and eventually England. Bobby Robson was the England manager and he would regularly come up to watch our games. He would seek me out and just ask, "Well, is the young lad ready yet?"

"No, not yet," I stated.

Back he came six months later with the same question. "Well is he ready?"

I told him again, no, but he was getting better.

The next season he found me again and didn't have to say anything. "Bobby, you can take him now," I suggested. They did and he managed to get in the squad for the 1990 World Cup finals.

He had improved enormously, so much that he became bigger than the Newcastle team and joined Spurs. I've been proud watching him from afar because he's a really good person. He would give his last penny away. He had a huge heart.

I recall he once won the Newcastle United lottery. He shouldn't have even bought a ticket because he was under age. Every week, though, he would buy a pound's worth while talking to the girls in the office at the ground. This time around he won £2,000. The club couldn't announce the winner because he had broken the law – he shouldn't have been allowed to purchase a ticket.

Everyone was panicking, especially the office girls, who used to look after him with sandwiches and cups of tea but also allow him to buy a lottery ticket. After being given the money quietly, he returned later in the week and threw it on one of the desks and told the girls to share it. They couldn't believe it but that was the way he was, so kind-hearted.

At the training ground we were having trouble with people coming in and playing golf on the pitches. There were holes everywhere – it was a right mess, so the club decided to invest in a night watchman who came complete with a mad German Shepherd dog. He kept it in a big kennel with a wire cage encircling it. It would be left by itself during the day.

One morning I could hear Gazza furiously knocking on the changing room door, which had been locked during the training session. He had been chased by the dog and bitten on the backside after one of the players, John Bailey, had let it out.

"I've been bitten on the arse, Suggy. Let me in, let me in!" he screamed. Bails had jumped out of the way on to the top of the kennel, leaving Gazza in the firing line.

Mind, that was only getting Gazza back for some of the pranks he pulled. He even did one on his own father, John.

Like his son, John loved fishing so, for his birthday, Gazza bought him a boat. He told his dad it was moored on the Newcastle Quayside full of fishing tackle and that he would meet him down the river at North Shields.

Little did he know that Gazza had drilled holes into the bottom of the boat, so John didn't get that far! He was soon having to swim to the bank as the boat slowly sunk. That was typical of Gazza's outrageous humour.

Brian Clark

Byker-born coach who was one of the first to spot the potential of a young Paul Gascoigne.

He was a little fat kid who no one else would touch. They used to call him 'corned beef legs' but I wanted him to go to Newcastle United.

An old boy, Davey Lloyd, told me he was taking this lad called Paul Gascoigne down to Middlesbrough. The lad was 13 and there's no getting away from it, he was plump. In truth, Davey was only taking him to Boro to keep a lad called Keith Spraggon company.

But the first time I saw him play it was obvious he had ability. When I finally managed to get him in at Newcastle it was obvious they didn't fancy him because they thought he was too fat. He also had a bad reputation as someone who messed about and was going to be more trouble than he was worth.

As far as I was concerned he was the real article and I managed to convince the club to take him on.

He went to a tournament with them and was voted the best player. After that he never looked back, even though he had a few run-ins. He was forever at our house, having tea, watching telly and messing about.

One of his joys was to take my daughter Lindsay out for walks in her pram.

Jimmy Nelson

Jimmy Nelson was a coach in the Newcastle United academy when Paul Gascoigne arrived and, alongside Colin Suggett, helped mould the precocious skills of the young midfielder. Jimmy still works for Newcastle and over the years has acted as a confidant for Gazza, who has always trusted and respected his opinions.

I was a part-time coach at Newcastle United working on Tuesday and Thursday evenings at the club's training ground at Benwell when Paul first joined as a 13-year-old. He was part of a really strong group of Under-14s. Most of them went on to eventually win the FA Youth Cup.

They really came to life as a team when we went to Aberdeen to take part in a tournament. We were even allowed to travel up to Scotland on the first-team coach. Joe Harvey, the former player and manager, travelled with us in his role as a director and keen supporter of the young players.

I can tell you that he was absolutely knocked out by Paul Gascoigne right from the beginning of his time with Newcastle. He was really delighted when we ended up winning the tournament. We were beating teams 8-0, 9-0. Joe really lapped it up. He just loved what he was seeing, especially Gazza, and would often shout out: "Look at the little bugger." Joe was absolutely transfixed by his play and cheek.

Gazza couldn't help himself. He was always up to some kind of mischief but it was never malicious. He just loved larking around. Nigeria had sent a team to play in the competition and before a game they all lined up for a team photograph. Quick as a flash, Gazza managed somehow to smuggle himself into the photo and so there he is right slap bang in the middle, the only white face, laughing his head off!

Gazza being Gazza also managed to get a lift back to the hotel in the Nigerian Ambassador's car, with the national flag unfurled on the bonnet, instead of coming back with the rest of us in our coach. Joe watched all this almost in disbelief before commenting yet again: "Look at that little bugger!" as Gazza gave everyone a regal wave.

If he had been fantastic in a game, I'd sometimes quietly give him a fiver, which was decent money for a kid of that age. I'd tell him if anyone asked, it was for his expenses, a taxi ride or something like that. In the years that followed, even when he came back to St. James' Park as a Tottenham player, if he spotted me he would without fail yell: "Anyone getting a fiver today, Jimmy?!"

I'd always had a soft spot for him. I could obviously see he was a good player but really it was the sort of person he was. He stood out as a daft, loveable lad and very kind-hearted. He brightened up the place. I never wanted him to leave Newcastle and certainly not for Spurs, where I thought he might be led astray. For me there were too many so-called personalities and hangers-on who could disturb his football focus and I think that's the way it turned out.

I persuaded an art teacher from Gosforth High School in the Newcastle area to produce a comic sketch of Gazza in a Spurs shirt fishing, and there's a shark who has got him right around his crown jewels, á la Vinnie Jones. The caption read, 'Don't let the sharks get you by the bollocks.' I handed it over to him and he loved it but the message was a serious one – not to be taken in by the many people who wanted a slice of him.

After one game between Newcastle and Tottenham at St. James' Park in which he and another ex-Newcastle player, Chris Waddle, had been in the Spurs side, I went into the players' lounge to have a chat with them. Of course, the first words from Gazza were: "Have you got a fiver for me, Jimmy?" Then he told me a story. Unbeknown to me, he was relying on one of my fivers just before Christmas time. He thought he would have received the money at the last training session before the festive period. He would have used the money to buy Christmas presents for the family.

I decided to cancel the session because there was too much else going on. I rang all the different schools where the players studied and asked for the message that there would be no training that evening to be delivered to the pupils. Paul never received it because he had taken the day off school. He told me he turned up at the training ground to find it locked and in total darkness. He thought at first he had just beaten everyone to Benwell and we would all eventually turn up. After half an hour he realised that wasn't going to happen.

So, knowing now there would be no money forthcoming from me, in desperation he decided to go carol singing! Believe me, the area around the training ground was never the most salubrious, but it didn't bother him. Off he went singing some of the Christmas carols he knew and knocking on doors. What a sight that must have been. And he added that he collected enough money to buy some presents and get the bus back home. He kept that as a secret for years until that day in the players' lounge when he had great delight in revealing his prowess as a carol singer.

Yet there have also been a few desperate occasions when you

discover that all has not been well with Paul. A few years ago I was at St. James' Park, just before Christmas, watching Newcastle against Reading. My mobile phone goes and Gazza is on the other end. All I hear is: "Jimmy, I'm fucked." I quickly asked where he was. He replied that he was in Bournemouth. I then got in touch with a number of people who knew him and said he needed help. I got the PFA involved and also notified Spurs, who were very good. Eventually, they managed to get Paul sectioned, which meant he would receive the best treatment for his alcoholism and depression. He would be in good hands, safe from doing anything stupid to himself.

On another occasion he was admitted to a rehabilitation centre in the USA after hitting another downward spiral. I was contacted, along with a few others, about filming a message that would be shown to him over there. But they didn't want a nice message, they wanted one that was hard and direct, one which would hopefully shock him. David Craig, who works for Sky Sports, set it up and told me I'd have to have a right go at Paul. He left me to face the camera, promising that what I was about to say would never be seen anywhere else. It was for Gazza's eyes and ears only. I sat down and started off by recalling the previous cry for help: "You said you were 'fucked'. Well, listen to me. You fucked up my Christmas you selfish bastard." I went absolutely ballistic, which is not me. I couldn't believe what I was saying. I had a real go.

When he had recovered, Gazza popped into the Newcastle academy to see his nephew, who we'd taken on. He told me he had watched and listened to my message and had almost wet himself laughing. He was telling the nurse that Jimmy Nelson had never said a bad word in his life. He was always putting his arm around me. Anyway, he had a shoulder bag with him and asked me what I thought he had in it. I said cigarettes. "Aye," he admitted. "I've got two ciggies. What else?" I hoped he hadn't brought a bottle of alcohol. No, thankfully he hadn't. "So, do you give in, Jimmy?" I said yes, I had no idea. "Well it's my poetry," he explained. I looked at him in amazement. Whether it was part of his rehabilitation in America, I don't know, but there it was. I don't think it would win any prizes but there were some dark messages in some of them, seriously dark. I asked him to consider getting some of them published. There were pages of them.

It was a far cry from the innocent, fun-loving kid who had been a standout player in the academy. I'd seen a few decent players pass through it. For instance, I coached Alan Shearer three days a week when he was 13, 14. We really wanted to keep him but he ended up at Southampton. I remember seeing him at his school one day lining up to collect his dinner in his South-ampton tracksuit. That was rubbing it in more than a bit!

The only worry Gazza had was his weight. He had to work on keeping it off in the early days. Often he would train with bin bags tied to his body under his training gear to sweat more. I don't think his diet was the best. I think sometimes the fiver I gave him went on bars of chocolate, which didn't exactly help.

But you couldn't get him off the training pitch at times. Once a session was over he would love to try and hit the crossbar from long range. No one told him to do it, he was obsessed with trying to improve his skills. To be fair, he was never in a hurry to get inside for something to eat. I think he only ate the wrong things when he was bored, when nothing was happening.

He loved other sports as well. My son James was a very good

tennis player who went on to play at Wimbledon and win the US Open boys' doubles title. Paul loved him, having watched him develop as a young boy. One weekend he even invited himself to a kids' party we had arranged for James. He scoffed loads of the birthday cake and started messing around. All the kids lapped it up.

At the age of 15, James left home to be coached at Bisham Abbey, which just happened to be the England team's usual base before games. One day I was with James sorting out a few contracts with the Lawn Tennis Association, who had taken him on. My wife Di and daughter Jenny were also with us. I discovered that England were training. I thought I'd go and say hello to some of them like Gazza, Alan Shearer, Steve Howey, players I had known as kids, but the security guy wouldn't let us get past. Feeling a little deflated, we walked back along the river but suddenly heading towards us is Gazza. He clocked me and yelled out: "What are you doing here you old sod?" Steve Howey then gets off the coach, which is parked nearby, with Jamie Redknapp. Gazza started talking to James about how he was getting on and then asked him if he would like the England training top he was wearing. James was delighted. He then said: "James, do you want my shorts?" "Of course," came the reply. So Gazza now looks at my wife and daughter before saying: "Di, Jenny, you'll have to turn around because I've got no under-kecks on," as he delved into his bag to find a pair of jeans to cover his modesty.

There were some tennis players nearby not believing what they were seeing. They also couldn't believe the sight of Gazza kicking spare balls into the River Thames, which ran alongside Bisham Abbey. It appeared one of his party tricks was to see how far he could kick a ball into the water. Goodness knows how many balls the FA lost.

After bumping into us and having a chat, Gazza announced he was going to see his partner Sheryl. He didn't want the media to see him leaving the training camp at Bisham. I told him I had my car and I'd take him if he wanted. He thanked me but said he had a taxi booked. The next thing, a Hackney cab turns up and he's climbing into the boot and ordering the cabbie to drive on while he's hidden from the media.

There had already evidently been some high jinks at Bisham with him and Steve McManaman. One of the groundsmen had left his tractor with the keys in the ignition, so the pair of them decided to take a ride – only to smash straight into a marquee.

James, who for some reason was a Nottingham Forest fan, was with me at Wembley when Gazza injured his knee in the 1991 FA Cup final. We were close to the players' tunnel and watched the Spurs players come out to sample the atmosphere and walk on the pitch as part of the pre-match preparation. You could see already that Paul was hyper.

James and I watched him pull down the goalkeeper Erik Thorstvedt's tracksuit bottoms. I turned to James and said: "Terry Venables had better get a grip of him." I'd seen what had happened in the past when Gazza was on one. The tackle on Gary Charles was naughty and he could have been sent off for it. It was obvious he was finding it hard to take control of what was a huge game. But that's him.

Look at Euro 96 and what happened surrounding the 'dentist's chair' incident in Hong Kong in the lead-up to the tournament. He then re-enacts it after scoring a sensational goal against Scotland. It was a case of, 'I'll do what I like. Nothing is going to stop me.' It was two fingers to those who have tried to curtail his character.

One day, I wanted to have some paintings that had been given to me signed by the likes of Gazza, Alan Shearer and Bobby Robson. Bobby put 'Best wishes Jimmy Nelson, from Bobby Robson.' Alan put 'Best wishes Jimmy Nelson – Alan Shearer.' Paul put 'Best wishes. Love and kisses. Tara for now. Paul Gascoigne.' It creates a laugh when anyone comes to the house and spots the painting and Gazza's typical original message.

He had outrageous skill but at times that had to be reined in. I'll never forget in the FA Youth Cup final against Watford when he nutmegged the same player twice before sending a fantastic pass forward. I'm shouting to him to behave himself. But we scored from it, so what can you do? Someone on the Watford bench looked at me and said: "He's got a chance, hasn't he?!" After that he went in the first team virtually straight away.

Colin Suggett was hard on Paul sometimes for his own good. I suppose I was mostly good cop and Colin was bad cop where Gazza was concerned. But it worked well. He needed disciplining. On the coach on the way back from games, Colin and I would discuss the game but we never felt it was necessary to speak to the lads there and then about what had gone on unless there had been an appalling display, which rarely ever happened.

We had a good team and Paul was at the fulcrum of it with his passing and movement. He rarely played the ball sideways or backwards. He wasn't afraid to try things. I get fed up watching much of today's football where the central midfield players are happy to pass back to the centre-half and then the ball goes slowly across the back line. That was never the case with Paul. I don't think, in all honesty, any player has matched him since he finished playing. He never had any problems on the field. The silliness and heartbreak came off it. I don't think he was ever able to handle the excessive amounts of money he was paid. So many people have tried to help him over the years. I'm just glad he is still with us – even if every time he sees me he asks whether I've got a fiver for him!

Tommy Robinson

Tommy Robinson was the coach of Dunston Juniors, where Gazza unleashed some of his precocious talent.

I am so proud of the young lad I knew – someone who was infectious, willing to help out and hugely gifted. All he ever wanted was a cuddle and to be loved. That was the way he played even in the days before fame came along. He played for the adulation of those who were watching, even at Dunston Juniors.

Gazza was a genius, a pure entertainer. We had him for two years before he signed YTS forms for Newcastle United. Before that he was on schoolboy forms and I had to get permission from Joe Harvey, the former Newcastle manager, who was then in charge of development, for him to play for us.

I remember a match against Wallsend Boys Club when Gazza picked up the ball from our goalkeeper, beat four, maybe five opposition players – and even a couple of his own who were desperate to join in the move – before lobbing the keeper.

Brian Watson, who scouted young talent for Newcastle, was just coming through the gate and asked who the heck was he? I told him that he needn't worry, he would become a Newcastle player.

Joe Allon

Joe Allon was the striker whose goals helped a Newcastle team which included his big mate Paul Gascoigne win the 1985 FA Youth Cup. In the early days on Tyneside they were inseparable, even if Gazza's antics often left Joe on the edge of despair. Both went on to play for the first team before Joe moved to a number of clubs, including Chelsea and Swansea City. He is now a football pundit and an entertaining after-dinner speaker.

We started playing together as 10-year-olds at Newcastle United during the school holidays. We would both get a bus up to the training ground in Benwell. In fact, a number of us stuck together through the age groups and became part of the side that won the FA Youth Cup in 1985.

Some of us, including Gazza and myself, went on to play in the first team. People go on about Manchester United's class of '92 – well, the Newcastle class of '85 wasn't bad. Brian Tinnion, Paul Stephenson, Kevin Scott and Ian Bogie all represented the Toon while others made a living elsewhere in the Football League.Paul and I were just glad to be part of a very good side which came together with that exciting and successful FA Youth Cup run.

We were a pair of likely lads, if you like – always ready for a bit of fun. Gazza was just mischievous all the time.

I was made head apprentice and given some responsibility to keep everything in order. That's hard going when you've got Gazza supposedly under your wing – and even harder when you've got all the apprentice jobs to supervise and you know he's going to struggle to do any.

One day, after leaving the training ground, the pair of us went into a café some of the first team would often use. It was halfway between Benwell and St. James' Park. We'd have Quiche and baked beans, bacon sandwiches, stuff like that. Whatever we could afford, to be honest.

There were a couple of well-to-do ladies sitting on a table with a young child who was probably around four or five years old. They were busily eating away while the kid suddenly made eye contact with Gazza, who started pulling faces, and the young nipper did the same. Then Gazza stuck out his tongue and the kid reacted in the same way.

Basically, anything Gazza did, the youngster would copy. Gazza being Gazza couldn't leave it at just pulling faces or acting silly, he had to go one step further. So the next thing I see him doing is grabbing hold of a pepper pot and pouring some of the contents on the table. Blissfully unaware of what was going on, the two women kept chatting while the child was also spilling pepper all over his table.

Then Paul dipped a finger into the pepper and pretended to lick it. The kid, though, wasn't so clever and stuck his hand into the pepper and promptly went on to taste it. That was it – cue bedlam. The kid started screaming and the two women couldn't believe what he had done.

Of course, Gazza put on his innocent face while I tried not to laugh but failed miserably. It was like a comedy sketch from 'The Two Ronnies'. I don't think that poor kid would have gone near a pepper pot again in his life!

Then came one of the most stressful days imaginable – the day Gazza left Kevin Keegan's boots on the bus. Kevin was due to make his Newcastle debut the next day at St. James' Park against QPR following his unbelievable signing for the Toon. Friday was pay day for the apprentices, so after training and doing our chores we would usually get the bus into the middle of Newcastle. He would go on the one-armed bandits and I would have a quid on a horse.

Paul was in charge of cleaning Kevin's boots and for some reason brought them with us. An old guy who supported Newcastle, Stevie, also came in with us on the bus.

So we all got off at Central Station while the bus went on to the depot at Worswick Street. While he was playing one of the slot machines, I asked him what had he done with Kevin Keegan's boots. He went white and uttered: "Fuck, I've left them on the bloody bus!" I couldn't believe it. Kevin Keegan, the former England captain, was making his debut the next day in front of a sold-out St. James' Park and at this rate he might not have any football boots.

With Gazza panicking, thinking this could be the end for him, Stevie decided to race off to try and find the bus at Worswick Street. It wouldn't have been good news for me either because I was head apprentice. Thankfully for Gazza, Stevie was able to find the bus we'd been on and managed to retrieve the boots. After that you've never seen Gazza move so fast. He raced off to St. James' Park and placed the boots in the dressing room ready for the next day as if nothing had happened.

I don't know to this day whether Kevin knew just how close he had come to losing his favourite boots 24 hours before his big Newcastle day. But it ended in true fairytale fashion as he scored the winning goal in a 1-0 victory.

Gazza scored twice and I got the other two in the FA Youth final which we won 4-1 at Watford after drawing the first leg at

St. James' Park 0-0. He had been amazing in every game and turned it on again in the final. He was particularly brilliant at Vicarage Road.

Elton John was the chairman of Watford at the time and he had watched the match. While we were in the communal bath in the away dressing room after the game he came in to congratulate us. Paul, completely starkers, lifted himself out of the bath and shouted: "Elton, give us a song." I told Paul to sit down because Elton was definitely not looking at Gazza's eyes!

We both made it into the first team under Jack Charlton, who was the manager, and it didn't matter which team he was playing for – the youth side, the reserves or the first team, Gazza always demanded the ball. There were England internationals like Kevin Keegan, Terry McDermott and Mike Channon playing for us, other internationals – it didn't matter to Gazza, he always demanded the ball. Nothing on the field fazed him. Even if he was having a bad game it didn't deter him.

In football terms he went from an ugly duckling to a beautiful swan. Off the field, yes he was hyperactive, always up to something or other, but also very kind hearted. He would give his last penny to anyone. He has a heart of gold. He's had his illnesses and his problems, but for me he is still a wonderful human being. He is always on the move. He never switches off but no one can take away from him those magnificent memories. For me, at Italia 90, was the best player in the world. Any doubters, ask the likes of Ruud Gullit and Lothar Matthäus. He tore both of them apart in the games against Holland and Germany.

That made it even sadder when he did his cruciate knee ligaments in the 1991 FA Cup final against Nottingham Forest. When he was at Tottenham recovering from that injury, I was at Chelsea and a group of us – Vinnie Jones, Dennis Wise, Andy Townsend and myself – went to White Hart Lane to watch a big boxing event which featured Chris Eubank against Michael Watson. We were all in one of the hospitality boxes. All of a sudden this guy bursts into the box with a crate of Holsten Pils complete with a huge brace on his leg while wearing the Tottenham kit. It's Gazza.

It's 10pm and I'm looking at him completely dumbfounded about why he was here at this time of night in his Spurs kit. He had been in the gym as part of his rehabilitation and the drinks were for us. He then insisted we followed him into the players' lounge to meet and greet some of the guests. It was a celebrity who's who. He took us over to meet Ray Clemence, who was a real gentleman. Terry Venables, who was the Spurs manager, came in. It was fantastic. Gazza then announced he was going back to the gym and wouldn't be watching the big fight. He was desperate to get back playing football again.

All this made my mind go back to those formative years when I first clapped eyes on this chubby kid who had bags of ability. In previous years some opposition fans had tried to wind him up by chucking Mars bars onto the pitch because of this reputation for eating chocolate. He didn't eat them every day, believe it or not, but he would scoff sweets whenever he could. Aware that he couldn't afford to put on any extra weight, he would often train with bin bags under his kit to sweat it all off. All that good work would go to waste when he trotted off for a full English breakfast after training. We all did, to be fair. It was all a bit different in those days before special diets and so on. Then there was also the local brewery, the club's sponsor, which would put on big lunches. They were fantastic and eagerly consumed.

Gazza was still aware of what could happen if he let his body go. Jack Charlton even threatened to sack him once, although it wasn't just about his feeding habits, it was about some of the antics he got up to off the field. He'd had a massive bollocking from Jack and when I came into the dressing room he was sat alone crying. I tried to console him but he thought that was it – he was finished, big Jack had read him the riot act. Football was his life and here he was thinking he was going to get the bullet.

As an apprentice you would have numerous jobs to do – not very pleasant ones like cleaning the toilets and the baths, hoovering the floor, getting the dirty kit in. At least if you could get them all done quickly you could be away by mid-afternoon and have the rest of the day to yourself. No, not Gazza. After the work had been done he would grab a ball and stroll into the gym and kick it around for ages.

In the past I've done some shows with him and really enjoyed being together again, recalling some of the great memories. Think of Gazza and you can't stop smiling. It's never been dull!

Jack Charlton

Jack Charlton almost brought a young Gazza's career to a halt shortly after taking over as Newcastle United manager.

Gazza was never vindictive or nasty. He would just go too far sometimes and had to be brought down a peg or two. I was first introduced to him when I spotted him fishing on the banks of the River Tyne with some of his mates. He asked me if I wanted a beer. I wondered where he was going to get one from. "Here," he replied as he dragged a crate of lager out of the river.

I think he later got the shock of his life, though, when as a 16-year-old I heard he had been making fun of some of the professional players. He was always cheeky but this time he had gone too far. I called him into my office and told him in no uncertain terms that if he didn't start treating the senior pros with more respect he would be out of the door and I would make certain he didn't get another club.

There was also another time when I looked at his stomach and told him he had two weeks to lose weight or else. He looked petrified. He probably didn't eat for a fortnight! But I knew how talented he was. I don't think he ever held it against me because he later sent me a signed photograph of him at Italia 90. It said, 'To Jack, my second dad. Love Gazza.'

When I was manager of Republic of Ireland and Gazza hadn't yet played for England, I asked him if he had any Irish blood in the family. No, he replied, he was 100 per cent Geordie. We discovered too late that he had an Irish grandmother, which would have qualified him to play for Ireland.

Brian Tinnion

Brian Tinnion was Gazza's team-mate from an early age and went on to play for the Newcastle youth team and also the senior side. He made more than 450 appearances for Bristol City.

I was good friends with Gazza, probably from the age of 14. We played together at Dunston Juniors. He learned to drive before me and one day gave me a lift home. He asked if I wanted dropping off at the door. I said, yes, that would be great. The next thing, he's driven onto the lawn and executed a wheel spin right outside the front door. As you can imagine, my parents were delighted! Gazza was the standout player in the Newcastle youth side. He played exactly the same way when he was 18 and in the Newcastle first team as he did when he was 14 and playing for Dunston Juniors.

Ian Bogie

Newcastle youth product Ian Bogie rose up the ranks alongside Paul Gascoigne, who was a regular guest at his family home. Ian played for a succession of clubs before stepping into the dugout. He is now back at the Magpies coaching the Under-16s.

We were both on schoolboy forms at Newcastle United. Gazza was a second-year apprentice and I was a first-year apprentice. I had the good fortune of playing for England Schoolboys at Under-14 and Under-15 level. We were from two different areas of the city. He was from Dunston and I came from Walker, and he used to stay at my house on a regular basis.

As a player you could see how good he was from an early age. Jack Charlton, who was the manager during his formative years, knew Gazza was a top, top player. He nurtured him and gave Gazza his opportunity at Newcastle. We also had experienced players in the squad who could try and look after Gazza, the likes of Glenn Roeder and David McCreery. It was good that a few of them would take Gazza under their wing and help develop the talent everyone knew about.

When we were both on schoolboy forms at the club we were often taken to the nearby Co-op for our dinner. There was a restaurant upstairs and we had a budget of about £2.50 to spend, which was enough to get you a good dinner and a pudding. We would all sit together on a big table. Often, Gazza would grab everybody's attention and whisper for us to watch one of the blokes on the next table. One of Gazza's favourite pranks was to loosen the salt and pepper shakers which were usually filled right to the brim. We all wondered what he was up to. Then we saw this bloke with his plate piled up with food reach for the salt and try to shake some of the contents over his dinner. The next thing, the whole lot emptied over his dinner. His face was a picture, not believing what he had done. We were now in stitches but trying not to laugh out loud because if he had known what Gazza had got up to he would have come over and chinned him!

At our house he was a nightmare because he couldn't sit still and found it hard to sleep through the night. He got bored too easily and was hyperactive. I mean, who else would be playing tennis with two hotel guests the night before the 1990 World Cup semi-final? But that was him from an early age.

One day, Gazza decided to take a look into my dad's wardrobe because we were going off to visit my grandmother and he fancied dressing up. There was gear that my dad had worn years back. Suddenly Gazza pulls out a suit from the 1970s and puts it on complete with a shocking checked shirt and gaudy tie. There he was walking to my grandmother's home in a suit with flared trousers. I couldn't believe it. Nor could any passers-by. There were even people going out for the day banging on the windows of their minibuses and laughing at a 1970s-style Gazza walking along the pavement.

As apprentices at Newcastle there were lots of jobs to be done. We were based at the old training ground at Benwell. You would have to clean the baths, look after the manager's office, tidy up the boot room and then it would be off to St. James' Park for more chores, which in the winter could mean shovelling snow off the terraces. You had to make sure the dressing rooms were tidy for the Saturday. There was also a little store room where the first-team players' boots were kept. Kevin Keegan, who had joined the club, had these fantastic Patrick boots which were hidden away. Gazza always wanted to look at them and feel them whenever he had the chance. So he would try and prise open this cupboard without breaking it. Then he would get this stick with a hook on the end and try to fish the boots out. Someone would be keeping a watch at the door to make sure no one spotted him. These were special boots mind, made of soft kangaroo leather. Gazza was obsessed with them and would do anything to have a feel of them.

It's strange now looking back, when you consider what happened to him in Italia 90, that just four years earlier a group of us including Gazza, myself, Jeff Wrightson – an ex-Newcastle player who went to Preston and who I still keep in touch with – and a lad called Chris Hutchinson, a Newcastle apprentice at the time, all went off to Corfu.

It was our first holiday abroad, young kids wanting to explore the world. The highlight was sitting in a bar watching the World Cup quarter-final between England and Argentina, the Diego Maradona handball and all that. There's Gazza quietly taking it all in, oblivious to what was going to happen to him in the next World Cup. Loads of people were in the bar, glued to the action, not knowing that sitting amongst them was someone who would become a household name in Italia 90. He had broken into the Newcastle first team by then and some people might have recognised him but he wasn't the personality which he would become four years down the line.

Sadly, I only played alongside Gazza in the Newcastle first team on one occasion, against QPR on the Loftus Road artificial turf. I was in the squad with him a few times, though, and for a game in London I was rooming with him in the hotel.

You could either get up for breakfast or forgo that and have a meal a bit later. It was either one or the other, never both. I got up and said I was going down for breakfast and asked whether he was going to join me. No, he said, he'd wait for his pre-match meal so off I went down to the restaurant.

Later, on my way back to the room, I was just walking along the corridor towards it when there's a real commotion outside the door. Gazza is standing there in the doorway in his boxer shorts yelling to some of the players who had come out of their rooms.

"Lads, I can't believe what he's done," he says, referring to me. The chambermaid was lurking outside the room ready to clean it. Gazza says to her: "Come in. Come and see what he has done." He was telling everyone that I was really nervous about playing later that day. So the chambermaid and a few of the lads followed him into the room. He then pulled back the bed-clothes to expose the white sheets which had been smothered in chocolate but looked like something else which you wouldn't want in your bed. "Look," he shouted. "He is so nervous he's shit the bed!" I didn't know where to put myself.

When he was transferred from Newcastle to Tottenham I played against him when Spurs visited St. James' Park. We had kept in contact. I was still living at home and some people had even called me the new Gazza, which was nice. It was going to be a full house and I'm up against him, so I had a few butterflies. Chris Waddle would also be playing. They had a decent side under Terry Venables.

On the morning of the game he was ringing me from the Gosforth Park Hotel, where Tottenham were staying. He said he was ready to absolutely murder me on the pitch, that he was going to run the legs off me and nutmeg me. In the end, he had an absolute nightmare. I think the occasion got to him. Spurs fought back from going 2-0 down to draw 2-2. He got pelted with Mars bars by the Newcastle fans – obviously goading him over his weight. They didn't give him a moment's peace and I think that got to him. He was shocked that fans who used to idolise him had turned.

That night he was staying over on Tyneside so we went out together to some of the haunts we used to frequent in our young years. We all used to go out together as apprentices and young professionals, living it up in the Bigg Market. Jimmy Gardner, Gazza's big mate, would invariably be with us. We had some great times.

After returning from the 1990 World Cup, where he had suddenly been elevated to superstardom, he joined us at a big barbecue which a few of us were going to in Newcastle. He turned up in a big sponsored Mercedes car, a real top-of-the-range job. He joins us and then starts handing the keys to anyone who fancies a drive in it. Anyone who wanted could go for a spin in it around the block. He honestly wasn't bothered that it was brand new and in pristine condition. In the end, they were queuing up to take turns in Gazza's fantastic car.

When I was manager of Gateshead a few years ago, he told me he was coming up to watch one of our games.

Grahame McDonnell, who had been Newcastle United's commercial manager, was now in that role at Gateshead. I told Grahame that Gazza was coming up and could he look after whatever requirements he needed. He said it would be no trouble, that he would sort him out with tickets and hospitality. Sure enough, he turns up on the Saturday.

Suddenly, Grahame is knocking on the door of the dressing room, where I am about to give the team talk. He says that I wouldn't believe it. Gazza had turned up with his two sisters, all the kids – about eight of them! – and some mates. I just told him to do the best he could.

I haven't seen him for a few years but I sometimes pop into the Gateshead Metro Centre where a big mate of mine, Micky Edmondson, runs a sports memorabilia shop called Back Pages, because Gazza's sister Lindsay helps run it. So I will have a chat with her and see how he is doing.

His problems have been well documented but he has a heart of gold and I love him. If I bumped into him I know we would get on famously. We've got a few stories to share from days gone by. When he came to stay with my family when we were making our way at Newcastle he was like one of our own.

We would travel to youth team games together and have a great laugh. I'm afraid it happens to a lot of footballers, when they lose what they love that's when the problems, including the boredom, arrive. It has taken its toll on a lot of people, not just Gazza.

2

'He somehow managed to open up a mate's car, which was parked on a fairly steep bank close to the Tuxedo Princess, and released the handbrake. He felt it was hilarious to see the car roll down the road and straight into the river'

– Paul Montgomery, former football scout and Newcastle nightclub owner

Neil McDonald

Neil McDonald was another up-and-coming young Geordie who played in the same Newcastle United side as Gazza. He has had a busy coaching career, joining up with Sam Allardyce at Bolton, Blackburn and West Ham in addition to managing Carlisle United, Ostersunds FC, Blackpool and Limerick.

I was 16, a year older than Gazza when I first got to know him. Jack Charlton was the manager. To be honest my first impressions were of a chubby kid who was eating sweets all the time. But you quickly began to appreciate all the football skills he possessed. Every time he came into training he was eating some kind of sweet. He would often have a mouthful of them.

That, though, wasn't his biggest problem. He drove into training – which was fine until you discovered he hadn't passed his test. He still only had a provisional licence and should have been on the bus. When Willie McFaul succeeded big Jack as manager he inherited the job of trying to look after Gazza. He warned him that he couldn't keep coming into training in his car until he had passed his test. It was against the law and he could find himself in terrible trouble. Willie told him to get back on the bus.

Gazza just ignored Willie's advice and kept on driving. One afternoon, Gazza and I had to go to together to a charity event in Newcastle. I parked my car at the football ground and Gazza told me to jump in with him. I didn't know what I was letting myself in for. He had a little black Mini but I soon discovered the windscreen wipers didn't work. Shortly after setting off it began to rain – and there was Gazza winding down his window and putting his head out, frantically wiping the moisture off the windscreen so he could see where he was going.

We finally got there and he parked up, and off we went to take part in the charity do. When we came out, there were a couple of cars parked either side of his vehicle. He was virtually hemmed in. It was such a tight fit I was wondering whether we would be able to get out of the cramped space. He got into the car and was moving slowly backwards and forwards with no end result. He was stuck.

Suddenly, there was a knock on his driver's side window. It was a police officer, which Gazza could have done without considering he still hadn't passed his driving test. The policeman asked him whether he had a problem. Gazza said he couldn't get out of his parking spot, so the copper offered to help him and eventually, thanks to his painstaking instructions, Gazza was able to get out.

I climbed back in the car and Gazza was a nervous wreck. "I thought he was going to pull me," he blurted out. "I've got no full driving licence, no insurance and I've already got eight penalty points on it." Don't ask me how he managed to get them! I'm now telling him to get me back to the ground as quickly as he can so I can get into my own car. You never knew what was going to happen next.

That was him because normally he never had a care in the world. He was just a happy-go-lucky kid who always wanted to please you and do things for you. As a young player he had all the skills, although at first he was a bit podgy and couldn't get around the pitch easily. But once Jack Charlton started ensuring he was fed properly he lost some of that weight, from then on he went from strength to strength. The penny dropped for him to stop eating all the sweets and chocolate he used to consume.

Jack was brilliant for him in his younger days. As well as helping on the diet side he taught him to save some of his money. He was basically a street kid whose family had known hard times, so Jack didn't want to see him getting carried away and wasting what money he was earning. He put him on the right track and made him more professional.

On the pitch there were no problems. Right from the start he displayed loads of skill, had confidence and played with his head up so he could see a pass. He could take players on, had loads of tricks. He had real upper body strength and was quick enough without being lightning fast. He could pass and move and score goals. He had everything.

Once he broke into the Newcastle first team he flourished with the experienced David McCreery alongside him. David was a bit of a destroyer and, being older and having played for teams like Manchester United and Northern Ireland, he would win the ball and pass it to Gazza, who would do the rest. They had a great relationship on the field and complemented each other.

It was an exciting time because we had a number of young Geordies in the squad. In addition to Gazza and myself there were the likes of Ian Bogie, Paul Stephenson and Brian Tinnion. We were all close and it helped make it a really good dressing room.

From an early age, Gazza was a livewire in the dressing room, laughing and joking. At times I'm thinking to myself that he shouldn't be saying certain things to the older professionals. That he was being too cheeky for his own good. They mostly accepted it because they knew he would go out on the pitch and deliver, although at times they had to have a quiet word and tell him he couldn't get away with certain things.

Mainly, he was just enthusiastic and wanted to make people happy, to make them smile. He loved doing pranks on people. That went on right through his career. We got to know his big mate Jimmy 'Five Bellies' Gardner – and poor Jimmy was often the butt of Gazza's jokes.

I remember when Gazza was signed by Lazio he bought a ticket for Jimmy to fly to Rome from Newcastle. What he didn't tell poor Jimmy, who I don't think had been abroad before, was that it included travelling to around 15 different airports before he could arrive in Rome. I think it took Jimmy two or three days to reach his final destination!

Gazza's full league debut was away at Southampton. He was a nervous wreck before the game. In fact, for most of his career he had a few butterflies before he got on the pitch. That was shown in his hyperactivity. He could never sit still, he was always fidgeting, grabbing a drink, laughing and joking. He would try and distract you and act the fool but really it was down to his nerves.

Once the game started, off he went – give him the ball and let him play. There were very few restrictions on him. He was allowed to express himself and when you're young you don't have any fear, any inhibitions. It was a free-for-all for Gazza to demonstrate his skills. He took the place by storm in that first season.

Although he carried on acting the fool whenever he could, the growing fame never went to his head. He was just a kid growing up – the difference being he was doing it in front of thousands of Newcastle United fans. It was his dream to be a footballer and he was being paid to do it. By doing it he kept all his family and friends happy. He often popped back to his old school because he had a great relationship with the teachers, and so if he could help with anything he would.

I think as young footballers we educated ourselves as we went along because your dream was to be a professional footballer and you left school at the earliest age you could. Even my kids now joke and say: "Dad. You've got no qualifications." Things like that. I left school at 16 and you try to learn things as you go along. Then there's learning about coaching and management in football, so education goes in different directions.

For Gazza, it was football, more football and acting the fool. He wanted to have people smiling and laughing all the time. He always felt he had to perform. At times you'd say to him: "Gazza, for Christ's sake shut up." But then you'd smile to yourself because you knew he didn't mean any harm. He was just a bundle of energy.

We were all different in the dressing room before games. Some players would sit quietly reading a newspaper and not get changed until later. He would always be messing around. If he couldn't play then no one would have accepted it but we knew he could.

Nowadays, it's completely different, you start building up to a game a couple of hours before kick-off with various stretching exercises. Can you imagine if Gazza was still active now? He would be at it for two hours before he had actually kicked a ball. The players would have been worn out by his antics. At least we only had to put up with him for an hour before the game started. He just loves to be in the limelight. That was the case right throughout his career.

The sad part for me is that even now it appears he can never relax and chill out in his own company. It seems he has to have people around him and to perform to them all the time, which must be hard. When you see some recent photos of him you can see how all this has taken its toll.

You never knew what was coming next with Gazza. On a Newcastle end-of-season trip to New Zealand he went missing for a few hours and everyone wondered where he had gone. Later, the answer was there for all to see. He had decided to have his hair dyed blond and at first most of the players didn't recognise him.

It was amazing to think that just a few years later he would be a household name following Italia 90. He had always been an emotional player and it all came out during and after the semi-final defeat against West Germany. When he was on his game he would take the you-know-what out of opponents, not in a nasty way but just typical Paul Gascoigne cheek. But at times everything became too much, as we saw when he was booked against West Germany and during the 1991 FA Cup final with that tackle on Gary Charles. In many ways that act against Nottingham Forest really damaged his career. He was rash at times and it could cost him.

But no one was more popular in any side he played for. I witnessed it at close hand at Newcastle, where if he did something outstanding or scored a goal everyone couldn't wait to join with him in the celebrations. It was the same with the other clubs he played for. He also wanted everyone else to do well. He is an exceptional person as well as an exceptional player. The supporters love people who show emotion and Gazza was never lacking in that.

The way he had advanced his career it was obvious that he was going to leave Newcastle. Coincidentally, we were both involved in moving on at the same time, although we didn't share the news about where we might be heading.

We actually travelled down to London in the same car – thankfully Gazza wasn't driving, although by now he had passed his test! We had been invited down to the house of Mel Stein, who was then a lawyer acting on the potential transfers. We were shepherded into different rooms. I discovered that Gazza was due to meet Alex Ferguson, the manager of Manchester United, who wanted to sign him. I was talking to Colin Harvey, the Everton boss, about moving to Goodison Park.

Bob Cass, a North East journalist who sadly isn't with us any longer, helped set up my transfer. He phoned me to ask if I would be interested in speaking to Everton. Arthur Cox, who had been the Newcastle manager, had just moved to Derby County and also wanted to sign me but I told Bob I did fancy a move to Everton. Who needed agents when you had good old-fashioned reporters with good contacts? Bob knew everyone.

Mel spoke to both myself and Gazza before we were sent into different rooms to speak about our respective potential moves. I didn't realise until later that Alex was actually in another room in the house. Mel did very well to keep the different parties apart so they didn't bump into each other.

It's incredible now, looking back, but in the car heading back to the North East neither of us mentioned to the other who we had spoken to. It was just assumed that we had gone down to see Mel to discuss the sort of contracts we should ask for.

There might have been even more people in that house – who knows? It was an incredible day. As we know now, Gazza didn't go to Manchester United. I think he would have been brilliant for United and they would have been brilliant for him. With all due respect to Terry Venables, who I know Gazza loved as Spurs manager, Alex would have looked after Gazza better in the long term. London was also a big place for a fairly young, impressionable kid from Newcastle.

Sadly for Newcastle, it was the break-up of a promising, good young side. Both Gazza and I had been involved in meetings with Sir John Hall, who was in the process of buying the club, and his ambition was to have a team of Geordies. I was up front with him about Everton's interest. He was desperate for both of us to delay any moves while he tried to get things sorted out.

In the end though, both Gazza and I left before things really got going under Sir John. That was also disappointing for the Newcastle fans who had seen other favourites like Chris Waddle and Peter Beardsley leave.

I haven't seen Gazza too often during the past years. One of the last times was when he turned up at Tottenham when they were playing Bolton Wanderers. I was the first-team coach under Sam Allardyce. The legendary Spurs manager Bill Nicholson had just passed away and they were having a special tribute to him, with many former players invited.

When I sat on the bench just before the game, I noticed Gazza who was standing close to the dugout. I tapped him on the leg and his immediate response was: "What are you doing here?" He clearly had no idea that I was with Bolton. You could see in his face it was a different Gazza to the fun-loving young player I had originally known. It was very worrying, to be honest.

I had another chat with him in the players' lounge after the game, when he appeared more with it. At first he sounded like he was drunk but he wasn't. He just seemed in a bit of a daze at what was going on around him. He told me about his brief experience of being a coach at Boston. What shocked me was when he admitted to me that he had been terrified of speaking to the players. I thought to myself, 'Gazza, you've got no chance of being a coach or manager if you're frightened of speaking to your players.' That was amazing when you consider how he'd been as a young player – giving cheek to the senior pros.

He was also asking about what a fitness coach should do, things like that, which made you think he really didn't know anything about coaching or management. He was asking about formations. He told me he felt he had a good chance of getting the Rotherham manager's job. 'Good luck on that,' I thought, because he hadn't shown to me that he was capable of taking something like that, even though you wished him well.

It also proved that beneath all this bravado and cheek there was a vulnerability about him – that he was nervous in some situations. I think that it all boils down to him not being able to relax, chill out or switch off. He is on the go all the time. That has been the case throughout his life.

Willie McFaul

Willie McFaul was the Newcastle United manager who gave Gazza his senior full debut at St. James' Park.

Paul was the same age as my son and they played their football together as youngsters. You could see straight away Paul had a lot of talent and that was borne out throughout his career. He could do things with the ball that others couldn't match. You have to nurture that sort of ability.

Jack Charlton, when he was manager, brought Gazza on as a substitute a few times and I gave him his full debut in an away game at Southampton. I didn't even tell him he was playing until the pre-match team talk. He never let me down. He had just turned 18 and he was already something special. In many respects he was still a young boy, especially off the field. He got up to antics probably more than anyone else of his age.

You had to appreciate that came along with his overwhelming talent. On the pitch he always liked to try to do something different. As a young player he needed to be controlled and, with that in mind, it was lucky that he played alongside some very experienced players like Glenn Roeder and Paul Goddard. They really helped him.

I remember people saying he was slow as a player but what they didn't realise was how strong he was. It enabled him to hold onto the ball. It wasn't just about his skills either, he had the confidence to go with them. He was bubbly and cheeky but he was also very kind. He was always willing to help anyone with anything. But it was quite an experience being his manager. Often he would pretend he hadn't heard your instructions from the dugout. I would tell him to pass, only for him to ignore me and go on to smash the ball into the top corner. He was an incredible player but you wonder if success came too soon.

It was sad when he left Newcastle United but in the end there wasn't much we could do as a club to stop him going to Spurs. I was really disappointed and hoped at first I could change his mind. It was difficult because he had the big clubs after him. I know Alex Ferguson was desperate to take him to Manchester United. That would have been interesting if he had landed there instead of Tottenham.

Paul Montgomery

Before he became a football scout working for the likes of Jim Smith and Sir Bobby Robson, Paul Montgomery ran two palatial Newcastle nightclubs which were popular haunts for several Magpies players, including a young Paul Gascoigne, who could count on Monty to keep a lid on most of his outrageous pranks.

When I managed Tuxedo Junction, a nightclub in Newcastle popular with the Newcastle United players, Gazza was a regular. I would welcome the Newcastle players and try and look after them. When I first met him he was a bit chubby but very chirpy and full of life. His mates, including Jimmy 'Five Bellies', would often be with him. His group of Newcastle players included Paul Stephenson, Ian Bogie and Alan Thompson, who had only just recovered from a bad car crash and would come in still wearing his neck brace.

Gazza, though, was terrified of the Newcastle captain Glenn Roeder, who seemed to have a hold over him. Gazza later tried to take Glenn over to Rome with him when he joined Lazio, but in his young days he was petrified of Glenn catching him out, doing something he shouldn't be doing as a professional footballer. Gazza would always ask me to give him a nod the moment Glenn came into the club. If I told him Glenn had entered the building, Gazza would race towards the back door and scramble down the fire exit. That would be the end of his night.

The big boss of the club, Michael Quadrini, knew what Gazza was like and would often say to me: "Why do you let that idiot in all the time?" He couldn't believe what I let Gazza get away

'Anyone getting a fiver today?' A picture from the early days at Newcastle United featuring Colin Suggett *(back row, far right)*. Gazza was 'hard work at times but he was worth it'

'Where are Keegan's boots?' Gazza nearly lost Kevin Keegan's boots on a bus before his famous debut for Newcastle in1982. Gazza won the FA Youth Cup in 1985 and made his debut for the first team the same year

'I'm teaching him English' . . . Gazza with Newcastle's Brazilian striker Mirandinha

'He had everything' . . . Gazza in a Newcastle team photo from 1986 *(back row, second from left)*. Team-mates include Glenn Roeder, Paul Ferris, Neil McDonald and Paul Allon

'There were six different shots of me grabbing Gazza's luncheon box' . . .
the famous picture of Vinnie Jones with Gazza during a Wimbledon
versus Newcastle United game at Plough Lane in February, 1988

'He wanted to make people happy'
... Clowning around at a Newcastle
restaurant *(above)* and *(right)* doing
an errand with Newcastle manager
Willie McFaul

**'The kid from
Dunston'** ... Gazza
returns to open a
stand named after
him at Dunston
Federation FC

**'Is the boy ready
yet?'** ... England
boss Bobby Robson,
pictured with fellow
Geordie Chris
Waddle, always kept
an eye on how Gazza
was developing

'Poor Jimmy was often the butt of Gazza's jokes' ... with big mate Jimmy 'Five Bellies' Gardner

'We've played together for two years and you could have done that all the time' ... Gary Lineker enjoyed a joke with Gazza after the famous 1990 World Cup quarter-final win over Cameroon

'Best player in the world' ... Lining up with the England team ahead of the crunch World Cup semi-final with West Germany at Italia 90. Gazza's performances made him a global name

'Like a holiday camp' . . . signing in at Spurs with boss Terry Venables and Paul Stewart, who often stayed in the same hotel as Gazza

'It flew past David Seaman' . . . scoring that free-kick against Arsenal in the 1991 FA Cup semi-final at Wembley (*above*)

'Long neck' . . . with Steve Sedgley after the Arsenal game. Sedgley saw the funny side after a famous prank involving an ostrich

knew straight away it was serious' . . . Spurs skipper Gary Mabbutt feared the worst after the famous tackle on Nottingham Forest's Gary Charles in the 1991 FA Cup final

When the year ends in one' . . . FA Cup final song with Chas & Dave and Spurs team-mates including Gary Mabbutt, Steve Sedgley, Paul Stewart, David Howells and Paul Walsh

'The Splash' . . . Images taken by photographer Richard Pelham of a behind-closed-doors game to prove Gazza's fitness ahead of the move to Lazio

'**Everyone wanted a slice of Gazza**' . . . breaking down in tears after the defeat to West Germany at Italia 90

with. "He's your mate so sort him out," he would add. I argued that he never meant any harm, but Michael felt he was crazy.

After one night at the Junction I was begging to agree with Michael. Suddenly, the fire alarm went off and we had to evacuate the whole place. Being a Saturday, it was completely packed, but everyone had to be shepherded out onto the street. There must have been around 1,000 people outside, not happy to have had their big night out interrupted. Very quickly, there were fire engines everywhere.

Eventually, one of the fire crew discovered one of the emergency glass cases had been smashed, which automatically triggers the alarms. You only normally break them if you know there's no other solution but to call out the fire brigade. He said this broken glass case was situated close to the dance floor. I quickly located it and then noticed someone nearby who was flat out on the floor. It was Gazza, absolutely out of it after obviously drinking far too much. He had obviously thought it would be funny to set the alarm off before collapsing. I got a couple of the bar staff to pick him up and take him outside in a bid to sober him up. The trouble was he had been spotted by Michael as he was being escorted through the door.

"Look," he yelled. "It's that idiot again!"

He then turned his attentions to me and told me I was to blame for the chaos for letting Gazza into the club in the first place. I still couldn't fall out with him, even though he would try your patience at times and I would have the owner in my ear about him.

In addition to Tuxedo Junction, we soon had another nightclub which was an old cruise liner, The Tuxedo Princess, moored on the River Tyne.

Newcastle had just signed their first Brazilian player, a striker called Mirandinha. Malcolm Macdonald, the legendary Newcastle number nine, rang me up and asked if I could look after him on a night out. I told 'Super Mac' it wouldn't be a problem. Mira was staying at a city centre hotel where I would collect him and take him out. Having just arrived he could only speak three words of English: 'hello', 'beer' and 'good'. He did have an interpreter with him, though.

At first I took him to Tuxedo Junction and he enjoyed that. I told Mira that, next time, I would take him to the boat. "Good, good, good," he replied. The next week he's on the boat, sitting at the bar. The interpreter informed me that Mira liked one of the girls sitting nearby, a brunette. I said he would find it hard having a conversation with her because he only knew three English words. The interpreter said he would help and for me to ask her whether she would like a drink. I introduced her to Mira and the interpreter, Carlos. She said she would love a gin and tonic. Mirandinha then makes a suggestive sign with his arms and blurts out: "Hairy pie." She is immediately taken back and asks me to repeat what he has just said. I tried to cover up for him and told her he had asked: "How are you?" She might have misheard because of his accent. Anyway, panic over, she takes her drink and there's a bit of conversation. A few minutes later he looks her straight in the face and again says "hairy pie" – which in Geordie terminology refers to the most private part of a feminine body.

It was too much for the poor girl. She whacks Mira with a punch which sends him flying off his chair. He's now on the floor, completely stunned and wondering what he had done to deserve that. The interpreter is confused and she storms off.

Once he got up, I explained to him what he had said, that he had insulted the girl. He just utters: "Fucking Gazza." It appeared his English had now incorporated an extra word.

I was still none the wiser until Gazza turned up a few days later at Tuxedo Junction. I told him I needed a word and related what had happened to Mirandinha. Gazza revealed he had told Mira in the dressing room one day that if he saw a girl he fancied to say "hairy pie" because it was another way of saying: "You are beautiful." The next time I saw Mira he had learned more English, informing me: "Gazza fucking loco!"

Despite some of the outrageous pranks he played, no one could fall out with Gazza. There was a night when he somehow managed to open up a mate's car, which was parked on a fairly steep bank close to the Tuxedo Princess, and released the hand-brake. He felt it was hilarious to see the car roll down the road and straight into the river.

Another time, at the Junction we had tables with old-style telephones where you could ring up another table if someone caught your fancy. One night, Gazza was in typical fun mood and he had heard a guy with a foreign-sounding accent sitting by himself on one of the tables. Gazza worked out the number of his table and rang a girl on a nearby table in the same accent, telling her how wonderful her breasts were. The girl slammed the phone down in disgust. Gazza quickly rang again and in the same accent told her what table he was on and adding that he would love to take a closer look at her breasts. The next thing the girl goes over to the poor bloke who hadn't got a clue about what had been going on and gives him a load of abuse after accusing him of making lewd suggestions. After witnessing the reaction, Gazza just fell about laughing his head off.

I've seen him on a few occasions in the past few years. I now run a hotel near Hartlepool close to the sea, which he likes because he loves to go fishing. He once came and signed a few copies of his autobiography for some of the locals, which was fantastic.

I was sorry to see him leave Newcastle when he did. Too many of the top players were sold during that era, stars like Chris Waddle and Peter Beardsley. The two nightclubs I ran were a bit quieter without him, mind, and there was less earache from Michael Quadrini!

John Gibson

John Gibson is a legendary football writer in the North East. Originally a Newcastle United correspondent for the local Evening Chronicle, he later became the paper's executive sports editor and also enjoyed a spell as owner of Gateshead FC. As a host of numerous talk-ins involving sporting personalities in the Newcastle area, he enjoyed a close relationship with Gazza.

I'd known Paul throughout his long and colourful journey, from a fresh-faced cheeky kid receiving a trophy from me at the local social club, through his great years when I visited him at his luxury villa in Rome and late on in his playing days when he came riding to my rescue to help raise funds to save Gateshead, his hometown football club. He was totally unpredictable, sometimes infuriating, but always fun. One night at Ponteland Social Club, Paul ended the session by sitting down at the organ which was on the stage and belting out rock and roll numbers like Little Richard. How the audience loved him.

I arranged to pick him up at Jesmond Tennis Club to do a chat show in Ashington. I emphasised the time and the importance of not keeping the audience waiting and Gazza agreed. When I walked through the gate, there was Paul still on court playing mixed doubles. He winked, won a couple of points to win the match, and ran across with sweat pouring off him. Inevitably, he had forgotten his suit. It was back home in Dunston, which meant a trip across town for him to get changed.

He drove like someone demented, waving cheerily to everyone on every street corner until we made it to his house. Upstairs, he ran about shouting to his mam for his newly-ironed shirt, only to discover that his dad had put it on and gone off to the pub. Eventually, Gazza emerged to inform me that we would have to go around to his girlfriend's – he had left the jacket of his suit there the night before. By now I was bordering on hysteria. The drive to Ashington seemed to take an eternity and we were met outside the club by a bunch of harassed officials looking in desperation for any sign of us. But on stage he was soon charming the audience with a succession of daft stories.

There was also a sensitive side to him. We did a gig at Morpeth which included another former Newcastle player, Paul Goddard, and as usual Gazza had them in stitches until someone asked him about the money he had supposedly been offered for him to stay at Newcastle.

"I'm an out-of-work miner who spends all my dole money to watch you on a Saturday," said the punter. "Yet you turn down £2,000 a week to stay at the club."

Gazza answered quickly and I wrapped the show up before we both left the stage. Gazza then went missing with a queue of fans waiting for autographs. I set off looking for him. He had locked himself in a toilet cubicle and there were tears rolling down his cheeks. The realisation that a fan could think a working-class lad like himself was too big for his boots destroyed him.

When he had moved to Lazio, I arranged to go and see him. *The Chronicle* had booked me into a hotel but Paul was having none of that. He moved me into his villa for the duration of my stay. He was obsessed by motorbikes. At that time in Rome he had nine! But Lazio quickly banned him from driving to the training ground on them. Not to be denied, one day he donned a German Second World War helmet and drove through the choking Rome traffic like a maniac, with his dad and me in a vehicle behind him. He then parked his bike in a garage just around the corner from Lazio's training ground and leapt into our car to finally arrive there, all sweetness and light.

I spent 11 years as owner of Gateshead FC and, during one season, we hit massive financial problems when our main sponsor pulled out. I unashamedly called on my friends in football to help bail us out. Alan Shearer did a talk-in free of charge and Gazza fronted a sporting dinner for nothing. He sold out 750 tickets at 30-odd quid a head in 24 hours. At the dinner I got the Gazza treatment. When my back was turned as I made announcements on the mic, Paul would move in, peppering my steak, spiking my drink and generally causing chaos, to the amusement of the punters.

During the build-up to the dinner, Gazza had got Stan Ternent, his manager at Burnley, to ring me at *The Chronicle*. I picked up the phone.

"John Gibson? I'm Stan Ternent. I believe you have Gazza up next week for a dinner. I'm afraid he won't be able to make it because it's international week and I'm taking all the players away to Spain for warm weather training." I almost burst a blood vessel until I heard guffawing in the background. Gazza had asked his boss to set me up as a joke. But later on, both Gazza and Stan were on the top table and Gateshead was saved.

Paul Ferris

Paul Ferris became Newcastle United's youngest ever player at the age of 16 years and 294 days and was tipped to be the new George Best until injury struck. He became a respected physio returning to Newcastle under Kevin Keegan. He qualified as a barrister and wrote a compelling autobiography 'The Boy On The Shed'.

The pass didn't come. There was no one-two. I was clear through on goal. Instead my team-mate just stopped and put his foot on the ball. He then stared straight at me and shouted: "Fuck off. If you don't pass to me then I'm not passing to you." With that he turned his back on me and passed the ball in the opposite direction. I'd never experienced that before or since on a football pitch.

We won the game and I knew I'd done enough to impress but I was still troubled by what had happened. We were in the old clubhouse and I brought my coke over to the table where he was sitting. He was younger than me, 14 maybe. He was sitting at the centre of the group holding court and telling stories. He seemed very popular with the other boys.

As I approached, he looked up. I was ready for the fight. He stood up so that he was in my face now. He was a little smaller than me, had chubby cheeks that were still red from the exertions of the game. His teenage spots were inflamed and looked like mini craters ready to erupt at any second. He had a crooked smile. He was smiling at me. He held out his hand. "Sorry about that before mate. I was just a bit pissed off when you didn't pass to us the first time. No hard feelings man. You played really well. Have me seat and I'll grab another one. What's your name again, mate?"

His apology was warm and sincere and his smile was infectious. I switched my coke into my left hand and shook his firmly with my right. "I'm Paul. Paul Ferris. What's your name?" He let go of my hand and dragged a chair and placed it next to the one he had vacated. We sat down. "I'm Paul, too. Paul Gascoigne. Me friends call me Gazza."

That was my introduction to Gazza. After that, despite all the many pranks, you couldn't help but like him.

Newcastle went on a trip to Bermuda and we were staying in a beautiful hotel. Outside there was a swimming pool and there were people in it and others lying either side of it. Gazza had his full Newcastle United tracksuit on. He then climbed onto the top of the diving board and dropped into the water. He didn't look at anyone or tell anyone what he was about to do. It was just him. He was excited to be there.

Alex Smailes

Alex Smailes was Liverpool's much-respected North East scout for years and helped various Anfield managers sign their transfer targets. One of his biggest signing coups was Peter Beardsley and it was so near and yet so far with Paul Gascoigne.

I was a regular visitor to St. James' Park on scouting missions for Liverpool and you saw straight away what a talent Gazza was.

I knew all about his reputation off the field but that didn't put me off. It just needed someone to sort him out and I had no doubt that Kenny Dalglish, who was Liverpool's manager, would be up for that.

I had already been involved in trying to take another Newcastle player to Anfield, Peter Beardsley, something which we were able to complete. Through my growing association with Peter I got to know Gazza quite well.

The interest in Peter had begun through chatting with Kenny and other members of the Liverpool staff when I met them in the team hotel on their trips up to the North East. I told Kenny that I felt Liverpool would have a chance of signing him because every time I went to the Newcastle training ground Peter was asking for Liverpool programmes and other things connected with the club. Sure enough, a few months later, after several phone calls between the interested parties including myself, Peter was on his way to join Liverpool. On a personal level, I was just pleased that the groundwork for the potential deal had been successful.

A little later Kenny's interest was extended to Gazza. He asked me how well did I know him and whether there was a chance of him meeting the player. Gazza was up for it and so I met him at the Washington Services just off the A1, close to Newcastle. I then took him to an office in Washington and set up a telephone conversation with Kenny which must have lasted around half an hour and proved that Gazza quite fancied the idea of joining Liverpool.

After it had finished I asked Gazza how did he feel about Kenny and he answered: "Absolutely brilliant." Both Kenny and I thought we were in to be quite honest, that he would soon become a Liverpool player. I think it all changed when Chris Waddle came up the next weekend. He was then a Spurs player and it appears that he persuaded Gazza not to do anything until he had spoken with the Tottenham manager Terry Venables.

These clandestine arrangements were common place in those days. The managers knew it went on even if they weren't happy. Willie McFaul, the Newcastle manager who I got on well with, once poured me a whisky and said I was a 'twat' for luring Peter Beardsley away to Liverpool. I retaliated by saying he had tried to tap Bryan Robson. "How do you know that?" he said looking as guilty as hell.

The non-league club I was associated with, West Allotment Celtic, were training at a stately home in the area called Back-worth Hall and that's where I made the call to Gazza's house after he had told me to ring him. His sister Lindsay answered and told me Paul was in London. I never gave it a second thought that we were on the verge of losing him to Spurs.

I then received a call from a national newspaper journalist asking me if I had heard Gazza was in talks with Tottenham. I had to keep quiet my disappointment and not to let on that Liverpool had been on the verge of signing him. Deep down I'm gutted wondering what had gone on but it was one of those things – you win some, you lose some – although I was really surprised after it had appeared to have gone so well with Kenny.

It didn't change my opinion of Gazza. He was someone you could never fall out with. He couldn't do enough for you at times. I remember one Friday night he had nothing to do and I asked him to come and watch West Allotment Celtic who were playing in a local cup final. He said he would love to. Not only did he come along but he did some of the physio massages and rubs on the players. You can imagine the surprised looks on the players' faces when they discovered who was their famous masseur for the day.

Another evening, Jim Pearson, a long time friend who used to play for Everton, was involved with Ian Rush on the sports gear side and told me they were meeting at the George Washington Hotel in Washington and did I want to join them.

There was a splendid buffet laid on for the hotel guests. Suddenly Gazza appeared from the snooker room where he had been playing and helped himself to a chicken leg. He went off with that cheeky grin like a kid who couldn't resist doing something he knew he shouldn't.

Of course, looking back, I wish he had joined Liverpool. I know it was a massive disappointment for Kenny Dalglish. I know Kenny would have been the kind of person he would have responded to and maybe prevented him from doing some of the daft things in his career. I still blame Chris Waddle for us missing out.

Gazza has always known how frustrated I was at him not joining Liverpool. One evening I was in the Metrocentre doing some shopping and, going past WHSmith, I noticed there were hordes of people milling around. I wondered what was going on.

I asked someone who explained it was Paul Gascoigne who was in there signing his book. I decided to go and buy one but two security guys wouldn't let me into the shop because the signing session had finished. The next thing I could hear Gazza's voice: "Let the so and so in!" came over loud and clear. He then signed the book: 'To Alex. I nearly signed for Liverpool. Sorry mate. Paul Gascoigne.'

Alastair Garvie

Alastair Garvie was Gazza's first agent after getting to know him in his earlier role as Newcastle United assistant secretary. He helped supervise his British record transfer from St. James' Park to Tottenham. But the pair soon parted and while many fellow agents went on to become millionaires, Alastair struggled financially and at one stage became a lollipop man.

I was the assistant secretary of Newcastle United when Paul Gascoigne signed as an apprentice with the club. His signing was pushed by Brian Watson, who had helped discover a few young players for Newcastle, and the former St. James' Park manager Joe Harvey, who was now the chief scout. It was very unusual for a young apprentice to be signed in the boardroom.

The club must have felt they were bringing in someone very special, despite the fact there were stories circulating that he was a bit lively off the pitch and was liable to be involved in a few pranks. Nothing nasty, just a few fun and games.

I saw him go into the boardroom because my office was close by and my door was open. I was initially surprised at all the fuss being made but I then quickly discovered a number of other clubs had been on his trail. I'd never seen an apprentice being given this sort of welcome before. Brian had raved about him and was desperate for Newcastle to sign him.

I didn't really have anything to do with him at first. I was friendly with Glenn Roeder, who Newcastle had signed from QPR, and had helped him out with a number of things. I soon decided to leave Newcastle and become Glenn's full-time agent. A little later he told me I should take on Paul. I also began to represent another Newcastle player, Chris Waddle. When I took on Paul I didn't realise really just how good a player he was and how he would develop. I did it because of my relationship with Glenn, who did see the potential in him.

I then started to get more involved with Paul. I took him out and about around the Newcastle area, getting him involved in a number of different activities. He enjoyed coming with me to the Durham ice rink, for instance, where Durham Wasps played. He did a number of presentations there and seemed to really enjoy the sport. We would go off to different colleges for various things. Despite still being young, nothing bothered him. He mixed well with people. Paul always had something special about him. He also liked other sports. He knew I played cricket at a decent level and that helped us get on. He had respect for people who were decent at other sports. It wasn't always about football for him.

Chris Waddle was older but, by contrast, was very shy and quiet at first. He wasn't as natural as Paul. But he eventually warmed to going out, like Gazza, to a number of events. I think it helped his football because he became more outgoing on and off the pitch. I believe the fact that Sunderland had originally rejected him stuck with him for a few years.

Luckily for me, I didn't fall victim to some of Paul's antics like other people around him. The worst thing that happened to me in those early years was having to go off and purchase a packet of condoms! He was playing for the England Under-21s against Scotland in Aberdeen. After the game he came over and asked me to do him a favour. "Can you get me a packet of Durex?" So off I went to the nearest pub and went into the toilets and duly bought a packet of condoms from the machine.

When he was with me I never had a problem with him. He listened then to people who he trusted. There were some good people around him during his Newcastle days, including his big mate Jimmy 'Five Bellies' Gardner. I used to help Jimmy out a few times. He never had much money so through my connections I would procure training gear and he would sell it on to make a bit of money. Jimmy would often come with Paul and I to the events I had arranged. They were great mates, inseparable.

His reputation on the pitch was quickly growing and it wasn't long before the big clubs started registering their interest in trying to sign him. Alex Smailes, a North East-based scout for Liverpool who I knew, informed me on a number of occasions that their manager Kenny Dalglish would love to take Paul to Anfield.

Manchester United were desperate to beat everyone to his signature – so much so that a secret meeting without Newcastle's knowledge was arranged in London at Mel Stein's house. Mel was a lawyer who I had got to know through arranging matchday tickets for him. Mel, despite being based in London, was a big Newcastle United fan. In any transfer we were going to use Mel's legal expertise.

Alex Ferguson, the Manchester United manager, was anxious to have a chat with Paul so we all got together at Mel's house. I never tried to persuade Paul what to do – it was left entirely to him about which club he wanted to join. But I believe that, unknown to me, Mel was in Paul's ear all the time telling him about Tottenham and their manager Terry Venables. Little did I know what would happen later on, Paul leaving me to take on Mel as his representative. I should have seen it coming.

In hindsight, Paul should have joined either Manchester United or Liverpool. There's no doubt in my mind that it was a mistake him going to London. Alex left the meeting thinking he had a chance of signing him but he also knew he still had to see off the likes of Liverpool and Tottenham. Spurs suddenly entered the race when I received a phone call from their chairman, Irving Scholar, who I knew from my days at Newcastle. Then came the regular calls from Terry Venables. It was obvious he wasn't going to take no for an answer. I sensed then that Paul was going to end up at Tottenham, especially if he was going to have the chance to meet Terry.

But out of the blue I was called to a meeting of the Newcastle directors in a hotel just outside Durham. They wanted him to sign a new contract. I imagine it was to try and increase the transfer fee. We didn't want that because by then Paul wanted to leave to further his career.

So it was off to Tottenham with a very favourable contract which included bonuses if he was called up by England – which happened early on in his first season there.

It started to become more difficult for me to look after his affairs with Paul now in North London while I was based in Durham. I made regular trips down south because Chris Waddle, who I still represented, was also at Spurs now.

Paul had surrounded himself with a few rogues and there were a number of incidents in the hotel Tottenham had booked him and his entourage into. There were so many pranks that they were advised to leave and find another hotel, which didn't go down too well with the club.

Even at Newcastle there had been a few escapades which had seen Gazza told off. Once, he and some of his mates decided to go shooting birds with shotguns at the club's training ground, which resulted in a severe ticking-off.

At times he just couldn't help himself. Being let loose in an upmarket hotel proved to be too much of a temptation. Nothing was done in a nasty manner, though. It was always just a bit of fun for him.

I never asked any of my players to sign a contract or legal bits of paper. I promised them if they ever wanted to move on then they were free to do so.

Around six months after joining Spurs, in which time he had made his England debut, he rang and said he wanted to leave me. I wasn't surprised, I knew what had been going on. Mel Stein had been slowly moving in on Gazza. Really, I should have had someone in London helping me, but I placed my trust in people like Mel.

Mel never phoned me. There was no letter from him explaining what had happened. I have never heard a single peep from him. I don't blame Paul. I was never going to stand in his way if that's what he wanted. It was a double whammy because Chris Waddle also left to join up with another agent, Dennis Roach.

After that, I was left to watch the pair from afar while their agents made loads of money off the back of them. What upsets me about Mel is that he would never have known Paul without me. He had no connections at all in the football world until I started getting Newcastle United tickets for him.

Yes, at times it was hard knowing the sort of money that would be circulating, especially when Paul left Spurs for Lazio, but by then I was resigned to my fate. I knew Mel and his associates would be receiving a nice fee but that's life. By then there was nothing I could have done.

It's been a real struggle financially at times, I don't mind admitting that. At one stage I became a crossing warden or, as they are more commonly known, a lollipop man. I wasn't ashamed at all – I actually enjoyed it. Yes, it might have been some comedown for many people but it placed a smile on my face trying to keep kids and their mothers safe.

If only they had known who was holding up that 'Stop' sign – a man who helped put Paul Gascoigne on the road to fame and fortune, someone who was involved in the £2.2 million move, then a British transfer record, of the player from Newcastle to Spurs. I only gave the job up because I suffered a bad fall and wasn't able to continue. Safe to say I wasn't a lollipop man for the money.

I can't stress enough that Paul for me was never a problem. His biggest problem is that there have often been people surrounding him whose objective is simply to make money from him. That's a real shame because he was just a likely lad who enjoyed playing jokes but was never nasty. I'm just glad I was able to hopefully help him in his formative years.

Alan Oliver

Alan Oliver was the football reporter for the Newcastle Evening Chronicle during the Gazza years and covered his emergence from the Magpies' FA Youth Cup-winning side into the senior team. As he quickly discovered, the player was as much of a handful off the field as he was on it.

When Gazza broke into the Newcastle first team, the chances of me getting off at the right train station when coming home from games in London were dramatically reduced. The media would always come back to the North East on the same train as the team after playing the likes of Tottenham, Chelsea and West Ham. Whereas they were all heading for Newcastle Central, my stop was Durham, the one before Newcastle.

As we started to approach Durham station, Gazza would suddenly appear, usually with another young player, Neil McDonald. They would then dive on top of me to try to prevent me getting off at my station. If they succeeded then I had no choice but to end up at Newcastle and try to get a lift or a taxi back to the Durham area. Gazza couldn't help himself, he just loved it if he kept me on the train. You just had to take it and look to get your own back if you could.

But these were great days when the players and the managerial staff would mix freely with the regular reporters on the Newcastle beat. There was a fantastic trust. As reporters we would turn a blind eye to some of the mad pranks – often started by Gazza. In return they would never refuse an interview. Even though he was still in his teenage years, Gazza was fantastic to deal with. He always knew we had a job to do and would always make himself available, so it was worth being on the wrong end of one of his japes.

One day we were coming back from Italy after an Anglo-Italian game. I fell asleep and when I woke up, as we were about to come into land at Newcastle Airport, I discovered I only had one shoe. It didn't take me long to realise who was behind this but Gazza continually denied he had taken it. I ended up getting off the plane and having to walk through passport control and customs wearing just one shoe, much to the amusement of the Newcastle players, staff and fellow media members.

A few days later I collared Gazza and asked him to come clean about what he had done with my shoe. "Ah, I didn't think you'd want it so I threw it in the Tyne!" he chortled. But you couldn't get upset with him. He didn't mean any real harm. It was just good, harmless fun to him. I got on great with him.

When he first burst onto the scene he didn't have a phone at home. If I wanted to do an interview with him in the week, I would ring the football club and pass on a message for Gazza to ring me later at home, usually in the evening. Sure enough, good as gold, Gazza would leave his house and walk down to Dunston Working Men's Club and use their phone to ring me. If my wife answered the phone, the voice on the other end would ask for me. She would then ask who was speaking. "It's Paul," he would reply very politely and respectfully.

As a player, even in those days, he was exceptional. I watched him make his debut at Southampton and, straight away, you could see he had something extra from the other players, nearly all of whom were far more experienced. He just went from strength to strength. The sad thing was at the time we just eventually said goodbye to the all the best players. Peter Beardsley left, Chris Waddle left and then inevitably so did Gazza.

At least I was able to get off at the right station when he headed for Spurs!

3

'The head groundsman was having problems with pigeons. So Gazza decided to climb up the main stand to get rid of them. The next thing we see is Gazza falling through a plank of rotten wood, hanging onto a girder around 40 feet up!'

– David Howells, former Tottenham Hotspur team-mate

Paul Stewart

Paul Stewart shared a hotel and a house with Gazza after the pair joined Tottenham at the same time. Tasked with being the playmaker's 'minder' at White Hart Lane, Paul is still someone he turns to in times of need.

After securing the move to Tottenham in 1988, I had a quick honeymoon in Cyprus during the summer, and then moved down to London. The club was obliged to put me up during the first three months of my move until we found a house, so they sorted out a room in the Swallow Hotel in Waltham Abbey. Gazza was staying with me as he'd arrived at the same time. With my wife still living in Blackpool, it meant that me and Gazza were often left to our own devices. Sometimes, we were joined by other players. We would get up to all sorts of antics. It was like a holiday camp at times; you can say it encouraged team morale, but there was a downside.

There was one occasion when we were staying in the hotel when Gazza ran up a £25,000 bar bill. I wasn't around but apparently he had invited all his family around to stay and then left the club to pick up the drinks tab. Terry Venables took us to one side and asked us to explain what had happened. Paul wasn't bothered. There were some mini milk cartons on a tray and he spent the time ignoring the boss and firing them over at a few of the press lads. Instead, the boss directed his questions at me, as often happened. "What's been going on – how are we expected to pay this?" As if I could do anything about it.

Every day he would be up to something, causing havoc with his jokes. I got on well with Steve Sedgley, who later joined us from Coventry City and who we both knew from the England youth and Under-21 set-up. He was nicknamed 'Long Neck' for obvious reasons.

One day, whilst Venners was taking training, all the players were on the pitch in a circle around the halfway line. Gazza was late. As always, the boss was asking me where he was, like I was his minder. Just as I was about to make an excuse, Gazza turned up with someone alongside him, carrying a brown sack. The sack was moving as if something was in it, and just as Venners was about to rollick Gazza for being late, the bag was opened and an ostrich ran out wearing a Spurs shirt. There was a number 7 and SEDGLEY written on the back. The lads just fell about laughing. This ostrich was running around our training ground in a white Spurs shirt, with the whole team watching. Everyone, the kids, the training staff, the apprentices, stood open mouthed or in hysterics. Venables' face was a picture. The bird went running off in a panic and he had some job getting it back. I am not too sure what the animal rights people would say if they knew that Gazza had a bird from the local zoo dressed in a Spurs shirt loose on the training ground. He claimed that he had 'borrowed' it from Broxbourne Zoo. We were never able to verify if that was the case.

During the summer of 1989, Ireland was one of Spurs' pre-season destinations. Gary Lineker was big news at the time. He had just joined us from Barcelona and he scored his first goal for Tottenham against Cork City at Musgrave Park. In the build-up to that game, we told the boss that we were going to take Gazza fishing. It was before Italia 90, so he was not at the peak of his fame, but he still loved to get away from it all. Of course, it just turned into an excuse to go for a drink.

We were in Mayo, in the west of Ireland. We called a taxi but when the guy turned up to give us a lift I thought, 'he's steaming drunk', which is never a good quality in a driver. But he was determined to give us the full tour and to get us to the three pubs in Bohola. There is a famous song about the place:

There's three pubs in Bohola, as everybody knows
MacDonald's, Clarke's and Roche's,
where the craic like honey flows.
And lovely Mary's here with me, I never more will roam
Mayo how I love you, Bohola my dear home.

He was giving us all the patter about the local sights and told us "Jack Charlton fishes here" – which I suspect you might get everywhere you go in Ireland. Then he said: "Let's go to see my mum first." We thought, 'You what?' But I think she must have been expecting the entire Spurs team – there was a massive spread of food, which was very good of her. Her son then wanted to take us around the famous 'three pubs' where everyone was desperate to get their photo taken with Gazza. We were a bit of a sideshow really, but it was a great laugh. By the end of the afternoon, we were all legless but we knew we had to go back to the team hotel for the evening meal.

The taxi driver/tour guide had been drinking with us through the afternoon and we asked him: "Are you sure you are going to be able to drive us back?"

"Sure, no bother," came the reply before he took another gulp of his drink. We just laughed.

Then we thought, 'what about the afternoon angling? The boss will be suspicious . . .'

We came up with a plan to stop at a fishmonger's on the way back, where we bought a frozen trout. It was so obvious we had not caught it – it had been gutted – but we took Gazza down to the river for a photo and hooked the fish on the rod. He was beaming with his prize catch. It was the one that didn't get away and indeed had not been away anywhere for some time – apart from a freezer compartment.

It was clear for everyone to see what we had been up to, but we took it back to the team hotel anyway. I am sure nobody believed us but it was such a funny story that they all just went along with it.

Off the pitch, Paul was a strange combination; shy, but a real practical joker; one of the brightest young talents in the game, but so insecure as a person; generous, funny, apparently happy-go-lucky, but riven by strange habits, doubts, medical conditions, quirks of character. In the early days, if we went out for something to eat together, he would finish off his main meal then he'd order three desserts and make himself ill. I never understood. It was hard for me to know even what to say. I had not seen anything like that before. It became an everyday aspect of life with Paul Gascoigne.

At home, Gazza's behaviour was just as bizarre. He was showing the first signs of his obsessive compulsive disorder. If we were driving to a game together – which we often did, as we were sharing a house – he would tap the rear view mirror all the time because it had to be exact, precise for him. He had to do things his way.

On other occasions, no matter how important the match was, he would want to return home. It could be Manchester United, but he would make me turn back to check if he had locked the door, or if the remote for the TV was in alignment. He would go upstairs to the bathroom to see if the towels were straight.

One day, we were running really late for a game. I was driving to White Hart Lane on the A10 and he said he had forgotten something and insisted we go back, which meant driving the wrong way down a dual carriageway. He had a wallet with a flap where he kept his credit cards. He was holding this wallet up in the front seat, pretending it was a police warrant card while I was flooring it because we were so late. We were meant to be at the ground an hour before the games but we were so late they had already been on the phone asking where we were.

Even after he left the club, and was living in Italy, Gazza would regularly come back for a night out. One of my favourite ever Gazza tales came after he had left Spurs for Lazio. When he returned to the UK, he would stay in a hotel near Hyde Park where the manager was a mad-keen Spurs fan. He loved Gazza so much that all the Tottenham players got to stay for free.

In one visit home, Gazza took the manager out for the night, got him drunk, somehow found his passport, flew him back to Rome and, en route, shaved off all the fella's hair and eyebrows. He woke up in Gazza's place in Italy not having a clue where he was, or how he had got there. Then he looked in the mirror to discover all his hair and eyebrows had gone as well. When he looked to Paul for an explanation, there came back the usual answer: "It was for a laugh."

Gazza could be friendly, generous to a fault, but fame could lead to trouble. And often through no fault of his own. One time, quite early during our time together at Spurs, he came up to Blackpool for the opening of Lineker's Bar. He was on crutches from the injury sustained in the Cup final and we were asked to go to the opening night as a favour. At the launch night, two lads came up to Paul and asked him if he would buy them a drink – but he explained he was not going to the bar because he was on crutches. Next morning at 9am there was a police officer at my door saying two men had reported an altercation with Paul. One of the lads claimed the two of us had beaten him up and broken his jaw. I told them: "Nothing could be further from the truth, Paul is on crutches."

They still took Paul into one room to be interviewed, and I had to go into another to face various questions about the night before. You would think that common sense would have told you Gazza could not beat up someone on crutches. But he still had to go through a police interview, albeit an 'informal' one at our home. It turned out the lads who had gone to Lineker's had left, gone down the road, got drunk, with one hitting the other in order to sell the 'Gazza brawl' story to the papers. Paul was being set up. It did make him paranoid and, in my opinion, understandably so.

Gazza's eccentric behaviour continued long after the Spurs days. He rang me one Friday night after I had finished playing – my daughter Chloe was still at school, it was around 2001. I used to go out on a Friday with my mates, so I turned the phone off. He called about eight o'clock at night. I did not phone back, then at 8am when I turned the phone on again I found I had been bombarded with calls from him and messages on the answerphone saying he was coming to Blackpool to see me. Then there were a series of messages asking: "Where do you live?"

Around lunchtime the next day, he arrived and I said: "How did you find me?" He got someone to drive him up to Blackpool from London, and went into the Tesco down the road. He just went in and started shouting: "Does anyone know where Stewy lives?" Unbelievably, there was a mate of mine in there who saw him and said: "I know, it is North Park Drive but I don't know the number."

So Gazza came to the top of the street, looking in windows to see if he could see any photos of my kids on the mantelpiece. One poor fella found a slightly drunk Gazza looking through his window first thing in the morning shouting: "Have you any idea where Stewy lives?"

When Gazza eventually turned up at my home, it was a lovely summer's day so we had a BBQ in the back garden. For a bit of fun, he started going through his phone ringing up famous people. Eventually he got through to Robbie Williams and made him sing his hit 'Millennium' down the phone to Chloe and her school friend, who could not quite believe it. Chloe recalls Gazza encouraging her to cycle down the drive, while he waited at the bottom to stop the traffic in case she came onto the road. He tried to take a photo. It didn't work, so he just threw away the camera. He was full of fun, full of laughs, a great fella just to be around when he was on form. But he was also completely unpredictable, hard to fathom and a nervous wreck at times.

When he was ringing random people on his phone, he could not get through to TV presenter Dale Winton. So he left a load of abuse on his answering service because he didn't answer straight away. I am still not sure why he had the number for Dale – but that was Gazza, totally unpredictable and capable of doing anything at any time.

Along with other ex-players, I was invited to Spurs' final game of the season in May 2017. They wanted the legends to reunite to say farewell to White Hart Lane – but Gazza wasn't there. The fans didn't forget him and it was touching when they chanted: "There's only one Paul Gascoigne."

I was honoured to be invited and it was a privilege to be there, to see some old friends and to say my goodbyes to a stadium that held so many happy memories for me. I was as close to Gazza as anyone at Spurs and it was a shame, but no surprise, that he wasn't there.

These days, Gazza still gets in touch. I can be in a meeting when I hear my phone go.

'NO CALLER ID' flashes up and I know exactly who it is and why he is calling. I know it is Gazza and he is back on the drink. If I can't take the call due to work or if I'm with someone, then I may get a text.

When he has been in rehab then it worries me. He will text me his new number, and I know there will be times when I cannot keep taking the calls because he is incomprehensible. The calls may start with "I love you, you are like my brother" to the other extreme, threats of violence, threats to knock me out. I can get annoyed because when he calls he will say things like: "I am going to end my life. I am 300 miles away and you cannot do anything about it."

The calls can be at three, four, five in the morning; you fear it could be bad news so you take the call and you have that desperate realisation he has been drinking again.

I know better than anyone that you can't subject your body to that sort of abuse. It means you will pay a price. When Paul is in drink, when he calls, I think he wants me to be a father to him. There are so many things I want to say, but under the circumstances, it is often difficult.

I want to say: "Look at me; I have managed to kick the drugs habit and don't end up feeling like I need to drink. What made you great was your ability to deal with any situation. You did it after battling with your knee injury for all that time. I cannot remember you ever letting anything beat you in your entire career – why are you letting this beat you now? I cannot believe you are giving in to this. You are a different man in drink, Paul, and when you call, you are too far gone to listen. I hope you listen to me now."

Doug Livermore

Doug Livermore was assistant manager to Terry Venables and spent many hours on the training ground with an obsessive Gazza who never wanted the sessions to end. He was often given the unenviable job of having to track down the England midfielder, earning the moniker 'The Detective'.

We signed him from Newcastle and you could see straight away that he was a lively character and a very good player who quickly turned into a top-class footballer – almost certainly one of the best in the world.

We knew there were other clubs in for him when it appeared that Newcastle were ready to sell but I knew once Terry Venables was able to talk to him that would be it. Terry was a great man-manager who would have convinced Gazza that Tottenham was the right place for him, where he could develop his game and also enjoy himself. I don't think he ever regretted that decision to join Spurs.

Gazza just wanted to get better and better and the biggest

problem was telling him to stop, that he had done enough in training every day.

Most of the days, once the first-team sessions had finished, Gazza wanted to stay behind and do extra routines. They would usually involve me working with him and so Terry would often say to not let him do too much. "Okay gaffer," I would reply – knowing that was easier said than done. So off we would go onto one of the pitches with a bag of footballs. Gazza would then practise his volleys, his headers, everything you can imagine. He had an obsession about trying to be the best.

If our first-team keeper Erik Thorstvedt was around, he would ask big Erik to go in goal while he practised his free-kicks. Then Gazza would tease him telling where he was going to put them. "Your top left, Big Nose," . . . "top right now, Big Nose," he chortled. Sure enough, poor Erik would be scrambling around unable to get near most of them.

After a while I'd have to intervene. "Come on Gazza that's enough. The gaffer doesn't want you to overdo it." He'd plead: "Just a couple more." "No, that's your lot," I'd reply. So off he would go while I collected the balls. But one day I looked over in the distance where Ray Clemence, who was then the reserve team coach, was putting his lads through their paces playing possession football. Who had sneaked onto the pitch? Gazza! He saw me advancing towards the pitch and suddenly tried to hide as far away as he could behind some of the players.

I told Clem that he shouldn't be on the pitch. "Dougie, I couldn't stop him, he just joined in," Clem replied. We gave him another five minutes and he finally reluctantly came off. He just loved his football.

He was great with the younger players at the club and would

encourage and help them whenever he could. Often he would challenge a couple of them to try and get the ball off him while he attempted to shield it. It was impossible for them – I don't think I ever saw him lose possession. He knew as well as helping them he was also improving his own game, being able to ward off his markers in actual first-team matches.

The happiest you ever saw him was on a football field. It was the one time he could be himself, unable to get up to any mischief. Besides being an outstanding player he was also a winner. He never accepted second best.

He was great with the fans who came to the training ground. Often you would see him taking his training gear off and handing it to the supporters. He was always very generous with an infectious character. He was a pleasure to work with. You couldn't have a more willing worker.

The main reason we went on to win the 1991 FA Cup was Gazza. We were in trouble in the fifth round against Portsmouth at Fratton Park. We were 1-0 down and not playing well. Terry and I were on the bench along with the substitutes. They were all shouting, "Give the ball to Gazza."

The next thing, Gazza pulls the game out of the fire and scores two top-class goals and we sneak into the sixth round on the back of a 2-1 victory. To be able to do that you've got to have some talent in the locker.

Yes, he was mischievous off the field at times but Terry and I never saw him as a huge problem. Gazza used to call me 'The Detective' because I was usually given the job of trying to track him down if Terry needed to speak to him. I'd get the call from Terry, asking me to contact Gazza because he needed to speak to him in the morning.

The nickname arose when one day I managed to find him playing snooker with some of his mates. When he saw me he just blurted out, "Oh, here he comes, the detective!"

On the field, Gazza certainly reaped the rewards of staying behind on the training pitch and pinging free-kicks past Erik Thorstvedt with that fantastic goal against Arsenal at Wembley in the FA Cup semi-final. It flew past David Seaman to help us on our way to a 3-1 win against our local rivals.

It's just a pity the way it went for Gazza in the final when he suffered that horrific injury. It was hard to put that to one side but in the dressing room as we celebrated the extra time victory against Nottingham Forest our thoughts quickly turned to Gazza. He had been taken to the Princess Grace Hospital in Marylebone and with Terry off doing his media duties, Gary Mabbutt and Gary Lineker came up to me and asked me to have a word with the gaffer about everyone going on to the hospital to visit Gazza with the trophy.

I saw Terry and he said straight away that wasn't a problem and to get it organised. So after gaining permission from the hospital I told the coach driver to take us all, players, management and other members of staff to the Princess Grace. We all walked into the room and handed him the trophy. He couldn't believe it. He was very emotional and seeing him like that got to us as well. It was a moment I will never forget. We knew that Gazza was the main reason we had reached the final.

Looking back, he couldn't help it because it was typical Gazza but the adrenaline was going in the build-up to the kick-off once we had arrived at Wembley. He was getting the other lads going, geeing them up. The whole occasion might have been too much – who knows?

After the injury it was a very difficult time for him but there was a determination to get back to how he was playing before the Cup final – form which, of course, was taking him to play in Italy with Lazio. You knew he would regain his fitness because nothing would ever put him off. I know from my experience of missing 12 months as a player through injury that, at times, it does your head in but you've got to be positive. Of course Gazza had his down times, but gradually he made his way back.

Just a year or so earlier he had been one of the stars of the 1990 World Cup finals. He had everything and for me, knowing his dedication to the sport, he would recapture most of those skills which would enable him to complete his move to Serie A.

After he finally arrived at Lazio, part of the agreement over his transfer was that Spurs would travel to Rome for a pre-season friendly. So we turn up at the Stadio Olimpico and there he was waiting for us. He hugged everyone as they got off the coach. It was great to see the love and affection he still held for everyone at Spurs.

We had a top class group of senior players at the time who would always watch out for one another and I think Gazza had appreciated that and had prospered because of it. It was down to how the club was run by Terry Venables. After moving up from being reserve team coach to become Terry's assistant I had a close-up view of Terry's people skills, which were simply the best.

His handling of Gazza was brilliant. Yes, he let him get away with certain things that maybe more disciplinarian managers wouldn't have, but then he clamped down on him. He would calmly pull him to one side and say, "Gazza, I need to speak to you." He would have a one on one, never losing his temper, and

that would be it. It's why Gazza loved Terry and fully respected him. Terry always talked constructively with Gazza and that
was the right way to treat him. It's why Spurs always saw the
best of Gazza.

David Howells

*David Howells played alongside Gazza in the Tottenham
midfield and was a member of the 1991 FA Cup-winning side.*

The best player I saw in my time was definitely Paul Gascoigne.
I'm sure most of the boys who were at Spurs around the same
period would agree.

I remember hearing Ally McCoist saying that Rangers got the
best of him. I'm not so sure, I think we did at Spurs. That season
following the 1990 World Cup, when we won the FA Cup, he
was sensational and dominated games more than anybody else
I've seen. He could grab a match by the scruff of the neck and
win it on his own.

He was also a one-off when it came to playing tricks. After
training we always used to go back to White Hart Lane and
spend some time there, maybe play a game of cards or have a
chat with the groundsmen.

One day the head groundsman was having some terrible
problems with pigeons making a mess everywhere. So Gazza
decided to climb right up to the upper echelon of the main
stand to get rid of them. At the time, the stand was being rede-
veloped and the next thing we see is Gazza falling through a
plank of rotten wood, then hanging onto a girder around 40 feet
up! Luckily, we were able to get him down before things turned
really nasty.

Gary Mabbutt

Gary Mabbutt was Paul Gascoigne's much-respected skipper at Tottenham and remains the man he often turns to during his darker moments. Gary also played for England and is now a club ambassador for Spurs.

I was captain when Gazza arrived at Spurs and he certainly kept me on my toes. He was one of the most intelligent players on the pitch. He could see things so quickly and make things happen. When we weren't playing well he could grab a game by the scruff of the neck and turn it our way.

He helped us reach the 1991 FA Cup final, which proved to be a day of mixed emotions. It started with Paul chipping a ball into the middle of the brass band as we warmed up on the pitch. We had seen him do things like this so many times. I thought to myself after he had sent things flying that he was on form and up for it but he started the game as if he was totally manic. People ask if we had noticed anything different about him in the dressing room but Paul was always manic before games.

As the match started he made two rash tackles, the first on Garry Parker. I blame myself in many ways for what happened later because I didn't see the challenge and if I had I would have been straight over to him and sorted him out. About 15 minutes later, Gary Charles ran across the box and Paul came and took him out at knee level.

Gary was lucky he didn't get badly injured but, of course, Paul did. I knew straight away it was serious.

I thought he wouldn't be able to continue. He did somehow manage to carry on after treatment and was at the end of the defensive wall after Nottingham Forest had been awarded a free-kick.

As Stuart Pearce went to hit the ball I was grabbed from behind and pulled to the floor. As I went down I saw the ball fly past me and I heard the cheer. The referee didn't see what had happened to me and gave the goal. Paul then struggled to get back for the kick-off. He collapsed and was eventually carried off.

A lot of people must have thought that was it – our chances of winning had disappeared because Paul had been the cog in the wheel of our Cup run. But we had a strong resolve in the side. We had a lot of characters and, to the surprise of some, we won it after extra time.

After the game, as everyone knows, the first thing we did was go down to the Princess Grace Hospital, where Gazza had been taken. We went up to the third floor.

The door opened and I gave him his medal and let him hold the Cup. It was very emotional. He told me that once he had settled into his bed, the TV was turned on just in time to see me lift the FA Cup.

It was a great moment being with him in the hospital. All the lads were there and Gazza wanted to find the surgeon because he wanted permission to join everyone at the after-match party. Of course, he wasn't allowed to come.

We saw the best of Paul Gascoigne that season.

Paul did eventually come back to a very high level but he was never able to surpass the form he showed in the FA Cup run. He was astounding in every single game.

It was known, though not discussed between us, that he would be leaving for Lazio at the end of the season – but it had no effect on him.

Paul Walsh

Paul Walsh spent a madcap few seasons with Gazza at Spurs and saw at close quarters the antics of the hyperactive England player. Walsh, who won the league title with Liverpool and was in Tottenham's FA Cup-winning squad, went on to become a popular pundit with Sky Sports.

I joined Spurs just a few months before Gazza arrived in the summer of 1988 along with Paul Stewart and a few others. I was staying in the same hotel as Gazza, The West Park Lodge, which England used to frequent, in the Cockfosters area. It was full on straight away although Gazza was soon asked to leave because he would upset people at breakfast by continually breaking wind. There was no stopping him – it was so loud. He would cock his backside into the air and let them rip before exploding into laughter. The hotel guests would stop eating and look at him in disgust although that just set Gazza up to do even more. He wasn't bothered one bit. With all the pranks and mischief going on, the hotel just wanted to wash their hands of him.

It meant Gazza moving to the Swallow Hotel at Waltham Abbey which had just been built. I stayed at The West Park Lodge until Terry Venables, the Spurs manager, told me I had a week to make alterative arrangements because I had remained at the hotel longer than my contract stipulated. I was in the process of renovating a house over the road from the hotel. Nayim had just joined Spurs and was also in the Swallow Hotel so I asked him if I could bunk down in his hotel room because he had a spare bed. This meant I would be joining up with Gazza and his gang again, which meant trouble ahead. It soon became absolute bedlam once more. It was one childish prank after another. If Gazza had been on the booze he would often shoot out the lights with his air rifle. The biggest priority was to make sure none of these stupid antics got in the newspapers.

His big mate Jimmy 'Five Bellies' was a regular victim of Gazza's fascination with his air rifle. He would use Jimmy's back as target practice and hand over £50 to try and deaden the pain as Jimmy rolled around in agony.

Another £50 was promised to Jimmy if he could suffer a lighted cigar resting on his nose for 10 seconds. I think Jimmy had a scab on the end of his nose for three months after that. Mental stuff was going on all the time. To be honest, I was glad to get away from it after two or three months. It was too much every day, although I was probably at my worst drinking and having a good time with the girls.

One day, I gave Gazza a lift back from the airport and we stopped off at a Wimpey for a double cheeseburger and chips. I went to pay and asked him if there was anything else he wanted. "I'll have a 99," he answered in his Geordie drawl. Within a few minutes it was dripping all down his face as he tried to get stuck into the ice cream. He had already entertained some kids looking through the window with his burger, making it fall out of his mouth on purpose. Now he was making them all laugh with his antics with his ice cream.

Eventually we both returned to the car and Gazza's in the passenger seat with what is left of his 99. As we were travelling up the road there's a cyclist, complete with his back-pack and helmet, which we are about to overtake. As we're going past I notice Gazza letting his window down and then, almost in slow motion, he's flicked his wrist and the remaining ice cream has hit the bloke full on in the face. All I can see when I look into the rear view mirror is this poor geezer covered in ice cream desperately trying to see where he was going. We're both chortling like a couple of schoolkids.

But suddenly the traffic lights we are approaching turn to red and I could see the guy frantically trying to catch up to us – and he's not happy. The bloke is getting closer and closer. Gazza is now crapping himself so he puts the window back up and locks his door which is now being punched and kicked by the furious guy. Luckily the lights finally changed and we could get away. Gazza, now believing he is safe, sticks two fingers up at him. He hadn't been so brave just a few seconds earlier!

It was just another day in the crazy life of Gazza at Spurs. It was a dysfunctional dressing room. There were the likes of Neil Ruddock, Pat Van Den Hauwe, David Howells – although the three real piss takers were Gazza, Paul Stewart and myself. You couldn't have Gazza around you all the time because it would send you mental.

I would always apologise to Terry Venables for my part in all of this because I didn't always act as a professional. But the reality is that because of everything going on I was probably playing at just 80 per cent of my potential during my time at Spurs.

If you speak to Alan Shearer or Teddy Sheringham, they love Terry. He is charismatic and if you meet him you can't help but like him. I understand that. But when I look at the four and a bit years I had there, I can only say that it was utter bedlam. The discipline was a disgrace. That's why I don't hold Terry in great esteem. He put all those players together in the dressing room. It was a volatile mix. Terry created that scenario and he let it grow. He let Gazza do exactly what he wanted. Looking back, I mentioned to Paul Stewart recently that it was like the film 'One Flew Over The Cuckoo's Nest'. Gazza played the part of Jack Nicholson. It was a load of lunatics behaving badly and Terry oversaw all that.

You can argue that we won an FA Cup and he deserves credit for that because he bought Gazza and Gazza won it for us. He got some things right but a lot wrong. I've said to Gazza that if he had joined Manchester United instead of Spurs then Alex Ferguson would have told him 'behave or else' and that's what he needed at times. Gazza would cause bedlam and he had a huge supporting cast.

As a player he could do absolutely anything. He could run, he could smash people out of the way, score great goals, pass and get it back, dribble. There's nothing he couldn't do. I felt that the only time he was completely happy and at peace was on a football pitch. Everywhere else he felt insecure and lost

The last time I bumped into him was at Anfield when Liverpool played Norwich City. I had a lovely photo taken with him. We swapped telephone numbers and kept in touch. He was in Bournemouth and I was in Southampton so we have attempted to meet up but I believe he is now living in the North West and I don't know if the number I've got for him is still in use.

He knows that I'm helping out at a local rehabilitation centre and have joined Alcoholics Anonymous. I would love to help him with some of his problems but he's not interested. Paul Merson is also making an effort but Gazza has got to want to do it, to want to change his life. You've got to have a bit of a clue that what you are doing is wrong. You've got to identify stuff within you and work out what has to change. People can guide you and help you but if you don't listen, nothing will change.

I believe he just rattles around. When he's got a big talking gig I think he probably says to himself, 'Oh no, how am I going to get through this?' He has a drink, does the gig and is probably very good and through the relief of getting through it, he goes on a binge for three days. It's a craving. Once he gets the taste, off he goes again.

It's hard for everyone coming out of football. But let's face it Gazza would have had more opportunities than nearly anybody else to be involved in something. He was Gazza and the whole world loved him. All he had to do was turn up, act normally and earn a fortune.

I didn't have that luxury. For instance, I think some people have forgotten that I have played for Liverpool but everyone knows about Gazza. Yet when you look back at his career he hasn't got any titles, something I managed to achieve before joining Spurs, unless you want to count those Scottish ones with Rangers! He could have achieved a lot more but sadly the antics often strangled the football.

Roy Reyland

Roy Reyland was Tottenham's kit man during Gazza's spell at White Hart Lane. He spent 29 years with the club and is now the equipment manager with Saracens Rugby Union Club.

In the space of a few years, Paul Gascoigne and I became very close. On one of Paul's earliest pre-season tours to Scandinavia we'd been given a day off and the local guide laid on golf, sight-seeing and various pastimes to keep the players entertained for the afternoon. "Have you got any fishing?" Gazza enquired almost immediately. I knew then we were kindred spirits. So me and the other Spurs fishermen, Paul Stewart and Steve Sedgley, were given some fly fishing rods and a lift to a nearby lake. Me, Stewy and Sedge hadn't fly fished before but Gazza was a seasoned fly fisherman, a very talented one. He was casting out 20 metres further than we were and it was one of the only times I have seen him calm, such was his usual enthusiasm and energy.

We stood on the bank fishing for an hour and that hour became two and still we'd not had a single bite. Gazza was getting restless. Then all of a sudden we saw this other fella out in a boat and he was catching loads of fish. Gazza was watching him reel in fish after fish, filling his net with some amazing looking specimens. We were all getting mightily annoyed staring at the lake while our flies remained motionless. Suddenly we heard: "Wey aye I've got one!" Gazza was nowhere to be seen. We looked up and down the lake and then we spotted him submerged in the water, fully clothed and reeling in a fish over his head. All you could see was his hair. Gazza waded back to the shore with this fish above his head like it was the FA Cup.

We took it back to the team hotel where the chef cooked it and Gazza proudly presented it to Terry Venables for his tea.

Gazza was the greatest player I ever put in a Spurs shirt during my time at the club. He had this fantastic lunging run and two great feet. He could drift past people, head it, tackle. Gazza also had a heart as big as a dustbin lid and didn't know when he was beaten. Kick him and he'd get up and laugh at you and pull that famous stupid face.

He would have played a million pranks at Spurs. For instance, he'd regularly burn Erik Thorstvedt's clothes. Every morning he would set fire to them because he used to say that Norwegians had no dress sense. So, to spare himself from that ritual, Erik used to ask me for three sets of training kit every session. He'd come in wearing one, put one on to train and go home in another set which was a nightmare for me. All this was to save his normal clothes from being burned to ashes by Gazza.

He was one of the liveliest players I've ever seen in a dressing room. He'd come in before a game and play pranks, even on a match day. He would come in at 1.30pm, pull his shorts up to his armpits and loon around. Then, just as suddenly, he would turn into Gazza the footballer. He'd be zoned in, do a warm-up, score three goals and then start messing around again. He was an awful loser and at the same time a great winner, albeit football or fishing. If the result didn't go his way he'd stamp around, throwing things on the floor and moping for days.

We used to have a secretary called Irene at our Mill Hill training ground. She had a soft spot for Gazza but he used to take the mickey out of her something rotten.

One day he came out of the dressing room stark naked and went into her office saying, "Irene, have you got a towel?" No way would Irene have a towel. It was just to embarrass her. Irene said, "Gazza, put it away and go inside. I don't find it funny." Everyday he would try and find something to wind someone up. He would put Deep Heat in people's pants and he'd find that funny. Gazza needed to be loved but sometimes I think he worked too hard at it. He was a folk hero amongst the staff, although Terry Venables and his assistant Alan Harris would often be pulling their hair out.

In the old days, when you walked into the main reception area at White Hart Lane, a receptionist would sit on the left hand side answering the phone. One day I was walking in with Gazza on the way to training when he suddenly jumped behind the desk and took the headset off the girl. He calmly sat down, put on the headset and started taking calls. It was hilarious. He'd pick up a call and say: "Wey aye! Tottenham Hotspur can I help yous?" Every call he'd say: "Of course, I'll pop you through." He'd forward them to the right department after adding, "it's free tickets. Putting you through." It's remarkable that Gazza's pranks never got him into more trouble.

But one day at White Hart Lane he nearly came a right cropper. It was a Friday night and Gazza decided he wanted to shoot the pigeons in the East Stand. His big mate Jimmy 'Five Bellies' was with him.

Gazza climbed up onto the rafters with his air rifle and was shimmying along towards the pigeon. He just didn't want to shoot it, he wanted to blow it to smithereens. Now just inches away from his prey and just as he was about to squeeze the trigger, the pigeon suddenly burst into life and flapped away. It totally shocked Gazza, who fell off the roof with an awful thump.

Jimmy dragged him over to the dressing room, where he arrived bleeding and bruised. We called the physio right away to patch him up so he could play the next day. Of course we had to keep all this a secret from Terry Venables.

That wasn't the only time Gazza brought his rifle with him to work. He used to take aim at my kit room door from 20 metres, shooting at targets he'd stuck on the door. You could see the pellet holes for years to come. Often he'd say to Jimmy to pick up a pair of shorts for him and when 'Five Bellies' crossed the dressing room Gazza would shoot him up the backside.

I used to say you needed two balls when he was playing, one for Gazza and one for the rest of the team. I lost count of the number of times I watched Gazza pick the ball up in his own 18 yard area and drift past three players. Before you knew it he was bearing down on goal. He was simply terrific and so strong. He would just shrug people off.

His best goal for me was that free-kick in the 1991 FA Cup semi-final against Arsenal. Just five minutes into the game I'm settling down next to Terry Venables on the bench as Gazza was placing the ball down for the free-kick. What people forget is that Gazza had just had his double hernia operation so we didn't know he was going to play, let alone last the game. He had missed the last few games and he was cramping up before the free-kick.

He must have been 40 yards out and I remember there was a huddle of players who all broke away and, of course, there was a long red wall in the way.

"Is Gascoigne going to have a crack?" the commentator asked a TV audience of several million. "He is, you know." This was a moment between Gazza and David Seaman.

We all knew Gazza could hit a ball but I can recall Terry Venables shouting from the bench: "Don't shoot, don't shoot." Gazza was now starting his massive run-up.

"Don't shoot!" Terry pleaded, now rising to his feet.

Soon Terry's warning changed from "Don't shoot!" to "great goal!"

It still stands as one of the best ever goals in the famous competition. Terry admitted to a newspaper: "I can't think of another player who could have done that."

That was Gazza.

Steve Sedgley

Steve Sedgley joined Spurs from Coventry City, winning the FA
Cup with both clubs. As an England Under-21 international he
played alongside Gazza before their paths crossed once again
with some interesting consequences at Tottenham.

I first came across Gazza when I was playing for Coventry and
he was with Spurs. I just remember him smiling at me and then
'bang!' I was on the floor after he had smashed me off the ball.
I think he had body-checked me. He just laughed at me while I
was trying to get up.

We next met when we were both with the England Under-21
squad for the Toulon tournament. He was eventually named
player of the competition. He showed what he was capable of,
producing on an international stage. Everyone was soon talking
about him on and off the pitch.

One day we were lining up for a team photo and I had the
misfortune to be standing next to Gazza. Just as the picture was
about to be taken he yanked at my blazer top pocket with the
Three Lions emblem embossed on it. When the camera lens
clicked all you could see was my Three Lions badge hanging off.
There was nothing I could do. But we got on well from that day.
He might even have felt a little bit guilty over decking me in the
Coventry-Spurs game, although on second thoughts I doubt it.

The next season when Coventry went up to St. James' Park to
play Newcastle I asked the manager John Sillett whether I could
stay in the North East after the game because Gazza wanted to
take me out on the Toon. The gaffer agreed that I could – as long
as I was back by Monday morning for training.

Of course, I told him that wouldn't be a problem. So Gazza and I had a great night out on the Saturday and the next day he convinced me to stay on the Sunday night as well. He promised me that I could lend his club-sponsored car to drive back to Coventry first thing on the Monday. So, come the Monday morning, I got up early and asked Gazza for his car keys. He then informed me he didn't have a car.

Instead he pointed me in the direction of the train station, told me the wrong platform and the wrong train and I ended up missing training. I walked into a rocket from John Sillett, who went absolutely bananas that I hadn't got back from a Saturday afternoon game until Monday afternoon. That was pretty scary.

So when I moved to Tottenham I obviously already knew Gazza pretty well. On one occasion we went off to play a pre-season friendly in Spain against Atletico Madrid. In the hotel just down the corridor from my room I could hear laughter coming from Gazza's room. He was sharing with Paul Stewart. I went to investigate and they were having a pillow fight on the bed. I wanted to join in, which Gazza agreed to. But unbeknown to me he had slipped something hard into his pillow before they both set about smashing me over the head. Eventually, a little dazed and battered, I managed to escape, racing out of their room only to bump into the manager Terry Venables, who must have wondered what had been going on.

Then there was the incident with the ostrich which is still remembered by everyone who was at Spurs at the time. I was a lot skinnier in those days and Gazza used to call me 'Long Neck'. There was a local zoo called Paradise Park near to where he lived. He would often visit it and if he saw an ostrich or an emu he would shout out, "There's Steve Sedgley."

One day, walking towards the Spurs training pitch I could see just ahead of me Gazza walking alongside what appeared to be a zoo keeper carrying something. When I got closer I could see it was a big sack. The next thing the sack opens to reveal an ostrich wearing a Spurs shirt with 'Long Neck' on the back. It started running around the training area just in time for Terry Venables to arrive wondering what the hell was going on.

Gazza was an absolute pest in the dressing room. You never knew what he was going to get up to next. He was always lively, unable to sit down. But that's what made him. I also don't think anyone could have handled him any better than Terry did. He allowed Gazza to be a free spirit. I don't think he would have been the same player if someone had cracked down on him. When he went to the 1990 World Cup I would argue that he was probably the best player in the world. A lot of that was down to how Terry treated him. He gave him freedom to express and enjoy himself.

During the run to the 1991 FA Cup final we had to play Portsmouth away. Unfortunately I had to room with him on the night before that game. Just a few minutes after we got into the room he was off, jumping on and off the bed, performing forward rolls, all sorts. He got bored easily and would have to do something to keep himself interested. Justin Edinburgh had not long signed and hadn't played many games for us. He was in the next room which was only separated by an inter-connecting door. Gazza insisted he left it open.

Gazza, who had only just recovered from a double hernia operation, then went out and played squash with John Moncur. He came back, called for room service at 10.30pm and started messing about because he never needed much sleep. The trouble was Justin and I did need our sleep but neither of us slept a wink because of Gazza's hyperactivity.

When we finally got to Fratton Park, Terry Fenwick got an injury in the warm-up and the coach Dougie Livermore called Justin over and told him he would be playing. He couldn't believe it. You could see him panicking. After having no sleep because of Gazza he was now being flung into an important FA Cup tie. But Gazza scored twice and almost single-handedly took us into the next round.

Gazza was brilliant again in the Wembley semi-final against Arsenal, scoring with that fantastic long range free-kick. It was mainly down to him that we reached the final. He was a great lad and no one has a bad word to say about him. And in football terms he was exceptional, by far the best player I have known. I might have been on the end of some of his jokes but that was him. He's a great, great lad.

Danny Baker

Danny Baker befriended Gazza during his Tottenham days and would often go out on the town with him and Radio DJ Chris Evans. Danny is a man of many talents, an erudite radio presenter, comedy writer and screenwriter.

Yes, Paul Gascoigne really did drive a London bus full of people around London's Marble Arch in broad daylight. And still he wasn't done! He brought the bus to a stop around 50 yards into Park Lane when the traffic had once again solidified. Jumping down from the driver's seat he stood arms out wide in front of the cheering passengers, most of whom didn't have any idea that he had actually been driving the thing and dicing with their very lives for the past 10 minutes.

Jumping back into the taxi with Chris Evans, Paul's face was now giving off sparks. It was clear the world had become his playground and that he hadn't felt so alive in ages. Suddenly he was off, exiting from the taxi. He had spotted a gang of council workers digging up the pavement. The group greeted him and Paul quickly outlined to them his latest idea. On went a hi-vis vest and ear protectors and one of the chaps hauled a huge pneumatic drill his way. Thundering the thing into life, Gazza began randomly digging up sections of London several feet from where work had actually commenced. It was pure Harpo Marx. In a communal panic the men eventually guided him towards the area that actually needed excavating. And for a couple of minutes Paul concentrated intensely on the task.

He then stopped as Chris and I watched from the cab. We thought this might be the signal for him to return to us. It wasn't. Gazza was merely negotiating a cigarette. One was provided, lit, placed between his lips and then he was off drilling again! Gas mains would have to look after themselves.

Then for the first time our taxi driver remarked upon the surreal events unfolding behind his back. "Your mate," he said dryly. "He's not all there is he?" Then, narrowing his eyes towards the drilling, he confessed: "You know, that's the one thing I've always wanted to do – what he's doing now." Fair play to him, plainly the bus episode was a bit downmarket for a cabbie!

Deciding to walk the rest of the way we paid him off and crossed to the far pavement where Paul was still jack hammering away. The watching workmen proffered both myself and Chris some power tools but we politely declined . . .

Image: Richard Pelham

4

'We came across him lying on the road next to his scooter. He was pretending to be dead. He'd even mocked up some blood. The next thing, he is getting up and laughing his head off, convinced he had fooled me'

– Dino Zoff, Italian goalkeeping legend and former Lazio manager

Glenn Roeder

Glenn Roeder hit it off with a young Paul Gascoigne after moving to Newcastle United under manager Arthur Cox. Such was the classy central defender's influence on the precocious teenager that Gazza asked Glenn to join him in Rome following his transfer from Spurs to Lazio.

The first sighting of this 'Jack the Lad' character I was starting to hear all about was when he appeared at the training ground in a pair of his mother's tights.

It's not a sight you expect to see and I quickly asked my new Newcastle team-mates Kevin Keegan and Terry McDermott why was this kid wearing tights. They said if he didn't wear them then his legs would go bright red within five minutes. They would easily get chapped. Not many kids would have the balls to do that, even if it was helping them. But here he was, this little fat kid, with a determination to be a great footballer.

The apprentices had to do all their jobs around the training ground and it looked like this lad who I had spotted wearing tights was the one organising them and bossing them around. I discovered he was still a first-year apprentice and yet he was ordering the older ones around. They weren't arguing so I thought he must be a decent player to earn this sort of respect.

I gradually got to know him. He was a complete extrovert and I was, if anything, more of an introvert. It's unusual for opposites to attract and get on so well but we did. I think he liked talking to me because it helped him experience what it was like to be a first-team player – something he aspired to be.

Eventually he did break into the first team and he enjoyed the best debut I've ever seen from a young player, down at Southampton. The Saints had obviously already heard about him because just a few months earlier he had run Watford ragged in the FA Youth Cup final. Such was Gazza's reputation, even though he hadn't played a single first-team game, that they put Jimmy Case on him. Jimmy was as hard as nails and had done plenty of marking jobs on top players, especially when he was at Liverpool. Jimmy never got near him.

Funny enough we played Watford later in the season and Tom Walley, who was the youth team coach, was helping Steve Harrison with the first team. He rang me up on the day of the game and said: "Is that genius Gascoigne playing tonight?" I said he was. "Fuck me," he said. "We'll have to do a job on him." To get the best out of Gazza, you need to tell him that someone connected with the opposition doesn't rate him. That is the fire that lights him. He always wanted to prove people wrong. So, on this occasion, I told him that Tom Walley had rung me up and said he hoped that Gazza was playing because he was useless. I said that Tom was normally a good judge of a player but had still insisted that Gazza was useless. He said: "I'll fucking show him who's useless." So, we're 3-0 up by half-time and he's been involved in all three goals. We ended up winning easily. The next time I bumped into Tom he told me that, in his opinion, Gazza was completely mad. I asked him why. Tom replied: "Every time he scored or made a goal that night he would run past the dugout, stare at me and point at my bald head and shout 'slaphead!' What was all that about?"

To be honest, I always felt that Gazza always enjoyed making goals rather than scoring them. Peter Beardsley, who played in the same team at Newcastle, was exactly the same. Gazza would rather skip past three players with his shimmys and dummies and slide the ball across the goal for someone to side foot in. He did that for me once against Sheffield Wednesday, even though I don't know what I was doing so far up the field. He did score his fair share of goals but undoubtedly he could have grabbed more.

After Arthur Cox left, one of his coaches, Willie McFaul, took over as manager. We were playing Spurs at White Hart Lane and Willie told me, as his captain the night before the game, that he was going to leave Gazza out of the team. I asked him whether he was sure he was doing the right thing. Willie said it was because he hadn't done well in the previous games. I said I'd back him but it was a huge gamble.

The next morning, there was a quick warm-up game between some of the first team and the fringe players who had travelled. Gazza was forced to line up against the first team and his hurt pride at being dropped came to the fore. The first team were 5-0 down after 20 minutes. Gazza had scored a hat-trick and made two goals. I told Willie to call the game off. If it had gone on much longer it would have been 10-0! He still didn't play him. I think we ended up losing 5-1.

Another time, we were due to play against Arsenal and Gazza was told he would be up against England international Kenny Sansom, one of the best full-backs in Europe at the time. "Gaffer, who's he?" asked Gazza. That was him. He was in his own bubble.

The only player who seemed to bother him was a fellow Geordie, Bryan Robson. We were playing Manchester United at St. James' Park and before the game I went into the toilet and there was Gazza shaking like a leaf.

"What's wrong with you?"I asked him. He said he was playing against Bryan Robson in 10 minutes. I said: "So what?" "But he's the England captain," Gazza replied. I admitted to him that Bryan was a great player but Gazza was going to be one as well. I finally managed to calm him down and for 60 minutes he gave Robbo the runaround. I don't think Bryan has ever forgotten that. Thankfully for him, Gazza – being a teenager at the time – eventually tired and Robbo got stuck into him big time.

On a pre-season tour in New Zealand, Gazza went missing for a few hours. When he returned we could hardly recognise him. He'd gone and had his hair bleached blond. He had been bored and decided to do something daft – not for the first time.

Gazza really enjoyed training. That was the problem. He would have loved it to have gone on all day but invariably it would finish around 12.30pm, so he would have the rest of the day to try and keep himself amused.

In his latter years, the Rangers manager Walter Smith asked me to join him and Archie Knox, his number two at Ibrox when Gazza was there. He knew of my friendship with him and I spent around two months up there.

Gazza would drive Walter and Archie mad because after training had finished he demanded they joined in playing head tennis. Once everyone else had changed and left, Gazza would put up a mini tennis net inside the dressing room and drag the pair in. Walter would look at his watch and say, "Gazza, it's gone 4pm." "Just one more game, gaffer," Gazza would plead. "Gazza, I've got to go into the office and do some work. I've been stuck here all afternoon," Walter yelled. It's a scary thought but if training had been all day, Gazza might have been even better than he was.

For a game against Aberdeen, he was due to report to Ibrox at midday, collar and tie, booted and suited and complete with his Rangers kit. I asked him beforehand what were we going to do in the morning. He announced that we would go fishing. He was some fisherman, by the way. Just like his 50-yard passes, he could drop a fly from his rod on any lilly you could point out. He was very talented in anything he tried. For instance, he was soon knocking up big breaks just weeks after taking up snooker. There was no coaching. He just picks things up easily.

So we went fishing. It's blowing a gale but that doesn't bother him. The one time he never gets bored is when he's fishing. He would stay by a river or lake all day even if he doesn't get a single bite. It got to 12pm and I said we had to get to Ibrox. He wanted to stay longer, saying there was no problem, everything was in the boot of the car and he could quickly get changed.

We finally got going and on the way he rang the groundsman who he was mates with, explained he was running late, and to let him into the corner of the ground where he could dump the car for the groundsman to eventually park in his allocated spot. By then he had managed somehow to wriggle into most of his suit but he still had his waders on as he got out of the car and rushed down the side of the pitch to join the rest of the squad. It was some sight but knowing Gazza he could have played even with great big waders attached to his legs!

At Newcastle, it became inevitable that he was going to move to one of the big clubs in the First Division. I love Newcastle – it's my club in many ways because I spent eight years of my life as player, academy director and manager. But there are clubs who enjoy a bigger stature and Gazza was always one day going to be drawn to one of them.

Tottenham came in for him and Terry Venables was the manager. I had worked under Terry at QPR and been his captain in the 1982 FA Cup final, ironically against Spurs, which we lost in a replay. I thought to myself, 'Gazza and Terry will get on like a house on fire'.

The Spurs chairman Irving Scholar knew Gazza loved fishing. There was a big fishing tackle shop across the road from Tottenham's ground. So when Paul turned up to sign, Irving took him to one side and said to leave all the paperwork etc. to the secretary and Gazza's agents and advisors, and to walk across to the shop with him. It was like taking a kid into the sweet department at Harrods. I think Gazza later emerged with two top-of-the-range rods and other assorted gear, all courtesy of Mr Scholar. The deal was then done.

I know that Manchester United had also been desperate to sign him. But there was no way he wanted to give the fishing gear back! In all seriousness, I know that Terry had already made a big impression on him and he wanted to go and play for him.

Terry was great for Gazza, always backing him, even putting up with the stupidity which followed him around. But again, just like at Newcastle, you knew with the talent Gazza had displayed for Spurs and for England, after being given his chance on the international stage, he would outgrow even Tottenham.

Lazio came calling and, because of our friendship, Gazza wanted me to join him when he eventually moved to Rome. To be perfectly honest, I also saw it as an opportunity to broaden my experience and learn a new language.

All that was almost wrecked by that shocking knee injury he suffered in the 1991 FA Cup final against Nottingham Forest. I don't know if I'm right but I would blame one lady for that

– Princess Diana. You could tell even in the warm-up that his mind was on other things. He couldn't relax. It was like he had hundreds of mosquitos all over him – unable to stay still. In the days before the game, he had been going on that he couldn't believe he was going to meet her when she was presented to the players and officials before kick-off. He was so revved up and carried that on into the match, exploding into that ridiculous tackle on Gary Charles.

As soon as I witnessed that, I left my seat in the stand and managed to get into the medical centre down near the tunnel area. I saw Peter Barnes, the Spurs secretary, who told me straight away that Gazza had damaged his anterior cruciate ligament – probably the most serious injury a top footballer can suffer. Peter said Gazza was all over the place, worried about his future. Peter said they were deliberately keeping the extent of the injury secret from Gazza. Peter explained that telling him would "crush him".

I went in to see Gazza and I obviously asked him how he was. He insisted that he could have played on! I told him it was best to continue sitting here and let the medics get on with the job.

In the following days, discussions took place about what was going to happen to the deal which had already been agreed to take Gazza to Lazio from White Hart Lane. Spurs were desperate for the transfer to still go through because they needed the money. The deal was renegotiated with Spurs getting £5 million up front, even though Gazza wouldn't be able to play for a year. If he wasn't able to prove his fitness in 12 months' time then an insurance company would pay the money back to Lazio.

Gazza was invited out there for a week before the start of the next season, even though he wasn't fit, to give him a taste of

Rome. It was also a dummy run for me because it was all sorted for me and my family to live with Gazza in Rome. Schools for my kids had already been allocated. It was all systems go. My job was to keep an eye on him and try to keep him out of any mischief. I'd never been out with him on a night out, although I'd read enough of what had gone on in the past through the front pages of the Sunday newspapers. I'm afraid, in my opinion, his so-called mates sometimes lapped up the attention from the paparazzi. They wanted their five seconds of fame, not thinking of Gazza. Anyway, with me around, hopefully those days would be numbered.

I enjoyed the week taking in the sights of Rome and spending time with Gazza. At breakfast one day, Gazza knocked a bread roll onto the floor. The next thing a cat pounces and places a paw on the roll. Quick as a flash, Gazza responded: "Hell, Glenn, even the cats here in Italy have got a great first touch!" It was an honour to be asked to join him, although I didn't like being called his minder by the papers!

But in the end it wasn't to be for me when Gazza finally joined Lazio a year after his injury. I felt he had let himself down badly through a Newcastle nightclub incident in which his injured knee was damaged again. And this after he had been told count-less times to keep any weight off the leg. For me, it's stupid as a footballer going into a nightclub where you are instantly recog-nised, never mind having just done your ACL. I wondered after this what else was going to happen. I didn't think it was fair to put my family through it so that was it, I decided I wouldn't be joining him in Rome after all. At first when I told him, he thought I was joking. But then he could see in my eyes that I wasn't.

Sadly, I still believe he could have achieved more than he did in Italy. He had his best periods when he was left alone to concentrate on his football but too often he would be surrounded by family and friends who treated it like a holiday. There were distractions all the time. There were still pockets of great play rather than extended periods but he was still the most gifted English player of his generation.

A couple of years ago we were together at a talk-in event. Being in Newmarket, the audience consisted of a few jockeys. He started off by saying how delighted he was to be in a famous horse racing area and told the jockeys that they could now sit down. "Oh you are!" he chortled. And off he went, vintage Gazza.

He's got a heart of gold. I don't know any ex-player who has come out and done a knocking story about him. There is nothing bad about him. Yes, he's done many stupid things but they are never malicious. They certainly don't make them like Paul Gascoigne any more.

Beppe Signori

Beppe Signori was a team-mate of Gazza's at Lazio, where he was a prolific scorer and much loved by the fans.

I don't believe anyone who knew him well could have wished ill upon Paul because he demonstrated an incredible generosity with all his team-mates. When he was in the right physical condition he also showed he was a player who commanded the big fee paid for him. Off the pitch, he was always pulling pranks. One day I found a gigantic ray fish on my windscreen. I quickly found out that Gazza had brought it in!

Dino Zoff

Dino Zoff was the goalkeeping captain of the Italy side which won the 1982 World Cup and was Gazza's first manager at Lazio following the player's move from Tottenham.

I loved that boy. He was a genius, an artist, but he made me tear my hair out. The big pity was we saw the beauty he was capable of only so rarely. He destroyed that beauty with his drinking and his eating.

He ate ice cream for breakfast. He drank beer for lunch. When he was injured he blew up like a whale. But as a player . . . beautiful. But he also made me feel depressed and frustrated. He was a great artist who lost his art. At times he made me crazy with rage. One year, after being on holiday, he returned to our training camp having put on 12kg in weight. At first, I had to ask who that was who had just walked into the camp. I didn't recognise him.

He played so many tricks on me. Once, when I was sitting on the front seat of the team coach, we came across him lying on the road next to his scooter. He was pretending to be dead. He'd even mocked up some blood. The next thing he is getting up and laughing his head off, convinced he had fooled me.

Another time he somehow managed to get hold of the whistle I used to supervise training and attached it to a live turkey he had brought into training. He then released it onto the training pitch, where it ran about for ages. It took ages to catch it.

Nobody's car was safe. He let down the tyres of Aron Winter's Porsche and Roberto Di Matteo found a dead snake in his jacket pocket.

Jim White

A leading newspaper journalist who recalls an interview with Dino Zoff shortly before the 2002 World Cup.

When we had finished the interview, when the photographs had been taken and the tape recorder switched off, Dino Zoff leaned forward and said: "Can I ask you a question. What has become of Paul Gascoigne?"

He admitted that having had a long association with him as his manager, he had never felt so much affection for a player. I explained that, the last I heard, Gazza was taking his coaching badges with a view to becoming a manager.

"A manager – Gascoigne?! Are you serious. No, no it can't be true."

Then he started laughing, his sizeable shoulders quaking with mirth. And he didn't stop. He just wept with laughter, so much so that there were tears tumbling down his cheeks. "I'm sorry, I'm sorry. Forgive me. But Gascoigne, a manager? Ha ha – now I've heard it all!"

Pierluigi Casiraghi

Pierluigi Casiraghi played alongside Gazza at Lazio and made 44 appearances for Italy. He also spent two years with Chelsea.

The Lazio coach Zdeněk Zeman was always seen on the training pitch with this wonderful whistle which he loved to use at every opportunity. One day it went missing after a session and he was beside himself. He thought he had lost it. Suddenly a goose appeared and waddled past us all complete with the whistle hung around its neck. Of course we all knew who had put it there – Gazza!

He was a great player but was unlucky with injuries. There were too many of them. He also had a number of off-the-field weaknesses that he struggled with. There was an obvious dependence on alcohol. Many of us tried to help him but when the issue is personal you also need the strength to get out of the habit yourself.

David Walker

David Walker was a prominent football reporter for the Daily Mail during much of Gazza's career before going on to become Leeds United's director of communications and sports editor of the Sunday Mirror. He broke the story that a three-year spell at Lazio was about to end for the England star.

Over the years I had in effect become the *Daily Mail's* Gazza correspondent. Although *The Sun* had him signed up for first-person pieces, I believe that over the years I had built up a trust with Gazza. The newspaper had increasingly looked to me on most things to do with him after I originally wrote that he was being sold by Tottenham to Lazio. After that, if something was going on in Rome with him, then I was the reporter nominated to cover the event.

Just three years into his time at Lazio I received a tip-off from Bill Fotherby, who was the managing director of Leeds United. He asked me if I knew that Lazio were trying to sell Gazza. I was surprised at that, although I assumed it was correct because Bill had over the years been a good contact regarding various stories. He mentioned that a few select clubs, including his own Leeds – who were then a top side having won the league title in 1992, had been alerted to Gazza's availability by Lazio. It was a great potential scoop and obviously I was keen to run the story immediately. But the sports editor, Vic Robbie, had other ideas. He asked me if I felt the story would hold – that no other newspaper would get wind of it. Vic wondered whether Gazza would speak to me about this shock revelation of him being sold. I felt because of the relationship we had Gazza would talk to me, providing I could track him down face to face. He'd started to change his mobile phone number quite frequently and the latest one I had was out of date.

So it would mean getting on a flight to Rome. It was a gamble to sit on the story but both Vic and I felt it was one that was worth taking. Of course we could have run the story and then gone to see him but by then everyone would have been swarming all over it. Vic felt to break the fact that Lazio were letting him go, plus an exclusive Gazza interview to go with it, would be the ideal package.

And to be fair to Vic that's how it worked out. I got the flight out to Rome and then headed for the Lazio training ground, a place I had got to know quite well. I waited at the end of the drive for Gazza to arrive.

Sure enough, he soon turned up driving his car with his stepson Mason, who was around five years old, also in the vehicle. Gazza stopped and asked me what I was doing at the training ground. I told him that I had come to see him and I needed a chat with him. He was very apologetic and said he couldn't do it there and then because he was due to have treatment on his latest injury. He promised that as soon as that was finished he would search me out and we would have that discussion.

I went for a walk, came back and was just hanging around when, true to his word, he came back along the road from the training ground to see me. He still had Mason with him and ushered me towards him for our promised chat. "Okay, what do you want to tell me?" he asked. I said I had to put something to him and it was quite sensitive.

I said: "Do you know Lazio are trying to sell you?" He looked absolutely stunned. He admitted that he didn't have a clue that was happening. "How do you know?" he replied. I told him that Leeds United had an interest in him but the bigger picture was that he was for sale.

I was taping his comments but I also said to him that if he wanted to ask more pertinent questions then I would switch the tape recorder off. He looked genuinely astonished by the news and, in addition to going away with a great story, I did want to help him as much as I could. He was astonished that no one at the club had the decency to tell him what was happening. No one had the courage to tell him to his face that his time at Lazio was about to end.

He'd had some fantastic games for Lazio and the fans loved him but he kept picking up injuries and that had worried the club's hierarchy, who felt they should cash in. Even though Leeds were a big club in those days I didn't get the impression he was exactly enamoured with going there, especially after being linked in the past with the likes of Manchester United and Liverpool.

But once he had grasped my words he was thankful that I had put him in the picture over his future. I then guessed his next move would have been to ring his agent Mel Stein, who would also have been in the dark about what was going on over Gazza's future.

I called my sports desk and informed them that I had two stories to file. The back page would be the exclusive 'Gazza For Sale' while inside there would be a big interview along the lines of Gazza saying that he wished someone at Lazio would have had the decency to reveal the club's plans. He also spoke honestly about his frustration at being plagued by injuries.

He mentioned that he assumed it was a *Daily Mail* photographer who had earlier been taking pictures of him and Mason. Evidently, Gazza had posed for action pictures of young Mason hosing him down. Typical of Gazza, he had his training gear on while a laughing Mason squirted him with water from the hose pipe. I informed him that there was no photographer with me and so it must have been one of the paparazzi who would often follow him around, much to Gazza's frustration. He'd been had – not for the first time. Thinking he had been doing me and my newspaper a good turn he had fallen into the trap of being openly photographed by a member of the paparazzi, who he despised.

That guy wouldn't have believed his luck. There's Gazza in his training gear larking around with Mason – brilliant pictures which would have been a nice earner.

After finishing the piece and despite him being genuinely stunned, he mentioned that he thought I had kids. I told him that was right, I had a boy and a girl. He told me to stay where I was and that he was off to the training ground laundry. He returned with his official shirt – not a replica – and asked what my son was called. I informed him it was Richard and so he signed it for me to give to him. He then stopped me again saying he couldn't just give me that because I also had a little girl who would like something. Off he went again before coming back with a few of his 'Gazzetta Italia' Channel 4 books which he signed to Rebecca.

I've now got the shirt on a hanger as a proud momento of that time with Gazza. In any case, I would look after it better than Richard would. It's a nice keepsake and proof that I did interview him.

As we know he didn't join Leeds, or indeed any Premier League club, and went off to sign for Rangers. Bill Fotherby would have loved him at Elland Road because they were in Europe and a top-five team but it wasn't to be. Bill's loss was my gain with a fantastic exclusive.

5

'After the semi-final, when everyone was distraught, a few beers were passed around and Gazza started singing, "Doe, a deer, a female deer …" it built up to a great big crescendo with everyone singing and lifted the spirits'

– Gary Lineker, broadcaster and former England and Tottenham team-mate

Alan Shearer

Alan Shearer, another Geordie footballing hero, was along with Gazza one of the main characters in England's Euro 96 displays which gripped the nation. The Premier League's all-time leading goalscorer, who won the title with Blackburn Rovers before returning to the North East with Newcastle, is now the main pundit on BBC's Match Of The Day.

In an England dressing room after a game you would go to put your socks on while Gazza was sat in the corner with his body shaking frantically with laughter because he knew he had cut the ends off, so you were about to pull them right up to your chin! If he wasn't messing around with your socks he would put Deep Heat in your underpants. He would burst out laughing as you dived into the showers to wash the stuff off. It didn't matter who you were, nobody was spared.

When I first joined up with England he was telling everyone he had booked this amazing holiday to South Africa. I said to Gazza, what about Apartheid? He said, no it was fine, he was staying in a hotel!

During Euro 96 we were often bombarded with him either singing Three Lions at the top of his voice or blasting it on his CD player. It could be the middle of the night or first thing in the morning – there was no let-up. I don't think the other hotel guests appreciated it either. Things were certainly lively with Gazza around. Fortunately, I never had to share a room with him. Unless there was a tournament I used to see him every couple of months, which was just about okay. You had to feel sorry for the guys who were with him all the time.

I was, you would say, an innocent bystander at the infamous dentist's chair incident in Hong Kong in the build-up to Euro 96. I saw that it was becoming messy and I managed to slope off, even though I couldn't have imagined it escalating like it did. It turned into a nightmare for everyone. When you look at the pictures now of what went on it's embarrassing. The shit really did hit the fan but to Terry Venables' credit he used it to his advantage.

Gazza knew how much Terry loved him and how well he had been looked after. We all did really and we knew he had been let down by the antics in the Hong Kong bar. It's something that shouldn't have happened.

We knew immediately afterwards that we needed to perform at Euro 96 because we didn't want to let the manager down again. Terry knew that and he pushed us on. We knew as players that he had protected us on many occasions and now we had to protect him. That meant doing well in Euro 96. I think we lived up to that. It was an amazing time for the country. It brought football and the nation together.

There are still loads of things which stand out from the tournament but for me there were two big ones.

There was Gazza's goal against Scotland, which was just genius. Few people, if any, could have done that. It was a piece of pure magic. There was also one of the goals when we beat Holland 4-1. Gazza to Teddy Sheringham to me and bang! Those two proved iconic moments in a never-to-be-forgotten tournament. It was great to be involved in it. The atmosphere for the Holland game was the best I ever experienced in an England shirt.

The dentist's chair celebration following the Scotland goal wasn't bad either. Looking back, I'm certain that had been organised before the game. I don't think that would have just happened. I can't be sure but I could hazard a guess who was behind it – the man himself. Anyway, I found myself squirting energy drink into his mouth, helping recreate what had gone on in Hong Kong.

It was the same with some of his pranks, they were incredible. But there again, only he would have been able to get away with doing them. Can you imagine someone else trying to put Deep Heat in your underpants? It wouldn't have been acceptable but because it was that cheeky chap Gazza, it was alright. That was him and we all loved him for it.

In the dressing rooms before these games he was Gazza – and everyone who has shared a dressing room will know exactly what I mean.

He definitely wasn't one to sit quietly in the corner reading a newspaper, a magazine, a book or whatever. He was hyper and excited but that was him and you let him get on with it. It's also where Terry came into his own in terms of how he looked after Gazza. He would always protect him. He handled him superbly well. He knew what made him tick and Gazza loved and respected him, which also helped.

As a player we know he was exceptional. The most important thing for me as a forward is you want to know when you make a forward run the ball is going to arrive. Gazza had the ability to do that. If a forward doesn't get the ball then he stops running. He could find and create a pass but that didn't detract from him also showing his brilliance.

He was an incredible player.

Gazza could do things with a football only a few could even dream of.

David Seaman

David Seaman was the unfortunate victim of Gazza's famous long-range free-kick in the 1991 FA Cup semi-final between Tottenham and Arsenal. He was also an England team-mate and shared Gazza's interest in fishing.

We both loved fishing and Terry Venables knew that. Often he would come up to me and say: "David can you take him fishing, he's getting hyper?" So off we would go but on one occasion, for some strange reason, Gazza decided to take a sleeping tablet before we set off. I'm thinking to myself, 'What's going on here?' Anyway, we started fishing off a pier and he spotted a trout and went for the big cast. In trying to get as far as he could he goes tumbling into the water. He's yelling for me to get him out. I dredged him out and told him he wasn't going to spoil my fishing. I was going to carry on while he tried to get dry. Five minutes later, I look back and he's fast asleep completely soaked.

Another time, again during Euro 96, myself, Ian Walker and Gazza were on a boat in the middle of a lake happily fishing. Another boat approached and then we heard the click, click of a camera. A man was taking pictures of us. Gazza said to start rowing towards him because he wanted to get his camera. We both made it to the shore and this guy was in his car but couldn't go anywhere because I'd phoned the owner of the fishing lake to shut the gate after explaining what had happened. Gazza told the guy to hand over his camera. He refused but Gazza managed to nick his phone. He then put his window up, so Gazza started letting down his tyres. The man then panicked and decided to drive off, smashing through the locked gate!

Gary Lineker

Gary Lineker enjoyed a fun and successful playing relationship with Paul Gascoigne for both club and country. The Match Of The Day presenter witnessed at first hand the birth of Gazza-mania – and many of his famous pranks.

Without that vulnerable side and all the things that come with Gazza, I don't think he would have been the player he was.

Training ground experiences, like everything else with Gazza, were always great fun. He was a practical joker beyond what anyone has ever seen in the game. There were times when he would cross the line, like the day at the Tottenham training ground when he decided to sort out the pigeon problem we had. That involved bringing an air rifle into training. He also tried to deny taking pop-shots at the famous cockerel symbol which was on top of one of the stands at White Hart Lane. Any excuse to use his air rifle.

We used to have a guy who would come along to the training ground, a nice chap who would do anything for you. One day Gazza had brought in this camper van and went to get one of those parking cones and then placed it on the roof. The chap appeared and Gazza shouted for him to do him a favour and take the cone off the top of the camper van because someone must have put it there.

"Yeah, sure," he replied. He climbed up the ladder on the back of the vehicle and just as he was doing that, Gazza got into it, turned the engine on and went for a ride with the poor guy hanging on for dear life. Gazza then drives out of the training ground, through the gates and turns right. There is a little mini roundabout 200 yards further down the road. This poor guy is now like Superman, horizontal and hanging onto the ladder at the back of the van. It's the most dangerous but also hilarious thing I've seen. Thankfully, after Gazza had negotiated the mini roundabout at high speed, the guy was still in one piece. So then Gazza screeched back into the car park and finally parked up. As he was doing this, Terry Venables, the Spurs manager, walked out of his office and muttered: "I don't really want to be seeing something like this, do I?!" He then immediately walked back into his office.

Another time a cyclist got the shock of his life when, while waiting for the traffic lights to change to green, Gazza drove up alongside him and stuck an ice cream cone in his ear!

For a time when I was playing for Spurs I used to immerse one of my legs into a hot bath to help with a muscle problem. Before a game against Manchester City, Gazza said it seemed a good idea and he would give it a try. After I returned to the dressing room after doing some warm-ups, there was Gazza up to his neck in scalding water in the big communal bath. Gazza didn't seem to have energy during the first half of the match and Terry couldn't understand why he had been so poor. That resulted in Gazza claiming that the bathing experience had made him dizzy. I pointed out that there is a big difference between dipping your leg for five minutes and lying in it completely for 20 minutes!

One night a group of Spurs players, including myself and Gazza, were on a night out in London and wanted to go somewhere but we couldn't get a taxi. Gazza then said why didn't we get a bus? The bus stops and it's full. Gazza jumped on first and had a chat with the driver. I was last on and I said to the driver that I'd be surprised if anyone had paid, so how much did I owe?

Nothing, he said. With Gascoigne and Lineker on his bus, no charge. He then asked where were we heading for. I replied that we were going to Piccadilly. He said no problem, it was just two blocks off his route and he would drop us off. Gazza then goes to the front of the bus and starts singing, "We're all going on a summer holiday." Within seconds the whole bus has joined in. It was just mad.

Out of everything in my career, the moment people ask me about most often was when Gazza got booked in the semi-final of Italia 90. I could see his bottom lip was going. I turned to Bobby Robson, the England manager, to ask him to have a word with Gazza. I didn't know the moment would be caught on camera.

The relationship between Bobby and Gazza was extraordinary in many ways. It was like a father and son – but a very frustrated father a lot of the time. He used to take Bobby to his absolute wits' ends a lot of the time. There was a lot of joy, a lot of love and a lot of tellings off! Gazza was a young maverick but what Bobby saw in him was what he could give to the team and what ability he had. It was worth a risk because to do well at a World Cup you need something a bit different, something above the normal, and Gazza provided that. Gazza always wanted Bobby to love him. He needed to be the centre of attention.

Even after the semi-final, when everyone was distraught, Gazza helped break the atmosphere.

On the team bus a few beers were passed around and then Gazza started singing, "Doe, a deer, a female deer . . ." Chris Waddle joined in and it built up to a great big crescendo with everyone singing, which lifted the spirits. It was typical Gazza, amazing.

The World Cup lifted him from being a great footballer to being almost a national treasure. A year later he almost singlehandedly took Spurs through to the FA Cup final. It then ended up with him lying in a hospital bed with all the various emotions going through his head.

There's no doubt that the injuries Gazza sustained impacted on his life on and off the pitch. The more time you spend injured, the more time there is to get depressed and perhaps turn to drink and drugs, or whatever else does you in these circumstances. They had a real negative effect on him.

David Beckham might have been given the nickname Golden Balls by his wife but Gazza beat her to it with me. Well, it wasn't quite Golden Balls, it was more Golden Bollocks. He used it after George Best had claimed that Gazza's IQ was lower than his shirt number. Gazza came up to me and said: "Hey, Golden Bollocks, what does IQ mean?"

I love Gazza to bits. He's got his flaws but haven't we all? His humour is infectious. He was sharp and witty before he lost his way and he was so intelligent as a footballer the only pass he'd give you is one he knew you'd have to give him straight back – unless he was knackered.

Late on in Naples, in the World Cup quarter-final against Cameroon, he suddenly put me straight through on goal. I said to him that we had played together for two years and that he could have done that all the time.

"I know, I know," he grinned.

I still speak to Gazza. He will suddenly text me or call me out of the blue.

The text always comes from a different phone because he's lost the last phone. That's him.

Terry Venables

Terry Venables took on the task of trying to manage Gazza, first at Tottenham then later with England. Despite his patience being tested to the limit, Terry's laid-back manner helped forge a close bond between the pair. It is one which has lasted beyond Gazza's playing days, with the former Three Lions coach often on the end of a phone ready to help in moments of distress.

I knew all about Gazza before we went up to play Newcastle at St. James' Park.

The changing rooms at the time were just cabins set up in the corner of the ground due to some redevelopment work which was going on. I noticed Gazza coming out with his team-mates with a beaming smile, taking the mickey out of everyone.

Even as a young player he was immensely talented so I decided to put the experienced Terry Fenwick on him, to try to smother him. Also being interested in possibly signing him in the future, I wanted to see what he was made of, whether he could stand up to the physical part of the game. So at the first opportunity, Terry went 'bosh', straight into Gazza.

It didn't seem to bother Gazza one bit. In fact, I noticed he wasn't slow to dish it out himself, especially when the referee wasn't looking.

That was it. I knew we had to sign him and that was also the view of the man I trusted about players, Ted Buxton. Alex Ferguson at Manchester United was after him so we had to move quickly. It was set up that I could meet him and hopefully persuade him to come to Spurs. But the first thing I saw when I walked into the room was Gazza sat on a chair with a big teddy bear on his knee. I thought to myself, 'What's going on here?' I had already been told that Gazza rarely behaved like your average footballer. To be honest, if it meant paying a big fee for the teddy bear as well to get Gazza, I would have done it! But once the teddy bear was placed to one side, I simply asked him if he wanted to play for me.

I knew it was between us and Manchester United. I could tell he was getting more and more interested as he listened to what I was telling him – that he would enjoy himself at Tottenham and, of course, the advantage we had over United was having Chris Waddle, a big mate of his, already at the club. Chris had also made the same journey from Newcastle to join Spurs so he would be able to help Gazza settle in.

I later heard that Fergie really got the hump after missing out on signing Gazza because he knew what he could have brought to his side at that time. To say he was pissed off is an understatement. It was a coup and a half to get him, it really was. Everyone says he gave me sleepless nights trying to control him. Yes, he had his moments, but generally we were in harmony because, don't forget, I hadn't exactly been a saint when I was a young player. We gelled immediately. At times I would get my father, who lived in London, to spend some time with him. He would take him down to his local pub to mix with the regulars, which Gazza loved. Everyone took to him. He just wanted to make people happy. I knew from early on at Spurs that he just wasn't a good footballer, he was a good guy.

Tottenham and Gazza were the perfect match. He was like a Rolls-Royce in a fluent attacking team with players like Gary Lineker and Paul Walsh. Gary Mabbutt also helped Gazza a great deal on and off the pitch.

One of the best moments, of course, was when we won the FA Cup – not that Gazza was involved in the game for too long after injuring himself with that tackle on Gary Charles. As we were leading the two sides out, Brian Clough, the Nottingham Forest manager, grabbed my hand. I couldn't do anything about it and so there we were walking out onto the Wembley pitch holding hands. At least we ended up holding the FA Cup.

In the tunnel before the game, Gazza was really worked up. He was hyperactive at the best of times but on this occasion he couldn't contain himself. I tried to calm him down and I thought I had succeeded until we saw what he was like after the match started.

During the warm-up on the pitch he had been up to his usual tricks, taking aim at the brass band as they walked around playing their music – or trying to with Gazza on their case. When I later became England manager he would do the same whenever we were at Wembley. He would ping a ball in the direction of the band and dissolve into fits of laughter if it sent a hat flying. Once I saw him somehow chip the ball into one of those great big trombones. I would say to myself, 'Oh no Gazza, don't do that.' But then you end with tears of laughter running down your cheeks. It was like watching a naughty schoolboy.

Against Forest, he was eventually carted off to hospital with a busted knee while we managed to maintain our concentration and win the Cup in extra time. Afterwards, some of the players insisted that we should take the trophy around to show Gazza, and that's what we did. It showed what they thought of him, even though his rush of blood could have cost us the game.

Many people say that Gazza must have been trouble, a real pain in the backside, but believe me I couldn't wait to be reunited with him again when I took on the England job. It was a real body blow when he left Spurs to go to Lazio. Don't forget, when I was the Barcelona manager I had been in charge of Diego Maradona. Again, the view was that he was a load of trouble. That was completely wrong. Could you imagine those two in the same side? Now that would be interesting.

I like to think I got the best out of him. I remember substituting him in one game, which didn't exactly go down well. "Fuck off, you bastard," he shouted to me as he walked towards the dugout. Later on, when we arrived back at the team hotel, he knocked on my door ready to apologise. He was holding a pint of lager. "Don't do it again," I said. Gazza replied: "I didn't mean it, those words just came out without me thinking." "No," I added. "Next time, don't come in with a pint of lager, fetch me a glass of wine!"

There was no need to punish him. He had been worried sick that he had really upset me. I knew it was heat of the moment because he wanted to stay on the pitch. If you let him, Gazza would have stayed on the pitch until midnight.

Lying in bed, there's hardly a night goes by when I don't think about Euro 96 and Gazza's outstretched leg in the semi-final against Germany. If he had connected with Alan Shearer's volleyed cross we would have been in the final against the Czech Republic with a great chance of winning. If only . . .

Not that many people had given us a chance of going that far after the so-called antics in the build-up to the tournament. There was a media frenzy over pictures of some of the players, Gazza included, enjoying a few high jinks in a Hong Kong bar. Honestly, it didn't bother me one bit. My attitude at the time was, so what? The lads were together, enjoying themselves.

There were calls to take them out of the squad. Ridiculous. If you are going to be successful you need to be together, a tight unit. That was borne out in the 4-1 hammering of Holland and then, of course, what about Gazza's goal against Scotland? That flick over Colin Hendry's head and the finish. Then came the dentist's chair celebrations. No one was bothered then about what had happened in the Far East.

Sadly, after he finished playing there have been many sad moments involving Gazza, and I've helped him out a few times. Sometimes my phone would ring and Gazza would be on the other end crying, threatening to do something stupid. He was a mess and it was breaking my heart but you can't be around him 24 hours a day.

I remember being shocked by his appearance when I was summoned to Kensington Police station to try to help him after he had been arrested for some drunken escapade. There he was in the corner of a police cell smoking a cigarette. Gazza asked the policeman who was guarding him to leave the cell for a few minutes so he could talk to me in private.

Once the officer had gone Gazza just stared at me and mumbled: "I want to kill myself." I knew he wasn't kidding, he'd had enough. I also knew he had to stop drinking the amounts he was consuming at the time, otherwise the drink would have killed him.

The problem was he didn't really have anyone really close to him at the time. A proper lady in his life, for instance. Most of the clubs he had played for tried to help him but eventually they all had to give up, it was an impossible task.

What no one can take away are the memories of his incredible talent. Gazza was a brilliant talent, one of the best this country has ever seen. What was equally important is the fact he was a team man. To be successful you need a real team ethic. He had a huge ego when it came to football but he knew he couldn't win games on his own.

Too often, though, he has been forced to live life on his own and that has been a continual struggle.

Ted Buxton

As Terry Venables' chief scout and confidant at Tottenham and then with England, Ted Buxton implored him to bring Gazza to White Hart Lane.

We'd heard about this outstanding young player at Newcastle called Paul Gascoigne, so Terry Venables said I had better go up and have a look at this kid. He was only 17 or 18 at the time. I watched him three times and thought, 'what a talent.'

After the third time, I told Terry that if he had the chance to buy him then do it, definitely take him. There were no doubts in my mind that he would be a great addition to the Tottenham side. I told him the boy was a genius.

For me, his football was on a par with today's top stars like Lionel Messi and Cristiano Ronaldo, maybe even better. Everyone who played alongside him or saw him in action loved him. For a start he had three lungs and two great feet. He could run all day and never wanted to stop playing. He could take any game by the scruff of the neck and turn it around. There was nothing you could fault him on. Football-wise, he had everything. I honestly don't think there has been anybody since who could match him.

Bobby Robson, who was the England manager at the time, invited me up to St. James' Park to watch a Newcastle game with him. Also sitting next to us was Gazza's dad, John, and we had a nice chat. I think Gazza appreciated that we had both made a fuss of his father and that probably helped when he was choosing which club to join.

I got to know him and his family well. Gazza loved his family being around him and I know he bought houses for some of them in the same street on Tyneside. That was the generous side of him, while at other times he could drive you mad.

When Terry was the England manager and we were staying in hotels he always had members of his staff, including me, in charge of the players whose rooms were on a particular floor. Gazza was always on my floor because he felt I could handle him, having known him at Spurs.

The night before one game I was told by Terry to get all the players on my floor up to bed. That included Gazza. I told him to have a good night's sleep and I'd see him in the morning. About 1am, my phone in the room rang and it was Gazza. "Ted, are you awake?" he asked. "Well, I am now!" I replied. He said he couldn't sleep. He wanted me to go down and have a game of snooker with him. I reminded him that he had a game the next day. I also warned him if he did go out of his room I'd drag him back in.

The problem was he always wanted people around him. He never liked to be alone. He needed people. It's why, whenever he had injuries which kept him from playing for some time, I worried about him. If he didn't get that buzz of people around him he could be in trouble.

Terry was brilliant with him, both at Spurs and with England.

He was like a second father to Gazza, although his patience was tested at times. Often, when we had finished training at Tottenham, Terry would call the players together for a meeting. We'd all sit down and then you would look around and someone would shout out: "Where's Gazza?" That would be my cue to try and find him.

More often than not, he would be over with youth team coach Pat Holland and his boys. He would regularly join in games and so I would have to grab him off the pitch and escort him to the meeting. He just wanted to play all the time and, as you can imagine, the kids loved playing alongside him. You just had to calm him down.

At the Spurs training ground you would get different people coming in trying to sell this and that to the players. One day, a fella asked me if I wanted any new jackets. I really fancied one of them so I said: "How much?" I think he wanted £110 or something like that. I told him to put it to one side and when I'd had a shower and got changed I'd fetch him the money.

When I eventually returned, he said everything had been paid for. I couldn't believe it. "Who has paid?" I enquired. "Gazza," he said. I went to find Gazza, who said that if I didn't accept the gift he wouldn't talk to me anymore. That was typical of him.

Terry had a great relationship with Gazza despite tearing his hair out over some of his escapades at times. Regarding man-management, Terry is the best I have known. I have always believed that 75 per cent of being in charge of a team is down to man-management, with 25 per cent coaching. That was Terry. I can't remember anyone, including Gazza, ever arguing back. He would call players in for a chat. They would have a discussion and that was it, finished.

For England games, Terry would insist that all the players had the best seats ahead of the FA officials. A lot of people from the FA weren't happy about it but Terry couldn't care less. He was always a players' man.

Not that flights, even with the players in the posh seats, didn't pass without incidents. If Terry got wind of anything he would always sidle up next to me and say: "Ted, sort it out."

On one particular trip I was summoned to deal with a problem. I arrived in the players' section of the plane to find a bearded bloke straddled across a couple of players and looking completely out of it.

I discovered he was a pilot – although thankfully not supposed to be flying our plane – who was en route to his next job. He had got talking to the players. Gazza, Alan Shearer and some of them decided to try and get him drunk. They had obviously succeeded. It got out in the media somehow that there had been a drunken episode on the plane. Terry got the players together and said they would have to take the rap but to keep the pilot out of it because if news came out about him being drunk he could get the sack.

Then, of course, we had the so-called dentist's chair incident in a Hong Kong nightclub in the build-up to Euro 96. This time I wasn't involved, thankfully. Bryan Robson, one of Terry's coaches, was put in charge of the night out. It got into the newspapers and could have been detrimental to our Euro 96 campaign. But Terry used it as a positive, saying the high jinks had helped bring the squad together.

That was proved with the fantastic celebration following Gazza's goal against Scotland. I'd loved that goal celebration so much that Robbie Fowler and Gazza helped me re-enact it, with them pretending to pour drinks down my throat. It was great fun.

They were a great squad, full of fantastic characters. I can still see Gazza stretching for that Alan Shearer cross against Germany. If only! It was a shame that Terry didn't continue as England manager because there was a great buzz around him, his coaching staff and the players. The biggest compliment I can pay everyone is to say that the atmosphere at some of the England games reminded me of the celebrations which followed the ending of World War Two. There would always be thousands with their flags and banners lining the route to Wembley for our games.

On the coach, as we approached Wembley Way, Gazza would always insist that the driver put on the tape with the England song 'Three Lions'. Football's coming home and all that. We had to simply have it on otherwise Gazza would be beside himself.

Before one game the tape wouldn't work. Gazza is now going mad along with some of the other players who by now, like him, have become superstitious. We didn't want anything to spoil our routine and the Frank Skinner and David Baddiel song was now a big part of the our pre-match tradition. Gazza insisted that the coach stop, complete with its police escort, as the driver frantically attempted to rescue the tape. The police didn't know what was going on. They must have thought the coach had broken down.

Thankfully, the tape eventually started belting out, 'It's coming home, football's coming home'. We're all singing and Gazza's happy again.

They were happy days all round, with Gazza often at the centre of it all.

Stuart Pearce

Stuart Pearce, like Gazza, wore his heart on his sleeve and played alongside him during Italia 90 and Euro 96. He went on to manage his country and took charge of Manchester City and Nottingham Forest.

Gazza was our talisman in the England squad, the one who could deliver a world class performance and win any game on the day. He was fortunate that in Terry Venables he had someone who knew how to deal with him. Terry would often treat Gazza as a naughty schoolboy. He knew how to handle him. He would stand in front of the England players and absolutely wipe the floor with Gazza for some misdemeanour or other. Then Terry would turn away and wink at the rest of us. He was very clever and was able to get the best out of Gazza.

I think Euro 96 was the tournament that Gazza enjoyed the most. He came into it with a few people doubting whether he could reproduce his form from earlier years. They thought he was over the hill. But he went on to deliver some fantastic performances.

As a bloke he was very generous. As a professional footballer he would train longer than anybody else. He would do anything for you. He's helped me out on many occasions when I've asked things of him. He doesn't forget. He is someone who is genuinely loved all over the country. Ability wise I have not seen anyone come close to him.

But having to manage him? That would be hard work! I would prefer to have played with him than managed him. But the likes of Terry Venables and Bobby Robson handled him fantastically.

He was the absolute standout player of his generation. His goal against Scotland in Euro 96 is something that gets played time and time again. His performance against the Dutch in the same tournament was scintillating.

Gazza would be priceless now. Injuries might have blighted his career somewhat but I would still struggle to find somebody over the past few eras who has made the same impact. You would probably have to go back to the 1966 World Cup-winning side, maybe someone like Bobby Charlton. He could comfortably handle going into any current side in the Premier League and would probably fit into the recent great Barcelona side.

During Italia 90 his displays and emotion probably made football more popular. He put English football back on the map. The ball was stuck to his feet, he could tackle, he could head it, he could score incredible goals. He had everything. It didn't matter who he went up against in the world. He always felt he was better than they were – and quite often he was.

José Mourinho

José Mourinho heard all about Gazza from Bobby Robson when they were together at Barcelona. He also saw for himself the outstanding skills when he sat in the Wembley crowd witnessing the outrageous goal for England against Scotland in Euro 96.

Paul Gascoigne was the special one. I worked with Bobby Robson and he was really in love with Paul and was always speaking about his talent and the pleasure he had in coaching such a talented player. Paul was aggressive, very physical but at the same time very technical, fantastic characteristics you need to be a top footballer.

I took my wife to the England-Scotland game during Euro 96, not something I did very often. She was six months pregnant expecting our first child. She was upset with me because I made her walk too far to get to Wembley but I couldn't have seen a better game of football. Paul was magnificent and he scored a wonder goal to add to his fantastic history.

As a man and a player he operated at 100 mph and when you go that fast it's dangerous. His career could have been better if he had been supported in a different way. Clubs now are much more ready to support players and to point players in the right direction. But I still think he enjoyed very much of his career.

Glenn Hoddle

As England manager, Glenn Hoddle sparked an infamous rage from Gazza in his hotel room after leaving the player out of his squad for the 1998 World Cup finals.

We had planned decision day for the final squad announcement to the last detail. It's the saddest thing I've ever had to do, leaving Paul Gascoigne out of France 98. It was purely because he wasn't fit and he wouldn't have been fit for the tournament. Physically and mentally, I knew deep down he had run out of time.

I thought about trying to talk to him but I couldn't, not when he was in the state he was in. He would never have taken anything in – he had snapped. I thought he was going to hit me. There was a lamp to my left, to his right, and he just punched it. The glass shattered all over the room.

He was ranting, swearing and slurring his words. He was acting like a man possessed. I stood there and he turned as if to go and then came back with a barrage of abuse. Physically, he wasn't 100 per cent. Mentally, he was all over the place. His eyes had welled up. I had chats with other players I had left out but he was too upset. That's why things panned out as they did.

There were five things he needed to do. Stop drinking, get fitter than ever before, change his diet, learn to control his emotions and stay injury-free. He needed to look inside himself and ask himself what he wanted. Where was he going and how was he going to get there? If he didn't do that then nobody could help him.

I had given him so many opportunities to get fit. Six or seven months earlier, I had said: "Look, you've got to be fitter. This is another chance. This might be your last World Cup."

Ian Wright

Ian Wright was the first to witness the damage caused by an angry Gazza who had just been told of his England France 98 rejection in manager Glenn Hoddle's La Manga hotel room. Wrighty, who was capped 33 times by England and won the Premier League title with Arsenal, is now a successful and popular TV football pundit.

Glenn Hoddle had done everything he could to try and make Gazza understand that England needed him for France 98. I think he told him a year before to get himself fit because he wanted to build things around him.

In the end it didn't happen and in La Manga where Glenn was due to announce his final squad for the tournament Gazza was still breaking curfews and doing stupid stuff. Even so there was still a massive furore about Glenn not picking him. People were saying 'how can we not take him?' Even Bobby Robson said at the time how brave Glenn had been because Gazza was one of the world class players but he wouldn't be involved.

I went into Glenn's room after Gazza had smashed it up after being told he wasn't in the France 98 squad. To be honest, I thought I was going in to be told that I wouldn't be part of it. But I found out that I was in the squad and he was telling me what he would want me to do. He was actually talking about me being in the squad while we both cleared the room up.

Glenn and I were fixing the mattress, putting stuff back on the table and he's telling me he wanted me to be effervescent as I normally was in games, that I might be used in such and such a game and here we were tidying the room up. The room had been smashed to bits. It was surreal.

I was quite embarrassed. I was imagining how Glenn had to deal with Gazza going mad in the room. How does someone deal with that? I didn't really want to say anything about what I was witnessing. I was asking myself 'why has he let me in with the room in such a state?'

Even when he was at the height of his game you still had to worry about Gazza. You could never predict what he was going to do next. I remember when I was living in Croydon and Gazza was at Lazio. It was a Sunday and about 4pm he just turned up at the house. We ended up going around the pubs of Croydon, playing everybody at pool while drinking. That's the kind of person he was.

To see him with his problems during parts of his career was sad. He was a footballing genius but deep down just a normal boy from the North East. Everything about his football was world class but he has never been strong enough to deal with the demons he often possesses. At some of the England camps he would wave drinks in front of Tony Adams and Paul Merson, who had admitted they were fighting against an addiction. Gazza would tease them, not taking in the fact that it was a serious problem for the pair of them.

You always hoped that Gazza would eventually go down the same path and fight his own failings but I never thought that the people around him were strong enough to help. It wasn't good to see.

6

'Gazza asked me to swap cars with him. I later switched on the radio to hear on the news that police were investigating a death threat against him. I was about to drive home in his car and someone was threatening to shoot the owner!'

– John Greig, Rangers legend

Ally McCoist

Ally McCoist, a Rangers legend in his own right, aided and abetted his big mate Gazza in some of the exploits which helped make his stay in Glasgow eventful and enjoyable. Ally went on to manage the club and also joined mentor Walter Smith on the Scotland staff. He is currently a successful TalkSport presenter.

What a football player, what a talent. I often think in many respects that we saw the best of him at Rangers. He was comfortable. He was happy. He could go off and do his fishing. The fans loved him, everyone did. He's probably the one player I've known who could actually win a match by himself – take the game by the scruff of the neck and win it through his sheer ability.

Without a doubt he has been one of the players who have lit up Scottish football in the past 30 to 40 years. There have been some brilliant imports, players like Henrik Larsson, Paolo Di Canio and Brian Laudrup, but to play with someone as talented as Paul Gascoigne was an absolute privilege and pleasure. There was never a dull moment. There are so many stories to relate involving him you sometimes don't know where to start.

It had been a tradition for something like 140 years that Rangers players had to report for every training session and match in a collar and tie. You had to be in by 10am.

One morning it was getting close to the deadline and there's no sign of Gazza. Suddenly the door gets kicked open and in he comes sporting a huge pair of fishing waders, but wearing a collar and tie, holding two of the biggest trout you've ever seen in your life.

We were falling about laughing. Walter Smith, the manager, couldn't do anything discipline-wise because he wasn't breaking any rules. After all, Gazza had his collar and tie on, and as far as I know there wasn't anything in the rule book about wearing waders!

As it happened, Gazza and I were injured so we were left behind in the dressing room when the rest of the players left to go training. He then told me he had an idea. He wanted to hide the fish in one of the players' cars. I asked him who was going to be the victim? He said why not Gordon Durie? So I fumbled about in 'Jukebox's' clothes to find his car keys.

Out we went to his car and opened up the boot. Gazza started unscrewing the spare tyre and I handed him one of the fish. I was then ready to give him the other fish but he told me "no, you don't do that." Instead he went into the car itself with the other trout and found a compartment to hide it in. He explained that once Gordon found this one he would think, 'that's it – job done.' I'm thinking to myself, 'what a brilliant idea – he's a genius at this sort of thing.'

Two or three mornings later, Gordon came in complaining there was an awful smell in his car. He said it was unbelievable. Every time he stopped at the traffic lights or at junctions, people walking by were looking at him in disgust at the smell coming out of his car. Eventually he found the fish that was in the compartment and said he knew it must have been me or Gazza who had hidden it.

But for the next two days he was still complaining that, despite finding the fish, his car was still stinking. He must have bought around 14 or 15 air fresheners. They were hanging everywhere in a desperate attempt to rid his car of the smell. In the end he sent it to be cleaned and the second fish was discovered. Never mind a good clean, it needed to be fumigated! I think not long after he actually got rid of the car.

Another time, I told the lads in the dressing room I was going to go out and buy some fireworks for my kids so we could have a bit of a display on November 5th. Gazza turned to me and winked, saying he was the man when it came to fireworks. He said he could get a £100 box of fireworks for £10. "Right," I replied, "I'll have two boxes." The only proviso was he couldn't let on where he was getting them from. I was told I would have to meet his mate Jimmy 'Five Bellies' up at the back of the stadium at 8.30am the next morning.

I agreed and turned up at the arranged time. Sure enough, Jimmy is waiting there and he opens up the boot of his car to retrieve two giant bin bags, massive things. I stuck them in the boot of my car, handed over the £20 and away I went.

That night, I thought I'd better open up the bags to take a look at the fireworks. Stamped all over the boxes were loads of warnings like, for instance, that spectators should be at least 50 metres from the detonation. You've never seen fireworks like those in your life.

The following weekend, my wife and I were coming back home from a do in Glasgow. It's about 1.30am. Gazza lived in the next village and he had told us that once we got in the house to let him know and he would send a couple of rockets he had left from Jimmy's boxes in the direction of our village. He wanted to know whether we would see them.

Nothing was happening so I thought I might as well go to bed. The next moment you heard this great big boom and the whole bedroom was lit up. It was one of the rockets he had let off. The story didn't have a happy ending because a few minutes later the local constabulary knocked on his door and took him away to spend the night in a police cell.

Another time he came into the dressing room, dropped his bag and shouted "right lads" and just smiled. He had a new set of teeth. The whole place was in uproar. When everyone had stopped killing themselves with laughter he came over to me and said: "Coisty, what do you think?" I said with those teeth he could chew an apple through a letterbox! I told him for a laugh to pretend that I was a blonde who he was going to chat up with his new teeth. He was up for it and so I sat down at a table with a glass of wine and he came up and introduced himself. "I'm Paul," he said and immediately flashed his new teeth. That was it then, you couldn't stop laughing.

We did have a bit of a set-to once in a game. I even chased him up the tunnel at half-time. It was stupid schoolboy stuff but once we got into the dressing room I clocked Walter and knew it was time to shut up. I'd had a few more experiences about how to handle Walter than Gazza at the time. Gazza, though, was still at it, pointing his finger at me and refusing to be quiet. The next thing, Walter has him pinned up against the wall and you can see the colour drain out of Gazza's cheeks. Then, in the second half, he went and scored two of the best goals you have seen in your life.

He also gave me one of the biggest frights of my life. At around 3am, when I was asleep in bed, my wife nudged me and said she thought there was someone in the house downstairs. I started listening and, sure enough, I could hear a noise which as everyone could imagine was quite disturbing. The first thing I grabbed was one of my golf clubs, a three iron. To be honest,

I don't know why because I couldn't hit a three iron at the best of times!

As I went down the stairs I could tell the noise was coming from the kitchen. I'm now faced with confronting a burglar. I kicked open the kitchen door and straight away I recognised the back of Paul Gascoigne, who is looking into my fridge. He didn't even turn around. I asked him what he was doing. Still not turning around, he informed me he was making a sandwich. I told him it was 3.30am. He said he knew that but he had woken up – he still lived in the next village – and was feeling hungry. He had no food in his house so decided to come over to mine. I asked him how had he managed to get into my house. He told me he had remembered me talking to my wife on the phone and that I had mentioned the spare house key being in a bag under the oak tree. So, when he was hungry, he decided to come over to my house, let himself in with the spare key and make himself a sandwich. I finally went back upstairs and my wife asked me what was going on. I replied that everything was fine, it was just Gazza making himself a sandwich!

Another story revolves around the Italian midfielder Gennaro Gattuso, who had just been signed by Walter. He's probably the most competitive player I've ever known, treating every training session like a full-blooded match and to hell with the consequences. There's the Old Firm game coming up at the weekend and just a few days before in training, in typical style, Gennaro is scything people down. Walter's going off his head, yelling that we have a game against Celtic coming up and to go easy on the tackling. He turned to Gazza, saying that as he knew a bit of Italian from his Lazio days could he tell Gattuso to calm down. That was a big mistake on Walter's part. Gazza went up to

Gennaro and, in his broken Italian, told him the opposite, that if he wanted to play against Celtic then he should show more commitment. Within seconds, Gennaro's studs are imbedded in my chest after a challenge which was nowhere near the ball.

Being hyperactive and unable to sleep, no one would room with Gazza before games. He was allocated a room all to himself. I used to room with Ian Durrant. Around 5.30am one Saturday morning, I couldn't believe my eyes. There playing a game on the telly in our room was Gazza. Durranty wondered what was going on as well. How had he got in and why was he using our telly when he had his own in his room? We discovered he had gone down to reception and asked for the spare key for our room. He needed company, Gazza explained. After that, Durranty and I would always have a different room to the one written down and on no account would Gazza be allowed a spare key.

Just before Euro 96, Gazza and Les Ferdinand were supposed to do an advert for a jet-ski company on the River Thames. Gazza couldn't make it and rang telling me he had the deal of the century. All I had to do was ride a jet-ski along with Les at the London Docks for an hour and the jet-ski would be mine – although there wasn't a great demand for jet-skis where I was living! But I agreed to do it as a favour to him. I met big Les and after putting on all the gear, including the wet suits, we were ready for action.

Two guys in another boat were involved, one driving it and the other taking the pictures of Les and I on the water. It was all going well but they finally wanted action pictures of us crossing right in front of their boat. No bother, we said.

The problem was, Les went first in front of me and the water from his jet-ski shot into the air and I couldn't see a thing. When I finally could see I found myself heading straight for the boat which was filming us. The two guys, one of them complete with £800 worth of camera kit, dived off their boat into the water while I went flying over it. It was like a scene from a James Bond film. I'm sure it was the sort of thing Gazza would like to have been involved in.

Stuart McCall

Stuart McCall was a team-mate and close confidant of Paul Gascoigne when the pair were together at Rangers. They faced each other in the iconic England v Scotland game at Euro 96 and, thanks to his friend's generosity, the McCall household has a few Gazza mementos.

When he arrived at Rangers I received the short straw when it came to where the players got changed in the dressing room – he was allocated a peg next to me. My peg was number three and I pleaded with Jimmy Bell, the kitman, not to give Gazza number four, which I knew was available.

But he was such a generous, fun-loving human being as well as an outstanding, talented footballer.

In modern-day football you talk about number 10s, luxury players or whatever. I used to say to Gazza that I would do all the dirty work and I'd get the ball to someone like him who could play and create magic. But he wanted to do his share of the hard work. Okay, he wasn't great at tackling, but he didn't mind running, putting his foot in, chasing back and winning headers.

I first came up against him in a League Cup game when I was

at Bradford City and he was at Newcastle United. We were both similar ages and I think Jack Charlton, the Newcastle manager, tried to buy me after this match to play alongside Gazza.

When you think of Gazza the footballer you see his outstanding ability, being able to go past people. But he didn't just want to concentrate on that – he didn't want players like me to do all the grafting. Despite his amazing talent he was no prima donna. He was always one of the lads, he didn't want to be treated any differently.

At Rangers he came into a really strong dressing room. There were a lot of characters in there. You had the likes of Ally McCoist, Ian Durrant, Brian Laudrup and Gordon Durie.

He was magnificent and it was just a pity it ended when it did – not even being able to finish off his third season and leaving for Middlesbrough. But no one was disappointed with his performances when he was there. He was at his best when he had a smile on his face and had the responsibility of his kids. Taking them to school and picking them up was something he looked forward to but when the family moved back down south, it left a big void which he found hard or almost impossible to fill. He didn't have anything to do at 3.30pm, he didn't have kids to pick up. He would take himself off fishing but that's really when everything unravelled for him.

When he had a stable family life I think that's when he was playing his best football. It was just a shame that didn't last long enough. I believe that if he had been on top of his game and had stayed to the end of his last season then we would have ended up winning a 10th Scottish title in a row, instead of finishing runners-up to Celtic.

Everyone knew of his injury problems at Lazio but the first

thing you noticed in training was how strong he was. There wasn't a lot of coaching done because the manager, Walter Smith, would say we were at this level and didn't need any intense coaching. But the five-a-sides we had were intense. They always meant something. There was no nastiness but it was really competitive. No one wanted to be on the losing side. Gazza was in his element and you didn't really want to be facing him. When his head was on it and he was bang in the zone, his body was ripped. He had the appearance of a really strong athlete. There were times in his career when things went wrong and he put weight on but at Rangers he looked perfect.

In five-a-sides he could collect the ball in tight areas and just roll you. Whereas Brian Laudrup would glide past you, Gazza went past you with a bit of strength. Straight away you could see he wanted to be part of what we wanted to achieve at Rangers. He wasn't going to sit back and bask in his big price tag and do some flicks and tricks. There was none of that.

We had to be in at 10am every morning for training. I think the fine was £10 for every minute you were late. There was also a tradition at Rangers that you had to report in a shirt and tie. The story has already been told that Gazza eventually turned up resplendent in a Hugo Boss shirt and Armani tie. That was the top half. Then we looked down at the rest of him and he's in some great big fishing waders, complete with a pair of wellies! Anyway, we went off for a good training session. I then went into the gym and I'm probably the last one back to the changing room. Gazza has long gone. So have my socks and shoes. My trousers have also disappeared and in their place are a pair of waders and wellies! I was due to pick my kids up from school, so in desperation I had to search out a pair of Rangers shorts and pick up some trainers. He had nicked pretty well every-thing. That's the price you pay for getting changed next to Gazza every day!

But in fairness it was a lively dressing room where it was tit for tat and Gazza would have pranks played on him in turn for him stepping out of line.

Gazza was very generous, probably over-generous at times. We'd just played a game on the Tuesday night, so the next day we were brought in for what is now called a cool-down. In our day it was to sober up. So we did a bit of light work and then we were off. It was someone's birthday and we were all going to meet up in what you would call an old man's pub in the middle of Glasgow. It was great because no one would bother you there. You could play pool. There was horse racing on the telly, you would often play cards. A brilliant place. You never got any hassle or bother.

So I jumped into a car with Ian Durrant and Gazza, then headed off into town. Durranty said he had to drop off a couple of tickets in one of the bars on the Paisley Road West. He told us both to come in and have a pint while he sorted the tickets out. It was quite busy. The lady behind the bar was obviously a huge Gazza fan and asked whether she could have the T-shirt he was wearing. He said she could as long as he could have her top in exchange. I think it was a Rangers polo shirt. Gazza took off his shirt and signed it and handed it over while accepting her top. He put it on and we're now back in the car heading for the pub where we have all agreed to meet. Soon, there was a horrible smell in the car. It was coming from Gazza and it was obviously the girl's top, which let's say wasn't the most hygienic.

We came up to some traffic lights which forced us to stop and

Gazza demanded to be let out of the car. He said he would be two seconds. The next thing, he's disappearing into a charity shop only to re-emerge in a blue and white floral dress! It was unbelievable. He had evidently handed over the stinking top and given a couple of quid for the dress. He gets back into the car and we're off again to the pub.

The strangest thing was that no one in the pub made a big thing of Gazza wearing a dress. 'Oh, it's Gazza' appeared to be the general opinion. Eventually he gave £100 to Jimmy 'Five Bellies', who was with us, to pop into a nearby Versace shop and grab him a top-of-the-range shirt to replace his dress. Jimmy comes back with one of the most lairy shirts you can imagine – it's horrific even though it's cost the earth. So Gazza takes the dress off and puts the shirt on. Later, people coming into the pub are looking at him and asking what the hell he is wearing. No one was bothered when he was wearing a dress but they can't handle this multi-coloured £100 shirt! Anyway, he just batted it all off and sat there.

Then a lad comes into the pub selling the Glasgow evening paper. I think they cost 30p each. Gazza asked for £10 off us all. We thought he was just collecting for the next round. There was now something like £160 which had come from all the lads. He called the young lad over and asked for a paper. I think he wanted to see whether he had got the star rating in the match report from the game the night before. I told him to save his money, that would have gone to me! To our disbelief he pushes the £160 into the kid's hand and told him to keep it all. The kid was obviously gobsmacked but off he goes.

Still hardly believing what we had witnessed, we spent the next hour or so playing cards. At the same time Gazza was getting so much stick about his shirt that he put his dress back on. Not long after that, the young lad who had been given the money pops back into the pub. We think he's come back to thank Gazza again. Instead he came over and pulled the zip down on his jacket to expose a Celtic top. He then shouts: "Hey Gazza, your team is a load of shite but not as shite as your shirt!" Gazza gets up to grab hold of him. But the kid wasn't hanging around and went racing out of the pub down the street with Gazza chasing him – or trying to chase him with a dress on. Needless to say, he never caught him. When he came back to the pub he was absolutely knackered.

There was Euro 96 and the England-Scotland game, of course. There had been plenty of banter in the build-up considering a number of us from Rangers – like myself, Ally McCoist and Gordon Durie – would be coming up against him in the match. The night before the game I gave an interview in which I mentioned that my daughter loved Gazza. She was born in England and wanted it to be 3-3 with her dad and Gazza each getting a hat-trick. There was no way I was going to get one.

I never thought anymore about what I'd said because I'm now fully focussed on trying to beat England at Wembley. There were some personal duels to be sorted – club team-mate against team-mate, like Alan Shearer up against Colin Hendry, Colin Calderwood up against Teddy Sheringham and the Rangers lads up against Gazza. I'd overheard some of the lads saying Gazza had promised them his shirt after the match. I was never one to get involved in anything like that, certainly not before a game.

It comes to half-time and we'd more than held our own against England, who had started off as favourites. Gazza had been quiet. Going off towards the dressing room, I heard these footsteps behind me and it's Gazza. He gets up alongside me and takes his shirt off, hands it me and says: "That's for your wee girl." I'd never mentioned anything to him but he had obviously seen the interview. All I had said was my daughter was a big Gazza fan. In the midst of that game, in which he had until then been largely disappointing, he could still think of me and my daughter. I didn't give him mine in exchange! I got back into the dressing room and just quietly tucked it into my bag.

The second half, of course, produced one of the most iconic goals scored at Wembley – the one where Gazza lifts the ball over Colin Hendry before firing home. After the match, we're in the coach going back to the Birmingham area where we are based. At the back of the bus, Ally McCoist gets out Gazza's shirt to show everyone. I think Darren Jackson, who played with Gazza at Newcastle, had another Gazza shirt. I said to Coisty that was a disgrace taking a shirt from someone who has probably knocked us out of the European Championships. I was straight faced. The other lads thought I was being a bit harsh. Then I dived into my bag to produce the one Gazza had given me. "Here's one that he hadn't scored in," I laughed.

We later discovered that Terry Venables, the England manager, was ready to take off Gazza if Gary McAllister had scored the penalty we were awarded. Instead it was saved by David Seaman and, from the corner, England broke away and Gazza scored.

In fairness to him he hardly mentioned it when he reported back for pre-season training. I can tell you now the stick he would have received from McCoist and me would have been serious stuff if one of us had done that. He was quite humble. We would have been rubbing it in his face, no danger. That said a lot about him. He had his daft moments but deep down he was very modest. He was so well loved by everyone. The problem was he would easily become addictive to things. At Rangers he went through a phase when he was downing slimming pills to try and regulate his weight. He would smoke to try and calm himself down. It was a terrible shame because all he wanted to do was to please people. You felt for him when he became troubled.

I returned to Bradford City shortly after Gazza had joined Middlesbrough. The first game Bradford City played back in the Premier League was against Boro. It was at Teesside but I was injured and didn't play. We ended up winning 1-0. Gazza came into the players' lounge after the game. I'm in there with my lad, who was celebrating his ninth birthday. Gazza must have been disappointed. They had just lost at home on the opening day of the season against a team they were expected to beat. He comes over for a chat and asks who the lad is. I told him it was my son and it was his birthday. He said he would see us later, all the best. A few minutes later we're heading out of the room and Gazza comes up with a signed shirt that he had just played in for my lad.

His first game for Burnley, with his career now going downhill a bit, was against Bradford City and I'm playing against him. At the end of the game we meet in the players' lounge and he comes up with his boots, which he's signed. "Here, give them to your lad," he says. They were probably one of the last pair he ever wore. He was so generous.

Later, he went to Boston to do some coaching in addition to playing. I had just joined Sheffield United and we're playing them in a pre-season friendly. He was asking me what he should do coaching-wise in the warm-up. He just wanted a few tips. Anyway, I wanted to know how he was keeping. He said he was having trouble sleeping. I said he was probably excited or maybe nervous about going into coaching. He replied that he would sleep for 10 minutes and then sit up bolt upright. I asked him if he was doing anything different. He explained that he was taking a healthy drink. "I'm drinking about 30 bottles a day of something called Red Bull," he said. "You're kidding me, aren't you?" I said. "It's a wonder your heart rate hasn't gone through the roof!" He was addicted to Red Bull. It was amazing he could sleep at all. He has this addictive personality. But he's so loveable at the end of the day. There's only one Gazza.

John Greig

John Greig spent his entire career with Rangers as a player, manager and a director. He is now an honorary life president.

I well remember the day Gazza asked me to swap cars with him. I was driving a club sponsored Honda Accord and he had a top of the range two-seater BMW but he explained that he required a roomier motor because he had his close pal Jimmy 'Five Bellies' and a cousin visiting, so I handed over the keys to my car. I warned him to look after the motor but moments later I was standing at the front door of Ibrox when Gazza flashed past me in it doing 70mph and honking the horn.

To be honest, I half expected that sort of reaction but I was totally unprepared for what happened next. I went off to the gym for a workout and later switched on the radio to hear on the local news that police were investigating a death threat against Gazza. Here I was about to drive home in his car – one you couldn't fail to notice, complete with tinted windows – and someone was threatening to shoot the owner! Needless to say I insisted on having my car back the following morning.

You could never remain angry with Gazza for long, though, even when you were detailed to act as his chauffeur – as I was when he was ordered home from a trip to New York by Walter Smith. Gazza had been given permission to take time off to recover from an injury but he was supposed to spend it relaxing away from the spotlight. Instead, he elected to fly to the USA for the weekend to watch the St. Patrick's Day parade.

That was bad enough but much worse was to follow when the Monday morning tabloids carried front page pictures of Gazza sitting with a bunch of Celtic fans and clearly enjoying a few drinks. Walter went ballistic and word was sent to Gazza to catch the first available flight home.

I was dispatched to pick him and his agent Mel Stein up from Glasgow Airport. I was fortunate enough to be given clearance to drive onto the tarmac to avoid the waiting hordes of journalists who had gathered. When Gazza and Stein emerged from the aircraft they couldn't understand what the fuss was all about. "What's he done wrong?" asked Stein. "The only way you could have beaten that was to lead the parade sitting astride a white elephant," I replied! Stein said that would be a great line for his book.

For all that, I admired Gazza. Alright, he had problems at times but would he have been the same player without the traumas that dogged his career? Possibly not. He might have started worrying about the game and not become the player he was at his peak. Perhaps Gazza didn't get as much from his career as he should have but, for a few years at least, he was the supreme entertainer and loved by the fans.

Andy Goram

Andy Goram was the Rangers goalkeeper during the Gazza years at Ibrox and was the fall guy for one of the most iconic England goals. Playing for Scotland during Euro 96, he was beaten by Gazza's volley against Terry Venables' side at Wembley.

The volley that followed after Gazza had danced around Colin Hendry was true and well hit but I look back now and curse myself because I feel I should have saved it.

Everyone knew that Gazza had been on that drinking spree in Hong Kong in the build-up to Euro 96, sitting in the dentist's chair and having drink poured down his throat. Now he was behind my goal lying on the deck with Teddy Sheringham squirting water down his throat. I felt sick but deep down inside from somewhere I managed to laugh to myself. Only Gazza could think of doing something like that. At the end, though, our pre-match agreement to swap shirts meant nothing to me. I just wanted to get off the pitch. He walked towards me with a big smile on his face but saw that a storm was gathering inside me. If he had said a word I would have smashed him. I would have had to knock him clean out because I was hurting too much. He took one quick glance, saw the thunder in my face and kept on walking. To be fair to Paul, he did seek me out afterwards when I had calmed down and gave me his shirt.

Then, on the first day of pre-season training he did me up like a kipper in the dressing room. I walked in and he had two traffic cones set up as goals at one end. In the middle of the room there was another cone with a white mophead stuck on it. That was supposed to be big 'Braveheart' Colin Hendry! Gazza was running up and down, flicking the ball over the mophead and volleying it in screaming "Gascoigne scores for England." Flaming lunatic. That was his moment of glory.

I was drawn to Gazza as a pal because I saw a little bit of myself in him. I never had his level of fame and I wouldn't have wanted it. He had a tremendous sense of humour. One time when he was in Rome he was at his lavish villa getting ready to go to the Lazio player of the year dinner. It was a black tie do and his mates were all running about having a drink and getting ready. But Jimmy 'Five Bellies' was making them late so Gazza took all the hair gel out of the tub and replaced it with something else. 'Five Bellies' slapped it all on in a mad rush. Halfway through the journey he ran his hand through his hair and suddenly massive clumps of it fell out. Obviously Gazza had inserted some powerful stuff! I used to wonder where all this came from. He was an insomniac and at times he must have lay there planning his next prank.

We were having a meeting after training on the pitch at Ibrox on a Friday morning before the Old Firm game. The gaffer, Walter Smith, had gathered us all in a circle. Nerves were fraught. You could feel the tension and everyone was silent because Walter was speaking. Then, all of a sudden, Erik Bo Andersen started squealing. Gazza was peeing on his leg. Gazza said he did it to try and lighten the atmosphere.

He was fortunate that he worked under Walter Smith at that stage of Walter's life. You can't underestimate the effect that Walter and Archie Knox had on him. They loved him and looked after him. Walter was like a father to him. The gaffer's missus Ethel is an amazing woman and she was the one who helped Paul when he was really lonely, having him around for

Christmas dinner. He had split up from his wife Sheryl again and he was alone around Christmas time. It would have been a recipe for disaster but the Rangers family looked after him. Walter drove to Cameron House on the banks of Loch Lomond where Gazza was staying and fetched him to the Smith house for his turkey.

Ian Durrant

Ian Durrant was also a team-mate of Paul Gascoigne's at Rangers and was part of a 'rogues gallery' which featured Gazza and Ally McCoist. He went on to become a coach at Ibrox under Walter Smith and McCoist.

I don't think we will ever see a character like Paul Gascoigne again. He has been a great friend over the years to me. He's a tremendous person. And what a player. Even in training he did some fantastic things. He would play every minute of the day if he could. On a Friday, the gaffer Walter Smith and his assistant Archie Knox had to drag him off the training pitch to save him for the game the next day.

Archie had a lot of responsibility at the club but one of the most important things he had to deal with was Gazza. The gaffer had too much on his plate to keep a watch on him. In fact, we all used to take it in turns to try and watch him. It was more like a babysitting job. Gazza was nuts but whenever he heard Archie's voice you could see the expression change in his face. Archie knew how to treat him and keep him on his toes. He knew how to get the best out of him.

He was absolutely priceless in and around the dressing room. At Ibrox there was already myself and Ally McCoist who loved to wind people up but then we had Gazza come along. He did me a few times. Once he nailed my shoes to the floor. Can you imagine grabbing hold of them to put them on and they wouldn't move! Often you would find that your clothes had disappeared. He would have hidden them. He loved to organise the Christmas parties. Often it would be some sort of fancy dress occasion. Gazza loved dressing up as royalty and always had a crown on his head.

It was sad to see him leave for Middlesbrough, although it nearly didn't happen. He was driven down to the Riverside Stadium by Jimmy 'Five Bellies' to sign but at one point he told Jimmy to turn around. But as he did there was another phone call from Bryan Robson, the Boro manager, and that persuaded Gazza to keep going.

Terry Butcher

Terry Butcher played with Gazza both at Rangers and with England. A powerful central defender who first came to prominence under Bobby Robson at Ipswich, he later went on to manage the likes of Coventry City, Sunderland, Sydney FC, Inverness Caledonian Thistle and the Philippines.

Gazza would often cover up things with a laugh and a joke. It was just a case of 'Oh, that's Gazza'. On the field he felt he had to be brilliant all the time. It's what people often expected and you can't live up to that expectation all the time. There's always that overriding fear as a footballer that one day your career will be over. You hope it will last forever but that day always comes when you have to retire.

He had real issues but you saw from time to time the real Paul

Gascoigne, the lovely guy that he is. Really, he never had the help that was needed.

One night we were staying at the same hotel. It had been an unbelievable night with plenty of drink flying around. Later the next morning, he looked out of his window and there were 10 Harley Davidsons parked on the lawn. He went downstairs and remarked to one of the hotel workers that he had noticed the bikes and that they were fantastic. "Was there a Harley Davidson show in the area?" he enquired. The reply stunned Gazza. "No sir, they are all yours. You bought them last night." He had managed to purchase them despite obviously being worse for wear through drink. They had been £100,000 each and he had secured 10!" He went off to search for the guy he had bought them off. He told him that he could only ride one – not 10 – so could he take nine of them back? The guy refused but in the end they agreed a deal. Gazza still ended up losing £500,000.

He's an amazing guy but he has lived on the edge for so many years. At times he has fallen off it but come back. That's been his life. If he'd had help at the right times maybe it would have been a lot different. He was hyperactive and couldn't sit still, something that was very apparent during Italia 90. One day, his room-mate Chris Waddle wanted to escape from him and hid in the room I was sharing with Chris Woods. If Gazza knocked on the door, I would have to pretend that I didn't know where the Waddler was.

If he was off the drink, Gazza would chain-smoke cigars. He would also drink Red Bull and get high as a kite. That was the wrong thing for him to drink. He needed stuff to calm him down. But you could never get him to read a book, for instance, because he would only make paper planes with the pages.

Walter Smith

Walter Smith took on the role of father figure when he managed Gazza at Rangers, helping in troubled times and even inviting the player to celebrate Christmas with his family, and signed him for a second time when he became Everton boss.

I bumped into him on holiday in Florida the year before he signed for Rangers. He was staying in the same hotel. He didn't know who I was, but that's Paul. I had my two boys with me and they certainly recognised him.

Later, on the beach, Gazza picked up an American football and deliberately hurled it way over my younger son's head so it would land on someone sunbathing nearby. It meant my son would get the abuse when he retrieved the ball while Gazza quickly disappeared into the sea.

Some time later, I read in the newspapers that his time was up at Lazio, that they were ready to let him go.

I sat down with Archie Knox, my assistant manager, and discussed whether we should try to sign him. Archie knew him from his days at Manchester United, when Paul was beginning to emerge at Newcastle United, and later when he was at Tottenham.

He'd had his injury problems but I said to Archie that I felt he was someone who could make a difference in our side. We needed a spark and I felt he could supply that. Archie agreed and encouraged me to try to do the deal. I then spoke to the chairman, David Murray, and he was all for it.

The chairman got in touch with the president of Lazio, saying we would be interested in signing him.

He was told they were selling him at the end of the season and we could speak to him, but there were also several English clubs interested.

The people at Lazio gave me his address so I flew to Rome, got into a taxi and door-stepped him. He had been out with a broken leg for much of the season so it wasn't a case of watching him play.

I heard this noise coming towards the gate and it was Gazza on a quad bike. He asked me what was I doing here. I replied that I was there to try to get him to sign for Rangers. He said "okay." The Lazio people hadn't told him I was coming.

We had an interesting day. I got a car back to the airport and returned to Scotland. His agents wanted him to join an English club but he said no to that and insisted he was going to Rangers.

At the start of life with us he was determined to show that he was back as a big player. It wasn't just about making an impression in Glasgow. He wanted to show London, everywhere, that Paul Gascoigne was still capable of making an impact.

You have to be able to deal with the other things that come with being Paul Gascoigne. One day, I bumped into the comedian Billy Connolly in Glasgow.

With that knowing look, he asked me: "How are you getting on with Gascoigne?" I replied: "Fine but there's always a wee problem here and there." Billy smiled and said: "Always remember this, Walter. You will always have to live with the genius. The genius will not live with you."

I really didn't think about it until much later. For the likes of Terry Venables, Bobby Robson and myself, that's what we've had to do. Any problems he had were outweighed by the tremendous football talent he possessed, so you have to put up with the genius. Sometimes you have to take action and rein the personality in. But you have to accept frailties. You have to accommodate them. I hear people in football talking about everyone being the same. They are lying. The majority of guys in the dressing room know that the ones who are exceptional will be allowed a bit of laxity.

With Gascoigne, I had to sit down with the whole dressing room and tell them: "This is what we have here. We have a boy who will win us games, so we all have to be able to handle him." Gazza didn't know what he had. He knew he was good but he hadn't a clue about being asked to do something. He didn't want to know tactics. He played in midfield and that was that – he didn't have a further thought. He had the genius for it and that was what Billy Connolly was talking about. The team and I had to work with that. You had to put up with the genius. You can become frustrated but then he wins you the game.

If you mention the name Gazza you immediately start to laugh. We had some real characters in the side like him, Ally McCoist and Ian Durrant. They bring a smile to your face when their names crop up. Gazza also had the capability of bringing a smile to your face through his football as well. He would be everywhere on the pitch. The only thing you had to make sure of was that you kept giving him the ball because if he didn't see it for a while, he got frustrated.

I thought for two and a half years at Rangers, until he got injured, he played some fantastic football for us.

At the same time we had another outstanding player in Brian Laudrup. In training for five-a-side or seven-a-side games I used to have them on different teams because if they played together they would just pass to each other all the time.

In matches they were unbelievable. You knew when Gazza was really up for it, he would be on his toes. When he wasn't dancing you knew he wasn't right. He could also gain or lose weight quicker than anyone I've ever known.

But it was always a challenge managing him. You take him knowing what you've got. I had to tell the lads that he would probably get away with a bit more than the majority of them but he would win football matches.

He was never bad in a malicious sense, it was always stupid things. Things would come into his head and I would have to handle the repercussions. Archie handled him fantastically and kept him out of my road whenever he could. I put an arm around him, to a degree, but I could go the other way with him as well when it was needed.

One Christmas he came over to my house for his dinner and to join in the festive celebrations. He was the life and soul of the party. He charmed everyone in all the different age groups. I wasn't surprised because whenever we needed players to attend a charity do he was always the first to take one step forward and volunteer, especially when kids were involved.

No one can take away the fact he was one of the most talented footballers of that generation.

When he eventually lost the Gazza persona, that's when you knew the problems could start.

He loved football and knew he was exceptionally good at it. He never bogged himself down with tactics or anything like that. It was just about playing.

That was Gazza and that was it.

When the footballing side was going to leave him, that's when you worried.

Everybody who knew him would have been sad to see some of the things that happened after he stopped playing. Many people have tried to help but obviously the problems have been deep rooted. Everyone wanted him to rediscover some aspects of normality.

Archie Knox

Archie Knox narrowly missed out on being able to coach Paul Gascoigne at Manchester United but that all changed when Walter Smith later managed to prise the player to Rangers. By then, Knox was Walter's number two, the role he enjoyed under Alex Ferguson at Old Trafford, and he would go on to work with Gazza again at Everton.

I remember going away on holiday one summer at Manchester United after Alex Ferguson had phoned me and said: "That's it – we've got Gascoigne signed." Something had obviously gone wrong because the next day he was on his way to sign for Tottenham. It was a big blow to Alex. Who knows, if he had gone to Manchester United then maybe the way his life panned out would have been different. I know he really enjoyed his time at Rangers, though, after Walter had gone over to Italy to doorstep him when it was known that Lazio were prepared to sell him. Walter told me that when he tracked down the house where Gazza was staying, he was met by Gazza riding a quad bike in the garden trying to run down Jimmy 'Five Bellies'.

Walter introduced himself and told him: "I'd like to sign you for Rangers." Gazza evidently said: "Oh aye, that would be great." That was the transfer pretty much done there and then.

Gazza was a one-off but somebody you couldn't help but like despite the stupid things he would often get up to. He had a bizarre pre-match ritual. In the dressing room, until Walter named the team, Gazza would be sitting there in his shirt and tie. When his name was mentioned, that was the key for him to take off all his clothes one by one while Walter continued talking. It was ridiculous, he could end up sitting there with his trousers down by his ankles and have no underpants, although he would often go home in some because he would steal a pair from one of his team-mates. It was a wonder that Walter could concentrate, although he would sometimes say to Gazza: "Is there any chance you could listen to what I'm saying?" Gazza would insist he was listening. To be fair to Gazza, he never took it for granted that he would be playing and I think this ritual was something to do with him being edgy and nervous.

He once had the lads in stitches when he turned up with a new set of teeth. He was quickly christened 'Red Rum' and 'Arkle' because they were more suited to a horse. After training he returned to the dressing room to find some hay and a bag of carrots next to his peg.

Quite often after training, Gazza loved going to a café not far from Ibrox on Paisley Road West. He loved the bacon rolls there. I'd join Gazza and some of the other players there on occasions. One day a group of us arrived at the café and outside there was a council worker sweeping the street. He was wearing a bright yellow jacket, complete with a hat, and was next to an old-fashioned cart as he brushed away. Gazza decided it would be great if the council worker came and joined us while he did his job for half-an-hour. Gazza asked him to take off his jacket and hat so that he could put them on. Within minutes, there he was sweeping the pavement and tipping the litter into the cart. There were people going past blissfully unaware that the council had a new sweeper, Paul Gascoigne.

Another time, it's the day of the Scottish Cup final at Hampden Park and we're playing Hearts. The kitman, Jimmy Bell, told me there was a problem – Gazza had arrived at Ibrox, where we were meeting first, without any of the right clothes for the occasion. He hadn't a clue where his club suit was and so he had turned up without a shirt and tie and didn't even have a proper pair of shoes. Luckily, I kept spare clothes in my locker, so Gazza was in luck. There was even a pair of shoes, although they weren't exactly fashionable. They had a big buckle on the front and were too big for him but, because all he had were trainers and football boots, they had to do.

When we reached Hampden the players went on the pitch for the traditional pre-match stroll. Typical Gazza, he began messing around with some of the ball boys, kicking a ball too and fro with them. I couldn't help but laugh when I heard the matchday commentator Jock Brown say: "There is Paul Gascoigne playing football with the young boys in his £400 Gucci shoes." If only he had known the truth!

7

'He must have thought he was Steve McQueen because at the training ground there were CCTV pictures of someone leaping over a hedge on a motorbike. If you looked closely, you could see it was Gazza. Robbo tore a strip off him'

– Craig Hignett, former Middlesbrough team-mate

Craig Hignett

Craig Hignett agreed to be Gazza's room-mate when the player returned to the North East with Middlesbrough. He played for a number of clubs during his career, including Crewe Alexandra, Barnsley and Blackburn, and managed Hartlepool United.

It was the 1998 League Cup final in which Middlesbrough were due to face Chelsea at Wembley and Gazza had signed just days earlier. He trained with us for a couple of days and then we went down to our southern base, Burnham Beeches Hotel. Because I had turned down the offer of a new contract, the manager Bryan Robson pulled me and said I wasn't going to play because he needed to keep happy the players who would still be at the club the next season. I was disappointed but these things happen in football, so you just have to go back to your hotel room completely gutted.

Around 10 minutes later there was a knock on my door and it was Gazza, who had been told by Robbo that he would be one of the substitutes at Wembley. He had heard I was being left out and he didn't think it was right that he was involved instead of me after not kicking a ball for the club. I told him not to be daft, the decision had nothing to do with him.

I normally roomed with Neil Maddison but Gazza suggested I switch rooms and go in with him. Rooming with him meant you got little or no sleep. The telly and lights would stay on because he didn't like the dark and he was scared if everything went quiet. After the first night I thought I was nuts for agreeing to it. It started off by us going down to dinner, during which he asked me if I played snooker. I said yes. He told me to eat my dinner as quickly as possible because there were two snooker tables and we needed to grab one. So I bolted down my food with him staring at me, willing me to go even faster.

It was no surprise Gazza turned out to be a very good snooker player because he was good at any sport he took on. While we were playing you couldn't help but notice that there were dents everywhere in the walls. There were hundreds of them, and just in passing I said it all looked peculiar. He said he would show me something after we had finished playing. That turned out to be around two hours later – he didn't want to stop. He then grabbed the two snooker cues, placed one on the wall and the other about eight feet away. He then snatched the white cue ball and bowled it, cricket fashion, at the snooker cues. It immediately thudded into the wall, making a dent. I asked him whether he was responsible for all the other dents and holes. "Probably around 80 per cent of them," he replied. He then explained that when he was here with England this is what he normally did after finishing his games of snooker.

Just as I was walking out of the room he said we hadn't finished yet and if we left now something bad would happen. He was very superstitious. We had to bowl more balls and try to snap the snooker cues with the force of the balls. When we had done that we could go. He was also moving the cues around because he didn't want the dents in one place. We must have been there until 1am before we managed to break both of the cues, which wasn't the easiest thing in the world to do. I was worried about the consequences but Gazza assured me that the staff would clear up the mess because they always did and nobody would say anything.

The next day we walked into the nearby village. Everywhere

we went, people knew him and were beckoning him into the shops for him to pile his pockets with loads of stuff. We went into a pub and when we came out there were some young lads playing football. He asked for them to give him a kick. They couldn't believe he wanted to join in and so they passed the ball to him – only for Gazza to boot it over about 10 gardens. He then produced a £50 note, gave it to one of the kids and told them to buy a new ball.

He later stopped an elderly woman in a car and said: "You couldn't give us a lift to the hotel, could you love?" She said yes and so off we went in the back of the car, two complete strangers to her. His life was chaotic but everyone enjoyed being around him and the public adored him.

The final itself saw Gazza come off the substitutes' bench but he couldn't prevent us losing 2-0 in extra-time to Chelsea. Afterwards, I was on the pitch and he came up to me and handed me his medal, saying he hadn't earned it but I had. I refused at first but later he signed it and gave it to me during the night do. He was the kindest, most generous person you could ever meet, even though it was never advisable to room with him!

To help Gazza settle in at Middlesbrough, Andy Townsend was asked if Gazza could live with him in a house he had moved into. Bryan knew Andy was a sensible lad and would look after him the best he could. Jimmy 'Five Bellies' would also be with Gazza.

One of their routines was for the three of them to arrive at the training ground with three identical mugs of coffee. One day, Robbo had told Andy to have a break and go and enjoy some quality time with his family in the Birmingham area for a couple of days. That left just Gazza and Jimmy in the house.

While he was in the kitchen just before bedtime, Gazza noticed that there were only five identical coffee mugs instead of the normal six on the coffee tree. Gazza flipped out and asked Jimmy where the other coffee mug was, that he couldn't go to sleep with it missing.

Jimmy said he thought Andy had taken it with him to use en route to Birmingham. It would be in his bag. Gazza told Jimmy to go and fetch it. Jimmy pointed out it was now 11pm, Andy was in Birmingham and they were in the North East. Gazza didn't care. He couldn't go to bed without that coffee cup being delivered safely to their kitchen. So Jimmy drove to Birmingham in pouring rain, having to climb over Andy's locked gates because by the time he arrived there it was about 1am.

Andy was fast asleep before being awoken by the door bell sounding. He went downstairs clutching a baseball bat, still in his boxer shorts, and opened the door to find Jimmy standing there. "What do you want at this time of night?" he asks Jimmy. "Gazza wants his coffee cup back otherwise he won't go to bed," was Jimmy's answer. Completely befuddled, Andy handed the coffee cup over for Jimmy to drive the two hours back to their house. Gazza was still sat up and he immediately asked Jimmy if he had the cup before placing it back on the coffee tree and then finally going to bed.

Another night we were in a pub in a village having a drink. We had joined Gordon McQueen and Paul Merson, who lived in the area, when suddenly everything went dark. Without the landlord noticing, Gazza had gone behind the bar and turned the electricity off so he could help himself to a packet of cigarettes, not wanting anyone to know he was smoking. After he had completed his mission he switched the electricity back on.

You never knew what he was going to do next. This, after all, was someone who had tricked a London bus driver to let him into his cab in the middle of Oxford Street to have a little turn at driving it. Recognising Gazza, the driver agreed. So after getting behind the wheel he tricked the driver into stepping off the bus. Gazza then shut the doors and drove off down one of the busiest streets in the capital, complete with passengers, while the driver looked on ready to have a heart attack. Thankfully, no damage was done, unlike his escapade on the Middlesbrough team coach.

As I say, no one could ever fall out with him because he would do anything for you. I remember Gazza donating a special pinball machine, which had been made to celebrate Italia 90, for Robbie Mustoe to auction off at his testimonial.

At Middlesbrough he probably wasn't what he had been in his earlier years, football-wise, but he was still the best one-touch player I've ever seen. He knew where everyone was on the pitch in a split second. He didn't have to look. I would have loved to have seen him in his pomp. He was so quick and powerful. Whether he was playing or not he was full of life, always ready for a joke or a trick. He would always have his medical bag with him – God knows what was in it!

One day Jimmy suffered from some of the contents. The pair of them were going to drive down to London and, before they set off, Jimmy wanted to put some Brylcreem on his hair. Unbeknown to him, Gazza had swapped it for Immac, which is a strong chemical used for removing hair. Jimmy ended up with a burnt scalp and Gazza had to stop off for Jimmy to have his hair shaved off, in addition to having steroid cream on his head because it was burning.

We had some great characters in the dressing room who all got on very well, players like Gazza, Paul Merson, Andy Townsend and Nigel Pearson.

It just had to be me who roomed with him, meaning many sleepless nights. You never knew what would happen. I don't think many people would last long sharing a room with him. He would often phone Jimmy up in the middle of the night making grunting noises down the phone, which would send poor Jimmy potty. Jimmy was a great mate who knew that when Gazza got bored he would become dangerous. So often he would go along with what Gazza wanted to do.

Some of the stunts he got up to were indeed dangerous. I think one day he must have thought he was Steve McQueen because at the training ground there were CCTV pictures of someone leaping over a hedge on a motorbike. If you looked closely, you could see it was Gazza. Robbo tore a strip off him, hardly believing a professional footballer would risk the sort of injuries you could suffer if you fell off.

Gazza also had these listening devices and would set them up in the dressing room. He would detail someone to go into the physio room and try to get the physio to talk about him. Gazza would be listening in and would later tell the physio, to his disbelief, everything he had said. He once came onto the team coach with a guinea pig.

The first day after signing from Rangers, he came into the canteen completely naked. He just bowled in with nothing on, calmly collecting his tray, helping himself to food as if it was the normal thing to do.

It was some entrance. He just wanted to play football and make people laugh.

Paul Merson

Paul Merson made his name at Arsenal before transferring to Middlesbrough for a short but inspiring spell in the North East in which he helped Bryan Robson's side win promotion. He also won a place in England's France 98 World Cup squad, unlike Gazza, who had become his housemate – with some chaotic consequences.

I don't know how I came to share a house with Gazza – I can't remember whose idea it was or when it was first suggested – but we were housemates within three months of my first season. We were the original screwed-up couple. Gazza was an alcoholic and a brilliant nutter. I was an alcoholic and a compulsive gambler with a history in Class A drugs. It was like a time bomb waiting to go off but it was a great laugh. Gazza was a great lad to be around. Most of the time it was non-stop laughter.

I travelled up on the train one morning after spending some time with the family. Gazza met me halfway. He had a bottle of red wine in his kitbag and started knocking it back while the other commuters sipped coffee and scoffed croissants for breakfast. I must have said to him a hundred times: "Oh, Gaz, you can't do that mate. Not when we're training and playing. You won't get to the World Cup." But it didn't stop him from draining the whole bottle.

I loved him, though. He was a bundle of laughs to be around, a lovely, lovely bloke. Honestly, if you were standing at the bus stop in the pissing rain without a penny in your pocket Gazza would give you his last tenner for a cab, then he'd walk home himself.

Something weird or funny was always happening when he was around. Whenever he was in the house he'd always be stark naked. It was a gorgeous gaff, very grand with big windows and fancy balconies. But when Gazza moved in I always found him kipping on the sofa first thing in the morning. "What are you doing Gaz. Why don't you go to bed?" I asked. He looked at me as if I was mental.

Gazza would do weird things just to lose weight. He'd take sleeping pills after training and then go straight to bed when he got home in the afternoon. It was the only way he knew to stop himself from eating. We also started a drinking game which involved sleeping tablets and red wine. Gazza would send Jimmy 'Five Bellies' to a fancy hotel to buy the grog. When Jimmy got back we all started knocking back glass after glass. Whoever stayed awake the longest won and scooped up a few grand in bets. It's a miracle it didn't end up killing one of us.

As a footballer I honestly think he's the best English player I've ever seen in my life. Whenever he played he set the place alight. But whereas I made it into Glenn Hoddle's England squad for the 1998 World Cup, Gazza wasn't so lucky of course. He was booted out of the group at the last minute because he'd been boozing hard and was having a personal meltdown. It all kicked off on the weekend that Glenn was due to announce his squad at our training base at La Manga, Spain. It was a Saturday night and after working hard we were allowed a few beers at the hotel. Gazza decided to get paralytic and was sat at the hotel piano trying to play a tune.

The next day we were allowed a golf competition on the local course before a series of individual meetings with Glenn that started at 4.15pm. They were being held so he could tell each of us whether we were going to France or not. The lads were a bag of nerves but Gazza took it as a sign to get rotten drunk again. He was paralytic on the golf course and when he got back to the hotel, me and Tony Adams tried to sober him up by stripping his clothes off and chucking him into the pool. God knows what the paying guests must have thought as they stared at us.

By the time Gazza went for his meeting Glenn's mind was made up. He must have looked at him and figured, 'No chance. I can't take him away for six weeks. Is he going to drink like this when we get to France?' When Gazza was told he was going home, he lost it, even smashing a lamp in Glenn's room. His world had caved in. It was a real shame and personally I think he'd got us to the tournament on his own. Leaving him out was a big decision but Glenn wasn't scared of making big decisions. The weird thing was, even though I was in the squad, Glenn's choice worried me. Gazza was a much better player than me and I couldn't lose the idea that I was only going because he'd been dropped. When I asked the boss he shook his head. "No Merse, you were both going to France," he said. Gazza would probably have gone crackers in the World Cup. Being in the finals of an international tournament can be really boring, especially if you're not playing.

The next season back at Boro the club had bought a brand new coach. It must have cost a gazillion quid because it had on it just about every appliance known to man.

We were all looking forward to making our first journey but as it sat there gleaming in the training ground car park, Gazza noticed that the keys had been left in the ignition. He hopped in. Then he fired up the engine and started the one mile drive to the nearest high street to put some bets on for a few of the lads.

He didn't get far. When he got to the end of the road that led out of the training ground, he turned right and crashed the bus into a concrete bollard. The side of the coach was caved in and the locks on the compartments that contained our kit for the next match had been mangled so the doors were wedged shut.

"Bloody hell, Gaz, what have you done?" I shouted as we all walked around the side of the coach to look at the damage. We ended up on another coach and having some new shirts sent straight to Birmingham for the game against Aston Villa. Gazza was now shitting himself. A big fuss had been made of our new bus when the club bought it and Gazza had wrecked it even before the team had made a journey on the motorway.

Shortly after leaving Boro to join Aston Villa to be nearer home, I got a call telling me Gazza had been taken into care at The Priory in London. Some of the doctors there thought it would be a good idea if I went in to talk to him. They figured a friendly face might do him good. Then the weirdest thing happened. As we were sitting in the room chatting, guitar legend Eric Clapton walked in. It turned out that 'Slowhand' was a volunteer at the hospital. I'd just finished reading his book so I was well freaked out. "Alright Eric, what are you doing here?" I stammered as he walked in.

Apparently when the story had broken in the papers that Gazza had been admitted, Eric had called up the hospital. He asked if he could talk to him because he figured he could give him some advice. After half an hour of bedside chat, Eric got up to buy coffees for everyone. Then Gazza rolled over in his bed and gave me a funny look. "Who the fuck is that?" he said. I couldn't believe it, one of the most famous men in rock history was bringing him a coffee and Gazza didn't have a bloody clue!

Andy Townsend

Andy Townsend moved to Middlesbrough towards the end of his career to become a team-mate of Gazza's. He helped Bryan Robson's Boro gain promotion to the Premier League. He also played for a number of other Premier League clubs including Chelsea, Norwich and Aston Villa and is now an erudite TV co-commentator and pundit.

I had some great times at Middlesbrough. It was often a lot of fun. Gazza was an amazing talent, a fantastic player and great, great fun to be around. I had my own little flat in Yarm and he rented the biggest, scariest house that has ever been built on the coast and was often in there on his own.

Those who know him well will have appreciated that he would panic over anything, so what he was doing living there, I don't know. The wind used to whip by at 100mph on a good day. The doors and windows would rattle continuously. He was a nervous wreck.

I ended up staying with him a few times and so I saw at close hand that he often suffered with OCD. Everything had to be hung up in its rightful place, nothing was allowed to be left in a different state. Sometimes I would get up in the morning, go into the bathroom and by the time I had returned, my bed had been made and I hadn't seen him. I thought I was going mad.

Gazza always had to be doing something. I was 34, 35, coming to the end of my career. I think he tried to finish me off in six months. After training he would ask if I fancied a game of golf. "Yeah, okay, maybe just nine holes," I would say, because we'd done a full morning's training.

Then he would plead to do another nine holes. After that it was 'should we have a game of snooker?' Never mind that, 'should we have a game of tennis?' No wonder I was often asleep at 5pm in the evening. Having a snooker table in his house we could be playing morning, noon and night. I think he must owe me around £4 million in bets because he wasn't very good and I'd played a lot when I was a kid.

One night a group of us including myself, Gazza and Paul Merson went out for a drink. We were quite late and when the cab driver dropped us off at his house, Gazza said to the cabbie that we would have to be back up in five hours for training. He said that if he gave him a few quid, he could stay the night and take us in to training the next morning. Once Gazza promised him £100 he literally ran up the stairs to his bedroom. Little did he know that there was a toilet in the room which had a big problem. If you flushed it then the water would just keep coming out. No one had remembered to tell him this little detail.

I got up in the morning and as I'm coming down the stairs I could hear what I thought was the sound of water coming from somewhere. I got to the bottom of the stairs and opened the door to the snooker room to discover that there was a three-foot hole in the ceiling and water was gushing everywhere. It had flooded the floor. There were soaking wet bits of plaster everywhere. There was water all over the snooker table – it was a right mess. Every time before we went off to bed after playing snooker Gazza would insist on brushing the table, ironing it before setting all the balls up. It was part of his OCD.

Now Gazza was coming down the stairs saying to get a move on because we were going to be late for training. He asked me what was going on in the snooker room. I told him if he could get a plumber in the next half hour that would be brilliant and if he could get one in the next 30 seconds that would be unbelievable. He took a look at the damage for himself. He couldn't believe what he was seeing. He was moaning about the cab driver flushing the loo but in fairness no one had warned him of the consequences.

The next thing, Gazza is paddling through the flood and making his way towards the snooker table. He then takes the triangle off the light compartment, despite the water continuing to cascade on top of him and onto the table and was trying to set the balls up. I couldn't believe it – but that was him.

He was an absolute scream to be around. He also had a big heart and would do anything for anybody. I've seen him do so many good things. We used to go to hospitals in the afternoons. He would go and cheer up people who were unwell, often kids. Often this was done off his own steam. It had been nothing to do with the club. A real genuine guy.

Bryan Robson

Bryan Robson and Paul Gascoigne enjoyed a natural rapport right from the beginning, which continued when they became England team-mates and Robbo was appointed the national team's assistant manager. Not put off by some of Gazza's pranks, Bryan even signed him from Rangers when he was in charge at Middlesbrough.

Manchester United played Newcastle United at St. James' Park and I think Gazza was just 18 at the time. He played so well in the first half that it was the closest I ever came to being on the end of the hairdryer treatment from the gaffer, Alex Ferguson.

I could see him coming towards me in the dressing room and he was raging. It was obvious he was about to unleash the hairdryer and, before he could do or say anything, I said: "Gaffer, the kid's a good player, I'll get a grip of him. Do you think I want to play this badly in front of my family and all my Geordie mates who are at the game?!" He just exploded: "Get him sorted then!"

To be honest, not knowing too much about a young player, you can't comprehend at first how to deal with them. He had so much ability and he was playing against me in central midfield. He was outstanding that day. People talk about my tackling, and about me kicking people and all that, but I used to go out to play football. Only if somebody started cutting up rough did I ever think about turning nasty and being physical. But in this instance, with Gazza, I didn't think about kicking the kid because he was so skilful.

In the second half I got a grip a bit and managed to tie him down but by then the damage had been done and Newcastle ended up winning the game 1-0. The quickness of his feet was amazing. He was always looking to get on the ball. He had so much confidence. I had so much respect for his skills, the acceleration and know-how in the first five yards with the ball.

The next season we all knew more about Gazza because he was being talked about as this brilliant young player. Mutual respect quickly grew between the two of us.

We were beating Newcastle in one game and were awarded a penalty. I took it and scored and, when running back towards the centre-circle for the restart of the game, Gazza shouted out to me: "Great pen, Robbo." I thought to myself, 'Have I heard him right?' We've just gone 3-0 up and Gazza's congratulating me on the penalty.

I discovered when we eventually started playing together for England that he had always respected me as a player, which was great to know.

It's just a pity we didn't play together at Manchester United. I feel not going to Old Trafford, and instead deciding to join Tottenham, was the biggest mistake in Gazza's career. He had a great career, despite people going on about his drinking and drugs problems, but I think it would have been even better if he had decided to go to Manchester United. My time there was almost up but you could see the Nevilles, David Beckham, Paul Scholes, Ryan Giggs, all that lot, coming through. It would have been great for Gazza. He was just a few years older than that group but he would have seen how they looked after themselves, how they prepared for games, their mentality. Then, with Alex Ferguson at the helm, Gazza might not have had the problems he went on to have.

Instead he went for the bright lights of London where you can hide yourself, do what you want to do and not get noticed. I also thought that at the time there were a few 'Jack the Lads' at Tottenham which wouldn't have helped him.

I used to visit the Manchester United coaches' room for a cup of tea and a chat, so I knew which players they wanted to sign because the gaffer would talk about them and ask our opinions. I know, for instance, that Alex was desperate to bring Alan Shearer to the club. He was also committed to signing Gazza. He was really disappointed when he missed out on both players. When you look back now you can see why he wanted them. I bet both of them, deep down, wished they had signed for Manchester United. Look at the success they could have enjoyed under Alex.

I started to get to know Gazza a lot better with England. He just wanted everyone to love him. He was forever prattling around, which I quite liked. I was a bit like that myself, taking the mickey out of the lads, doing stupid things.

At training, all he would try to do before we started was to kick balls at the back of your head when you weren't watching. He loved spraying water on people at every opportunity, which he felt was hilarious. If there was a bucket of water lying around you knew you could be in for a soaking.

He got away with it because he had that cheeky chappie look. The players loved him. At times he would go too far and some of the lads would snap before peace was restored – because we were all team-mates after all.

Then there was Italia 90. It was great being part of the squad but I ended up snapping my achilles tendon, so that was the end of my competition. But I firmly believe we had a great chance of winning the tournament. We had a great goalscorer in Gary Lineker, Gazza was at the peak of his form and I think I could have been so helpful to the team and also to him. We had that understanding. I could tell him to calm down on his tackling and he would listen. I told him I'd do his tackling for him and to make sure he was on the move so I could get the ball to him. Then it was up to him to do what he was best at, which was creating and scoring goals.

I'd always respected the ability he had but I knew he could be rash in his tackles and challenges. It was always possible that he could badly injure himself.

We had other players who could take care of the physical side. It was a good, all-round team and no wonder England reached the semi-finals. It was just then our failure at penalties once again which stopped our progress. I think if we had knocked out West Germany, then we would have won in the final against Argentina.

Even though we never won the World Cup, everything changed for Gazza. It just wasn't his football which captured the public's imagination, it was the emotion he brought to the game. I think they saw how natural Gazza was. He wore his heart on the sleeve and they lapped it all up. They identified with him. He wasn't a robot, he was completely natural. Most of the country took to him and couldn't get enough of him.

He couldn't always handle it but you have to understand that if you do well at a World Cup where everyone is watching, fame will follow you. The spotlight is going to fall on you even more. Sometimes, that's where you need a strong family around you or a group of players who keep you grounded. If he had been at Manchester United, I think we could have helped him cope better with all the sudden adulation.

I remember returning from the 1982 World Cup finals, where I had done well. I was getting all the headlines. Then I was made captain, so there's even more focus on you. I had a wife and two girls, which immediately gives you more responsibility. You don't want to let them down. I don't think Gazza had that. He was often left to do what he wanted.

When he did his cruciate knee ligaments in the 1991 FA Cup final, it's probably the worst injury a professional footballer can have. He did well to come back from it. I returned from broken legs but that's far easier than the recovery from a cruciate knee job. The specialist has to be top class, the physio has to be great and you've got to really knuckle down and do the remedial work. I don't think he was ever the same Gazza again. He was still an outstanding player but just lost a little bit which had propelled him to be one of the best players in the world.

Playing in Italy was an experience for him. I know some people won't believe it, because of some of the tricks and scrapes he has got himself into, but he is an intelligent lad. For instance, I know he picked up the Italian language inside six months. He had lots of ups and downs in his life but that's him. It's why we're talking about him now, years after he finished playing.

Euro 96 was a fantastic time with Gazza at the forefront of things. I was the Middlesbrough manager at the time and assistant to Terry Venables with England. Terry was a great manager and coach, top class at man-management. I don't think it's any coincidence that when England got to the World Cup semi-finals in 1990, Gazza was on top form, while he had a renaissance for Euro 96 when England again reached the semi-finals.

Without a doubt, Euro 96 was a competition we should have ended up winning. We were a better team than Germany in that semi-final. If only Gazza had stretched a bit further to that cross, it would have won us the game. Darren Anderton went close too, so on both occasions we were just inches away from going into the final. We had an excellent team and Terry got the tactics spot-on.

It hadn't started so well with the media frenzy when we were in Hong Kong preparing for the tournament. The players hadn't had a drink when we played in China. When we got to Hong Kong we were all having a meal together with the Hong Kong XI we had just played.

It was about 11pm when we finished the meal. It was Gazza's birthday and he asked Terry if he could take the lads out for a drink. We were flying home the next day. It was around midnight when we ended up leaving the restaurant. Terry said to me: "Robbo, if you're going with them I want everyone back in the hotel by 2am." I said, "No problem, Terry, I'll make sure of that."

So we went to a bar called the China Jump. They all started off with just a beer. We had a cordoned-off area where some of them started ordering these cocktails. I was just talking to the bouncers with a beer in my hand. Gazza suddenly appeared and shouted: "Robbo, come into the dentist's chair." I said no, because I didn't drink shorts. I told them the rest of them could do it as long as they only had one go each and then came back to the protected area. They were back within 20 minutes. But then this barman placed a big bowl of drink on a table and handed out straws. So they started sipping the stuff with the straws. Myself, Alan Shearer and David Seaman were just watching them.

I don't know what the hell was in this bowl but they are now all completely leathered, absolutely drunk. Whether they were drained from the game and the drink added to this, I don't know. Now they started spraying bottles of beer over one another and ripping each other's shirts. I asked one of the bouncers to calm them down. They wouldn't listen and the next thing I know they're ripping my shirt. Eventually, some sort of calm ensued but there they were, all standing with ripped shirts.

Of course, then they've got to go to the toilet and then they are easy prey for people taking photos of them. That was how those photos were made public.

At 1.30am I told them it was time to climb into taxis and get back to the team hotel. Gazza wanted to stay for a few more drinks. I wouldn't let him. I know for a fact that all the players were back as Terry had requested by 2am. There had been a bit of stupidity but the photos made it all look a lot worse. All hell broke out, of course, when it got in the papers.

That was why it was brilliant when Gazza scored that wonder goal against Scotland and they all re-enacted the dentist's chair. Who could blame them, because they had been absolutely hammered in the media for having a few drinks. That was Gazza, though, his brain never stops. Quick as a flash, he organised the goal celebration. There had been no talk between them of doing it before the game.

They never got a bollocking from Terry for what went on in Hong Kong. It was me who got the bollocking! "I'd sent you to keep an eye on them," he blasted. "Gaffer," I replied. "Houdini couldn't have kept them safe!" In a way, that incident had brought them even closer as a unit. They were a tight bunch as it was but that helped tremendously. They knew the media were against them so they wanted to display a united front.

We also had some really good players. Before the tournament, Terry had told them he wanted them to play the Dutch way, able to alternate positions. Some people doubted that was possible but I think we managed to do it, ironically beating Holland 4-1 en route to the semi-finals. We were the best side without a doubt. Our toughest game was against Spain when we needed a penalty shoot-out to get through.

My biggest regret in football was turning down the chance to succeed Terry as England manager.

It was a really good squad and I'd witnessed it build. I don't know whether I was still in shock when Terry wasn't allowed to carry on. I was really looking forward to the 1998 World Cup alongside Terry.

I had learned a lot from the European Championship. His intention had always been to leave after France 98 and for me to take over. So when Terry left after Euro 96, it was a bit soon and I was also manager of Middlesbrough. I didn't want to leave Boro at that time. Sadly, Gazza didn't go to France 98 and that was all down to a lack of man-management. Glenn Hoddle, who took over from Terry, always seemed to be at loggerheads with Gazza instead of trying to control him.

Gazza's antics didn't put me off signing him for Middlesbrough. We were going for promotion into the Premier League and we had loads of games in hand on our rivals. We had a number of international players so our games were postponed when the international calendar came around. We'd managed to get to the League Cup final but the priority was promotion and to win these outstanding matches.

I felt we needed a real boost so I enquired about Gazza, who was at Rangers. I wasn't bothered if he still had a little problem with his knee. An 80 per cent Gazza was better than any other player in the First Division, as it was then. With the forwards I had like Marco Branca, Paul Merson and Craig Hignett, I thought Gazza feeding them could make all the difference. That's the way it turned out. He got on the ball, dictated things and we ended up winning five of our last six games.

The lads took to him because the moment he arrived he was full of enthusiasm. He was always passionate about his football – playing provided him with the most enjoyable moments of his life. He did the job for me.

The next season he started off brilliantly, only to get injured just before Christmas. When we went to Old Trafford to play Manchester United we were third in the Premier League. He was out for some time and we started dropping down the table. We ended up finishing ninth, which wasn't bad.

But the danger for Gazza comes when he gets bored or he wants to stage a prank. One day at training he decided to jump onto the team coach and take it for a ride. He ended smashing it up! It was a brand-new bus that the club had purchased. Gazza couldn't resist it because it was so new and had that lovely 'new vehicle' smell. He intended to drive to the local bookies to put some bets on but didn't get out of the training ground. Instead, he went headlong into a big rock.

When he came into my office all sheepish-looking after the incident I told him I hoped all his horses would come in first because he was paying for the damage to the coach and would be forking out two weeks' wages in a fine. I knew when I signed him he would be up to something but I suppose not many managers have had to punish a player for crashing the team coach.

There were a few minor run-ins. The most difficult time you have with Gazza as a coach or manager is when he's injured. When he misses his football, that's when he goes off on one. On the football side of things he helped us win promotion and settle in the Premier League. But after his injury during that season I felt I needed to move him on. He had done his job. We have always been honest with one another and I knew it was time for him to leave. I got the best 18 months out of him anyone could have managed.

Everton came in and showed their interest. I said to him I felt it was the right time for him to move on. He didn't disagree.

8

'He challenged Big Dunc to see who could complete the most press-ups. The loser would have to hand over £50. Gazza gave it everything. Sweat was pouring off him. "Beat that Dunc." Duncan didn't flinch. "Nah. Can't be bothered. Here's your £50."'

– Ian Snodin, Everton legend, broadcaster and media pundit

Ian Snodin

Ian Snodin briefly shared an England camp with Gazza, although injury prevented the Everton legend gaining a cap for the senior international side.

I'd just arrived at Everton and we went to St. James' Park to play Newcastle United. I was alongside Peter Reid in midfield. I'd heard a lot about this special young talent that was Paul Gascoigne. After around 10 minutes, Gazza nutmegged Peter. He had shouted out beforehand that he was going to do it as well. There was smoke coming out of Reidy's ears! A few minutes later I couldn't believe it – he did it again! Then he overran the ball slightly so I thought: 'Here's my chance.' I won the ball and got him. He's there on the ground holding his leg and so I leaned over him and said: "Show some respect."

A couple of minutes later, without any of the officials seeing, he clipped me around the ear as he was running past. I thought fair enough, he's got something about him. He's not going to be intimidated. I'm ashamed of myself now but I asked him how much a week he was on. I knew he wouldn't be on much because he had just got into the first team. He looked shocked.

Around three years later he was playing for Tottenham after his big move. I'm thinking to myself, 'how much is he on now?' I thought, 'he's not going to miss the chance of mentioning it after what I had said a few seasons before'. Sure enough, we're lining up in the tunnel before the game at Goodison Park when I hear this voice boom out: "Snods, how much are you on a week?" It's a wonder that he didn't hand me £20 and say I needed it more than him.

I was in Albania with Gazza and the rest of the England squad. The staff had handed out bars of chocolate for us to eat while we were there. I was rooming with Tony Cottee. We went past Gazza's room and there's loads of the squad in there. I wondered what was going on. Gazza then asked Tony and I whether we had any chocolate bars in our fridge. We hadn't touched them. I said we had loads. So he asked us to fetch them. We discovered he was throwing them out of the window to a group of Albanian kids in the street. He was cutting the bars up and chucking the bits to the grateful kids. They started chanting, "Gazza, Gazza." But when he ran out of chocolate he couldn't help himself. He told us to go to our rooms and grab bars of soap. Oh no, I could see where this was going. We did what he said and he chopped them up and flung bits through the window. The kids thought they were bits of chocolate and started eating them. To their horror they had been hoodwinked and were now spitting bits of soap onto the road.

At Everton, he was fun to have around. He loved playing table tennis. We'd set up a table tennis table in the gym and, one day, Duncan Ferguson sent the groundsman off to pick up six buckets of KFC. Instead of playing for money we were playing for chicken wings and Zinger burgers, much to Gazza's delight.

He could never keep still. After training, he challenged Big Dunc to see who could complete the most press-ups. The loser would have to hand over £50. Gazza typically gave it everything he had after going first. He was just about ready to collapse after reaching 50. Sweat was pouring off him. He just had enough energy to remark: "Beat that Dunc." Duncan didn't flinch. He just carried on reading his newspaper and said to Gazza: "Nah. I can't be bothered. Here's your £50."

Darren Griffiths

Darren Griffiths is Everton's Broadcast and Liaison Manager and has collected a number of Gazza stories from his time at Goodison Park.

Gazza used to stay at the Redbourne Hotel when he was with us. One day he arranged for the hotel staff to have a game against the Everton staff at the training ground. After watching the match, Gazza suggested they should all go for a drink, and they all went off to a pub.

When they walked in, there was a guy at the bar in an Everton tracksuit who they didn't recognise. There was also a guy in a hi-vis jacket with paint-covered jeans and big working men's boots. They sat down and wondered where Gazza had got to. Suddenly, this guy in the hi-vis jacket turned around – and it was Gazza! He had decided to swap clothes with the first person he met in the pub. This random bloke was suddenly wearing an Everton tracksuit and Gazza had the working man's gear on.

On another occasion, after Everton had signed David Ginola, Gazza came out of the dressing room sporting a blond wig on what was the Frenchman's first day of training. He wore it for most of the session, much to David's amusement.

Another time at the training ground, Gazza told our kit man, Tony Sage, that he had left his boots at Goodison Park and asked him to drive over and fetch them for him. Unbeknown to Tony, Gazza had removed the whistle from the old kettle at Bellefield and placed it in Tony's exhaust. The noise coming from Tony's car as he headed towards Goodison could be heard all over the city!

Gazza also became friendly with another kit man at the club, Dave Flanagan. He used to take the mickey out of him, often mocking his pop-out eyes, and decided to buy Dave a catfish with similar-looking eyes. He brought it in happily ensconced in a big bowl, announcing to Dave that he had discovered one of his relations!

Gazza would often buy things from the magazine *Exchange and Mart* at a whim. He once sent Jimmy 'Five Bellies' to Birmingham to buy a parrot he had noticed was for sale. Gazza took himself off to Owens, a restaurant not far from our training ground, and told Jimmy to meet him there later with the parrot, which by then would have been in a cage in the back of Jimmy's car for a couple of hours. As soon as Jimmy arrived, Gazza opened the flap in the cage to allow the parrot out. It went absolutely berserk and flew everywhere in the restaurant, which sent plates and dishes tumbling to the floor and smashing. There were waiters diving for cover. It was absolute pandemonium.

Everton used to go to Italy during pre-season. The players were in a bar and one of them, Stephen Hughes, wanted to go to a nearby store to get some bits. Gazza asked him to get some local cheese. He said that he loved this special cheese when he was in Italy with Lazio. Stephen asked Gazza what to say in Italian so Gazza told him. A few minutes later, Stephen returned to the pub beetroot-faced. Instead of asking for the local cheese he had asked for a blow job, courtesy of Gazza's Italian!

But Gazza also had a big heart. After coming back for pre-season training following the summer break, Gazza asked the club masseur, Jimmy Comer, if he had managed to get away for a holiday. Jimmy said he hadn't been able to because he had undertaken a masseur course which had taken three weeks.

Gazza was perplexed that Jimmy had not had a proper holiday. Unbeknown to Jimmy, he arranged with the manager, Walter Smith, to give Jimmy a week off and booked a big lodge for Jimmy and his family next to Loch Lomond. He paid for everything, including the travel.

Alan Stubbs

Alan Stubbs faced Gazza in the Old Firm derbies when he was at Celtic, and the pair were later team-mates at Everton.

Gazza would get obsessions over things. I remember at Everton he had this craze for having to do things in threes. One day he came back from the tattooist having had three tattoos done. He'd eat three bags of wine gums. On another day it would be packs of ham or tins of baked beans. He couldn't finish until he had eaten three of something. Then he would usually make himself sick.

As an opponent he was a genius but always on edge. He would show you up with a bit of skill or wind you up something rotten. There aren't many players who would happily shove a finger or even their tongue in your ear or feel your backside. You would turn around to say something and he'd have a great big smile on his face.

At Everton he used to come in to training wearing really scruffy tracksuit bottoms and T-shirts. He would then make sure he was the first one in the dressing room after training so he could swap his clothes with someone else's and go out looking like a million dollars. Luckily enough, my clothes were a little bit too big for him, so I managed to avoid it. But there were at least six or seven players who felt the wrath of Gazza doing that trick.

Alan Myers

Alan Myers was the Everton press officer when Paul Gascoigne signed for the club. From the moment Gazza arrived at Goodison Park, Alan's life was never to be the same again. They formed a close friendship, one which has survived the course of time – the pair staying in touch during Alan's many years as a leading and authoritative Sky Sports reporter.

Michael Dunford, the Everton secretary, called me into his office and said the manager Walter Smith had made a signing and they wanted me to look after him when he arrived. So I asked who it was because there appeared to be a bit of mystique surrounding this new player. He replied it was Paul Gascoigne. I thought 'oh no' because of some of the stories we had all heard about him in the past.

I was told that if I went down to the car park at Goodison Park he would be there waiting. Sure enough, there was a Range Rover parked near the players' entrance and Gazza was sitting in it all alone. I expected him to have a huge entourage but there he was all by himself. I beckoned him over so I could introduce myself. "Aye, man, how are you?" he said, "can you do me a big favour?" I asked him what he wanted. "Will you go and get us 20 tabs?" I replied "Sorry, what?" "Can you get us 20 tabs?" he repeated. I told him I didn't know what tabs were. "Cigarettes you dickhead!" I thought this was just part of the Paul Gascoigne wit I'd heard about. But he was serious, he was demanding a packet of fags. He gave me a fiver and I headed across the road to a shop nearby and purchased 20 Embassy cigarettes for our new signing. I returned with them and he got out of his car and together we headed towards the room where his unveiling before the media was about to take place. Safe to say life was never quite the same after that introduction.

In addition to the increased media attention, it was virtually a full-time job trying to look after Gazza – with some help from the players' liaison officer. One day, for instance, he just turned up at my office and presented Mason and Regan, his two young sons. So I started talking to them and after a while I noticed Paul had disappeared. I asked them where he was. "Gone to training," they both replied. So he had just dumped them on me as some kind of childminder because he was supposed to be looking after them for a few days. In my office all day, as I'm trying to do my day job, were these two kids.

Every single day with Gazza around at Everton was an event. Together with Jimmy Martin, the kitman, away trips meant we were responsible for making sure Paul was in his room by 10pm the night before a game. As most of us know, his comedic value is up there with the greatest comedians – the Ken Dodds and Jimmy Tarbucks – of all time. We would walk out of the lift in the hotel on whatever floor he was on at 10pm, and all we would hear from a room further down the corridor was, "I'm here!" We didn't even have to knock on the door.

I remember arriving at the training ground one day and seeing Alex Nyarko, a player we had signed from Lens, standing in the corridor in just in his underpants, clearly unhappy. He was remonstrating with Sue, the receptionist. "Gazza has gone off with my clothes," he was shouting. Sue confirmed she had seen Paul going off dressed very differently than normal. Funnily enough, I'd seen him in the car park looking very smart, wearing fashionable brown cord trousers and other designer gear.

Evidently, he had turned up for training in his Everton track-suit but had forgotten he had an important business meeting in the afternoon. Without telling Alex, he stole his gear, leaving poor Alex with Gazza's scruffy training kit. The kitman had to come to his rescue and find him some unused training stuff so he could go home. You never knew what Gazza was going to do next.

I copped for it the time I had to take him to the Question of Sport studios in Manchester. I knew the producer of the pro-gramme and he had said he'd love to have Gazza on. I'd asked him and he replied: "Yes, I'll do it for you Myers." That's what he would always call me, 'Myers'. Walter had given him permis-sion to appear on the programme but he didn't want any fooling around and, once again, the onus fell on me to make sure he didn't get up to any mischief.

So I picked him up in my car to make the journey from Mer-seyside to Manchester. Paul would always insist on sitting in the back, never in the passenger seat. I never liked it, saying it was making me look like his chauffeur. "Just drive, Myers," he insisted. He jumped into the back where there were also bits of shopping I'd done in the morning, together with boxes full of photos of the players ready for them to sign and hand out.

We were now bombing along the M62 towards Manches-ter and I asked him to sign some of his photos. When he had finished, he asked if I wanted him to sign the other photos. "No, they are to be signed by the rest of the squad," I said. I was wasting my breath. He signed all the Gary Naysmith photos. Then he said he was going to sign David Weir's photos. He must have ruined seven or eight other players' photos. I couldn't do anything about it because I'm driving in the fast lane trying to get him to the Question of Sport studios. He then started signing my headrests in the car. So now all the pictures of the players were ruined and parts of my car had been scrawled with the name Paul Gascoigne. He's just gone mad!

The problems continued when we reached the Green Room where everyone congregates before the shows are filmed. I'd promised Walter that he wouldn't be drinking. My cause wasn't helped by one of his big drinking buddies Steve Watson being with him. Gazza was downing champagne. I got really fed up with him and told him he was now on his own, I was washing my hands of him for the night. I told him to get his own lift back.

Three programmes are filmed on the night but he wrecked two of them. After finishing his programme he kept walking on set while the other two were being shot, which I don't think the Question of Sport producer felt was very funny.

I was also fuming with him because he had let me down. I was worried that I would have a lot of explaining to do to Walter if Gazza didn't turn up for training after the amount of alcohol he had been downing. I couldn't sleep. Anyway, the next morning I was up and about when my wife asked me why had every piece of bread which had been amongst the groceries on the back seat of my car been signed, 'Best wishes, Paul Gascoigne.' He had taken every slice out of the wrapper and signed them, then neatly placed them back in order inside the wrapper.

But no matter what he did you could never fall out with him for very long. As soon as I walked into the training ground, I heard that infectious laugh. He knew he'd got me. And nobody was any the wiser about what had gone on the night before because he was in training and up for it.

'He was full of pranks' . . . giving photographers a soaking before a derby clash with Roma in the Stadio Olimpico

Divine Ponytail' . . . Gazza goes for a new hairstyle during his Lazio days

'Could you imagine those two in the same side?' Gazza meets Sevilla's Diego Maradona in 1992 – Terry Venables managed both

'He ate ice cream for breakfast' . . . a cheeky grin for the cameras while on the bench at Lazio. *(Far right)* boss Dino Zoff who was the victim of many tricks and treated him 'like a naughty son'

'You always have to live with the genius' . . . Rangers boss Walter Smith, pictured with Gazza and assistant boss Archie Knox, was a father figure to Gazza and even invited him to Christmas dinner

'Plenty of banter' . . . there was rivalry between the Scots in the Rangers dressing room like Stuart McCall and the English players like Gazza. *(Above left)* Gazza with 'sparring partner' Ally McCoist and comedian Bob Monkhouse

'Three of everything' . . . Alan Stubbs faced Gazza in Old Firm games but they were later team-mates at Everton

'Did me up like a kipper' . . . keeper Andy Goram *(far left)* was the victim of a Gazza wind-up after Euro 96. Rangers team-mates are pictured here on a fishing trip during a tour of Denmark

'He just wanted everyone to love him' . . . Bryan Robson struck up a natural rapport with Gazza and teamed up with him at both England and Middlesbrough

'The goal has remained in everyone's memory ever since' . . . Colin Hendry looks on as Gazza scores his famous goal at Wembley in Euro 96 – just minutes after Gary McAllister's missed penalty

'I saw it becoming messy and managed to slope off' . . . Alan Shearer was an 'innocent bystander' on the night of the 'dentist's chair' in Hong Kong but joined in the fun after the Scotland goal. Photographer Richard Pelham was perfectly placed to capture the moment

'Creating havoc' ... Another Richard Pelham pic – this time of Gazza with David Beckham and Paul Ince after they had sealed World Cup qualification in Rome in 1997. Richard with Gazza (below)

'David, can you take him out fishing, he's getting hyper' ... Gazza, David Seaman and Ian Walker go fishing during Euro 96 – a trip which ended with Gazza confronting a photographer

'I had given him so many opportunities' ... Gazza in happier times with Glenn Hoddle – the man who dropped him from the France 98 World Cup squad

'I'll do it for you Myers' . . . With Sky reporter and former Everton press officer Alan Myers, also pictured left *(far right)* as Gazza is unveiled at Goodison Park

'To Jack, my second dad. Love Gazza' . . . reunited with first Newcastle manager Jack Charlton at a book signing

'Your mate – he's not all there is he?' Danny Baker and Chris Evans saw Gazza drive a bus full of people around London

'It was a short stay but very sweet' . . . signing in at Burnley with manager Stan Ternent. One of Gazza's jobs was to make the tea for his team-mates

'It was like a time bomb waiting to go off but it was a great laugh' ... Paul Merson shared a house with Gazza when they played for Middlesbrough – and chaos often ensued

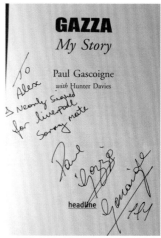

GAZZA
My Story

Paul Gascoigne
with Hunter Davies

To
Alex
I nearly signed
for liverpool
sorry mate

Paul
'Gazza'
Gascoigne

headline

'I nearly signed for Liverpool' ... special note in the autobiography for former Anfield scout Alex Smailes

'At his best when he has a smile on his face' ... back home and enjoying the Bobby Robson Trophy match at St. James' Park with his two nephews Joe and Cameron in 2009

'People do care for him and like him but no one can change him' . . .
pictured in relaxed mood in Bournemouth in January, 2020

Image: Adam Gerrard

A couple of weeks later I received a cheque from A Question Of Sport for his appearance (or appearances!). We were on a train going down to London when I handed it over to him. He said, "You have that, Myers." I didn't want it. It was his money. "If you don't have it, I'll eat it," he stated. He promptly screwed it up and swallowed it.

But seriously, I wouldn't have it any other way. When I returned to Everton in 2013 after working elsewhere, I was quickly confronted with four players coming up to me armed with their briefcases wanting to discuss image rights. It was certainly a lot different the day I left Everton with Paul Gascoigne playfully trying to shove a window wiper up my backside. Players in Gazza's day had fun while now many of them are businessmen.

When he was at Everton, Paul lived in a hotel in the Woolton area of Liverpool. One day, a woman came on the phone saying she wanted to make a complaint about one of our players. She said she thought it was someone called Paul Gascoigne and he had driven past and knocked a small boy off his bike. She had seen him throw a packet of sweets at him, which had caused the boy to fall off. I had to ring Gazza. "I knew that was going to happen, Myers," he answered. I asked him to explain himself. "The kid was shouting at me, wanting to know if I had any sweets, so I threw some jelly babies at him which hit his head and he fell over."

It was non-stop. But there was another side to him. We went up to the North East to play his old club Newcastle United. I would always stand by the tunnel at games. Anyway, I saw a wonderful flick from Paul which set up Kevin Campbell to score the only goal of the game. Gazza shouted over to me: "Myers, did you see that?" There were probably around 45,000 inside St.

James' Park but he was just concerned that I might have missed his trick which led to the goal.

Afterwards, the rest of us are on the team coach which was ready to leave the ground. But the gaffer and Gazza were still to get on it. So Walter's number two Archie Knox shouted: "Myers, (everyone is calling me this now because of Gazza) can you go and find Walter? We need to go." I got off the coach and found the manager leaning against the wall just inside our dressing room. "I'm waiting for him," he said. "Who?" I replied. "Him!"

I went to look around the corner of the room and there's Paul sat on his own in floods of tears. I wondered what the hell had happened and asked him if he was okay. "I am, Myers," he said. "I'm just made up that we've won." It was such a privilege to see what football meant to him. He had genuinely broken down because Everton had beaten one of his former teams. The three of us then walked out and down the steps to the waiting coach and by now he's all smiles and playing up to the cameras. That was the real Paul Gascoigne and that's where the love for him comes from. I know he has his critics and he has done some stupid things but you can't help but love that honesty and sincerity he has. He was a lad who just wanted to play football and to please people. It was hard to digest the fact that when he crossed that white line he became a genius, but when he returned from it he often became an idiot. I have never been able to work that out.

He was injured at one stage and unable to play for a spell when he rang me. "Myers, can you get me some tickets for something at the weekend because my family and friends are coming down from the North East?" I asked him to give me a clue as to what he wanted. "Anything," he said and put the phone down.

I rang a friend I knew who worked for a local radio station. He said he could get me some tickets at the Manchester Arena for a Westlife concert. I rang Gazza back and told him and he was really pleased. I just needed to know how many tickets to request. "Eleven Myers." 'Bloody hell', I thought, 'eleven!'

In the end my mate promised to get eleven tickets and another three for myself, my wife and daughter. We got to Manchester Arena for the concert and I bumped into Gazza's big mate, Jimmy 'Five Bellies' Gardner. I couldn't see Paul and the concert was about to start. "Where's Paul?" I asked. Jimmy immediately pointed to the stage and there was Paul walking out with Brian McFadden from Westlife. The group had discovered that Gazza was in the building and beckoned him to join them on stage.

A couple of weeks later we're at the training ground and Gazza says to me: "Myers, tell your daughter to be ready to be picked up with two of her mates. They will be taken to a hotel to meet up with Brian." "Brian who?" I asked. "Brian McFadden. He has sorted out some tickets for her." Evidently, Westlife were due to be in concert again in the area. Anyway, Westlife's limo came to pick up my daughter Jade and two of her friends, and took them to the concert. They went backstage afterwards to meet the band. They couldn't believe it. Gazza had arranged all this as a big thank you for what I had done for him. His generosity knew no bounds. He would always look after people.

When I switched to working as a Sky Sports reporter he came back to haunt me when I was sent to Everton's training ground to interview Abel Xavier, who was leaving Everton for Liverpool. We had started the interview when suddenly a window opened close to where we were filming with this voice booming out: "Abel, don't go. Abel, don't go." Of course it's Gazza.

We aborted the interview and went around the corner to get away from him. We started off again only for another window to open and Gazza yelling: "Please don't go." In the end his head popped out of five different windows and we couldn't complete the interview. But he was great for me when I was with Sky Sports. He would always agree to do interviews, which of course was a feather in my cap due to his fame.

I have also been involved in some of his low moments – when he must have felt the world was caving in on him. One morning I received a call from one of his therapists who was trying to sort out his alcohol addiction. Gazza was on the way to his clinic in Arizona. He was in a bad place. The therapist wanted people close to Gazza to send him messages via a TV link and, with me working for Sky and also knowing Paul, I was the man to organise it. It wasn't always going to be a 'nicey nicey, hope you get well' sort of stuff. Paul had to hear the truth and what he was doing to people close to him. I asked my boss at Sky if we could use the recording facilities of the company. He said yes, for me to take a camera and take as long as I wanted because Paul had been good to us over the years.

It's not right for me to reveal who was on it because to this day it all remains confidential, but I managed to conduct around 15 interviews with people at the top of their game in football and the entertainment world, very famous people. It had to be private and the footage was never to be made public. There was some hard-hitting stuff. It was what his addiction was doing to family and friends. It was probably the most powerful 20 minutes of television I've ever been involved in.

There were two copies of the interviews. One went over to the clinic and I have kept the other one under lock and key.

The contents shocked him and helped him enormously. Shortly afterwards, he returned to this country and I went to see him. He wanted a tape of the interviews but I had sworn not to release it and so he never got his hands on it. What was great was that so many people wanted to plead with him to get his life back on track.

What is sad is that Paul could have got so much more out of his post-playing career. There is a long list of people who have tried to help him carve out new opportunities. Then, of course, there are the agents who have used him and shafted him. I've shared some really dark moments talking through things when he has been in a mess. He has often suffered at the hands of people in social media who insist he hasn't helped himself, that he has brought his problems on himself. I get all that but if they knew the real Paul Gascoigne they would discover a real complex human being. He is a psychologist's absolute dream, trying to work out what he really is. To me and those who really know him, he is a very special person.

I can't resist him, good or bad. I still get the odd phone call. Not so long ago, I went up to Ibrox to do 'A Night With Paul Gascoigne'. When we got there I was shocked to see only around 80 people had turned up. We would normally do shows for a lot more people than that. I asked him why the low turnout, and he told me these were the ones who hadn't wanted their money back when he had let them down the last time by not showing up. I thought this could be a hostile audience ready to give him hell but he soon captivated them. That was him. He would never want to purposely upset anyone. Anyone who has spent some time in his company will know that. Thankfully the laughs have outweighed the tears. There's only one Paul Gascoigne.

9

'While he knew in his mind what he wanted to do, the rest of the body wasn't capable and he shed a few tears on the pitch and was eventually taken off, which was really hard for him. We all wanted him to do well but, sadly, it didn't happen'

– Matt Murray, Sky Sports reporter and pundit and former Wolves goalkeeper

Stan Ternent

Stan Ternent has managed a number of clubs, including Black-pool, Hull City, Bury, Huddersfield Town and Burnley, where he signed Gazza for a brief spell when the player was coming to the end of his career.

I had been trying to sign him for a while when he was at Everton but Walter Smith, who was in charge at Goodison Park, wasn't for letting him go. We were going for promotion from the old First Division, which was then the second tier.

Walter lost his job and so I thought that was my opportunity, and I managed to get a deal sorted out. First, though, I had to take Paul to see my chairman, Barry Kilby. So he came with me to Barry's house to meet him and his wife, Sonja. I'd talked to Gazza's agent to make sure he was on the straight and narrow and at the time he was with Sheryl, which usually meant he was in a better place. If he fell out with her then it would be like World War Three. No, he was fine, his agent said, he had turned over a new leaf. It was getting on towards the end of the season and I thought he would give us a lift and possibly help us clinch promotion. I had done the same with Ian Wright a couple of seasons earlier.

So he was dropped off at my place with Jimmy 'Five Bellies' and I took him to see the chairman to sort some bits and pieces out surrounding the signing. Anyway, everything was going well when Sonja asked me if I fancied a glass of wine. I said yeah, I would love a small one while we continued talking with Barry and Gazza. Then she turned to Gazza and asked: "Would you like one as well, Paul?" "Aye, I'll try one," he answered. The chairman is now giving me a real knowing stare. "No, he's okay, he's off the big drinking," I assure him. Two bottles later, Barry says to me: "Are you sure?!"

Although he didn't stay long at Burnley, the other players learned a lot from him and thought he was terrific. Gazza stayed at my house, as did Jimmy, because obviously I needed to keep tabs on him. One evening one of my sons, Chris, announced he was going up to The Drum. Gazza asked what it was. I told him it was our nice local pub, out in the country and out of the way, but he couldn't go. I told him if he went it would be packed inside 60 seconds because word always spread quickly about anything happening in the area. Jimmy said he would go up with Chris and would let Gazza know if there was anyone in there. The phone goes a little later and it's Jimmy telling Gazza that there is hardly anyone in and to come up. I told Gazza it was up to him but I was betting it would soon become swamped. In a place like that, everyone hears what's going on and if there was a chance of drinking with Gazza then the floodgates would open. But off he went. Within a few minutes he's ringing me. "Can you come and pick us up, it's madness." I had to sneak him out of the back door. The pub was rammed within two minutes of him ordering his first drink.

You could never fault him, training-wise. He was always first in every morning and he would make a pot of tea for the squad. The players couldn't believe it. Paul Gascoigne, *the* Paul Gascoigne, making them a cup of tea. They weren't thanking him one day, mind, after Gazza discovered somebody had done something to his football boots. They were killing themselves laughing while drinking their tea. Gazza turned around and said: "I don't know why you're laughing. I've put all kinds of shit in the tea!" He was a great lad to have around the place and, although he didn't play many games, he almost helped us win promotion.

We played Coventry in the last game and were winning 1-0 but we were still one goal worse off than Norwich on goal difference for the last play-off place. In the final minutes there were two good free-kick situations, ideal for Gazza. To his and our horror, the Coventry goalkeeper Magnus Hedman made two fantastic saves, which cost us in the end. It was really disappointing and hard to swallow at the time. But he more than paid his way because the attendances shot up. We were often sold out and we also did well on the commercial side with the sale of replica shirts. The chairman agreed an incentive deal with him. In fact, if I ever bump into Gazza these days he quickly tells me he's still owed a few quid from his Burnley shirt agreement. I never regretted signing him for one minute. Even now the older Burnley fans can always say they have seen Gazza in the claret and blue of Burnley.

In training he was still skilful even if he was coming to the end of his career. Some of the players told me they couldn't believe they were in the same side as Gazza. Without doubt he's one of the best players this country has ever produced.

To have him and Ian Wright at the club was tremendous. Ian was at Celtic and things hadn't worked out for him there. I knew him well from my time at Crystal Palace, where I was assistant to Steve Coppell. I let it be known that he was always welcome to play for Burnley and that's how it all started. It was a similar sort of deal as Gazza's.

With Ian we got promoted from the third tier to the second. Ian gave us a lift and I knew Gazza would do that as well. So within a matter of a few years we had one of the greatest goal-scorers playing for us, in Ian Wright, and one of the greatest players of all time, Gazza. They both have infectious personalities and are outgoing lads. Of course, I wasn't scared to take them on. I've never been overawed by players with big personalities. Show me a good player and I'll show you a good manager. Yes, they can be tainted, but that's what you often get with a genius. At least I managed something that the great Sir Alex Ferguson – who has been very good to me over the years – couldn't, and that was to sign Gazza. I know Alex would have loved to have brought him to Manchester United. Instead, as we all know, he ended up at Spurs.

I know he got up to some pranks with the players but to be fair to him he never bothered me. He was at it all the time with them. We would have loved to have kept him but the collapse of ITV Digital affected our budget, as it did with lots of clubs outside the Premier League. It meant we couldn't afford him so eventually he went off to play in China. It was a short stay but very sweet.

Gordon Armstrong

Gordon Armstrong spent most his career in on-field battles with Gazza only to finally play for the same side, albeit for just a short time, when the pair were together at Burnley. Gordon spent 11 years at Sunderland, making 349 appearances, before moving on to a number of clubs including Bury and Burnley.

His signing for Burnley came totally out of the blue although the gaffer (Stan Ternent) had also pulled a rabbit out of the hat in previous years bringing Ian Wright to Turf Moor. That had been really successful. With Gazza it was a bit different. It was right at the end of his career and he'd had a few problems but he still possessed those touches of magic in training. He also still loved the dressing room banter and was accepted straight away by the other players.

Gazza loved to join in with Footgolf which a few of us put together at the training ground. We used to play for a fiver a game. It got really serious. There would be the likes of Gazza, myself, Paul Cook, Kevin Ball, Ronnie Jepson, little Robbie Blake. It was great fun. It wasn't a proper golf course, it was one we hastily put together. For instance, there was a gas meter in the middle of one of the fields that you had to hit. There were certain trees you had to aim at. There was a gate at the end you had to drill the ball through. I think, in the past few years, proper Footgolf courses have been set up. Maybe we should have patented the idea! I think a few people must have heard what we were doing, nicked the concept and modified it to what is around now. It was great for Gazza because he could show off his skills, although he wasn't too keen when it came to paying out if he lost. I think he'd had a bad time with his missus and didn't have too much cash when he came to Burnley. He didn't want to lose anymore.

His arrival lifted the whole club and raised the profile. With Gazza on board, the expectation level went up which tested the players who were already there. You knew you had to up your game. Of course, having the opportunity to play alongside him was something we had all looked forward to.

Funnily enough our paths had first crossed when we were both at school in the North East. I was the same age as him and we first played against each other in under-14s football. He played for Redheugh Boys and I played for Montagu and North Fenham Boys. We both got sent off for kicking each other in one game. There was always a fierce rivalry over the years whenever we met.

In this particular game, we went into a tackle and slid into each other. Once we got back onto our feet we started fighting. There was some pushing and shoving and the odd kick, two young footballers full of testosterone. We always used to argue who was the better player. He also played for Gateshead Boys and I represented Newcastle Boys. In one game we both scored. After he scored he ran past me pulling faces and mocking me, and so after my goal I gave it back to him. We were always in close proximity on the pitch with him playing right midfield and me left midfield. He was then a chubby little kid with bags of talent but clearly wasn't looking after himself properly. He used to eat all the wrong things. He was someone who loved to wind you up. I think it was all part of making him a better player because all that would get him going.

Strangely, despite his immense talent, he was overlooked when it came to being selected for other squads. I was picked for Northumberland Boys, being on the other side of the Tyne from him. He was qualified to play for Durham Boys but he didn't get a look in. He didn't get anywhere near the England Boys Under-15s side either which, when you consider what he eventually achieved, is pretty incredible.

We would always clash on the field but off it was completely different. Whenever I met him he was great. We'd bump into each other in Newcastle and he'd invite me to join him and his mates for a drink. We got on really well.

On the field, the rivalry continued – I signed for Sunderland and he joined Newcastle. There were some heated affairs and there was no let-up when he went to Tottenham. He was so hyped up when he had to play against Sunderland due to his loyalties to bitter rivals Newcastle. He really lost it in one game against us at White Hart Lane. He'd only just come back from the 1990 World Cup and was desperate to rub our noses in it. He played brilliantly but there were a number of flash points all involving him, he was making gestures and crashing into you with late challenges. We had a few argie bargies over the years but he's a great lad, a real diamond of a bloke. When he came to Burnley, to my surprise, he never mentioned any of this. Mind, since those games he would have experienced a million different things in his life.

Once, he actually stopped a game to come over to me. He was playing for Middlesbrough and I was in the Bury side. The second half was just about to kick off when he came running over to me and gave me a hug. "Fucking hell, I never realised it was you!" he yelled. I obviously hadn't made much of an impression in the first 45 minutes if lining up for the kick-off to the second half was the first time he noticed me! But it was a class act and I can tell you the Bury boys were very impressed. So for me it was great, after all those years, to actually have the opportunity to play in the same side – even if it was for just a few games.

When he was at Burnley he'd carry this kind of doctor's bag everywhere with him. There were all sorts in there – I daren't hazard a clue what it contained.

We went to Southampton for a game on the Easter Monday. It's a long trip and so all the isotonic drinks and health stuff was being handed out on the coach to help keep the bodies in shape in readiness for the game. Unbeknown to the mana-gerial staff, what he was doing was filling his bottles with vodka from his doctor's bag. He was drinking all the way down to the south coast and so by the time we arrived he was completely pie-eyed.

Matt Murray

Matt Murray had just established himself as a first-team goal-keeper at Wolves when a 36-year-old Gazza arrived at Molineux desperate to extend his playing days. Injuries curtailed Matt's career at the age of 29 and he went on to become a popular match reporter and pundit with Sky Sports.

Gazza came in to train with us in October 2003 because he knew Paul Ince well from their England days together. The manager, Dave Jones, also wanted to give him a chance to play in the Premier League again. You immediately warmed to him because he was so friendly. I remember giving him a lift from Molineux to the training ground because he had got all mixed up on the timings for training. Just in that short space of time in the car, he was so honest about himself, opening up about different things. You could see straight away he had a good heart.

He just loved being around people and brought energy into the dressing room. And for me, Gazza was someone I had watched as a teenager in Italia 90. So to have him, Paul Ince and Denis Irwin – two other players I admired – at the club was incredible. The likes of myself and Joleon Lescott were like, 'what's going on here?' These are people who helped us fall in love with football.

He wasn't the player he used to be but every now and then he would produce this great bit of skill in training and slot the ball through my legs. He would shout: "You should have shut them, keeper!" and he would produce a great big smile. That was him at his happiest, doing cheeky stuff like that.

He wasn't so happy one day when we were getting changed. We used a tennis club for changing purposes. You could go from the dressing room into the toilets but to get back into the dressing room again you needed to know a code to unlock the toilet door. The next thing, you heard this banging on the door and screaming. It was Gazza, who had panicked because he couldn't get out of the toilet. He felt trapped. It was like he was almost having a panic attack. He told us he suffered from claustrophobia which went back to an incident when he was at Rangers. He had evidently got locked in somewhere and couldn't handle it.

We'd all heard stories of some of his pranks in previous dressing rooms, like nailing someone's shoes to the floor and putting Deep Heat in underwear, but we escaped, although he was still the life and soul in there. He immediately commanded everyone's respect because he was Gazza. You got a buzz from just being around him.

He was playing in the reserve games trying to prove that he could still perform in the Premier League. I wasn't playing in a second team game against Everton but I heard he found himself up against some committed Scousers who wanted to impress against a legend who, of course, once played for the club. While he knew in his mind what he wanted to do, the rest of the body wasn't capable and he shed a few tears on the pitch and was eventually taken off, which was really hard for him. We all wanted him to do well but, sadly, it didn't happen for him and he never played in the first team. Dave Jones had given him the chance to train with us and show what he had. It was still amazing to have him with us, even for a short time.

I think he knew deep down that he didn't have it any longer to play in the Premier League. After all, football at that level is a hard business. He trained well and regained his fitness but couldn't get anywhere near the standard of the past. It's a hard fact of life that everybody's career comes to an end sometime. It's harder for some players to let go and I guess that's been the case with Gazza. It was his life and you still see that when he's on form in his after-dinner speeches. You can also see there's a lot of love for him from the nation. He's definitely a legend of the game and would be a great player in whatever era he played in. I also believe Gazza would have had more protection over his off-the-field problems if he was playing now. There is a better understanding of the mental issues that can affect players. Instead of using him to create headlines, I'm sure today there would be more time spent looking at the underlying issues which he clearly had.

For me, the fact I got to train with him was really good. I also played against him in a reserve team game at Middlesbrough. We had a young side with the likes of me and Joleon Lescott. They had an experienced team out, Alun Armstrong was up front and scored a hat-trick, Marlon Beresford was in goal and there was Gazza. Joelon and I were just 16 or 17. Their new stadium, The Riverside, had just opened. I came to punch a corner clear but was wiped out by one of their players. There standing over me laughing his head off, was Gazza. "Don't worry, you'll be alreet keeper!"

10

'As a player, if you wound him up saying he couldn't do this, couldn't do that, he would be seething inside, ready to show us all. So that's what he should do with his life now, prove us all wrong. I would love to see him in football again'

– Chris Waddle, fellow Geordie and former Newcastle, Tottenham and England team-mate

Harry Redknapp

Harry Redknapp never managed Gazza but admired him from afar. When living in the same area of the country, the pair bumped into each other on occasions. In addition to managing the likes of West Ham, Tottenham and Southampton, Harry became a reality TV star after being crowned king of the jungle on the hit show I'm A Celebrity . . . Get Me Out Of Here!

I've got to know him better in recent years, with him at times living in the same area on the Dorset coast.

I obviously followed his playing career closely. He was an absolutely amazing player. I was at Wembley during Euro 96 and saw him score that iconic goal against Scotland. Really, I was there to watch my son, Jamie, who was in the squad. It wasn't going great in the first half and Terry Venables made changes which included Jamie coming on for the second half, with England going on to win the game. The Gazza goal was special and has remained in everyone's memory ever since.

Jamie used to tell me stories about Gazza, about when they were together with England. Gazza would often ring Jamie or someone else at 2am for a game of table tennis. According to Jamie, Gazza would be up to ridiculous things simply because he couldn't sleep. And if he couldn't sleep it would be hard luck on somebody else. Gazza always wanted to play one game or another. He was just so hyperactive.

I remember talking to Walter Smith, who told me about the time when Gazza would go to a rifle range and ask his big mate Jimmy 'Five Bellies' to bend over. He would then shoot Jimmy up the backside with a pellet gun. As a footballer he was an amazing talent and possesses a heart of gold but can be, in the nicest sense, a real pest at times.

A few months ago I was in a Chinese restaurant in Bournemouth with my wife, Sandra. We sat down and ordered our food, and suddenly Gazza appeared from nowhere and sat at our table. I think he'd had a few drinks. It appears that he has his good and bad days. Let's say this wasn't one of his good days! He kept taking his false teeth out and plonking them on the table, as well as showing us his gums – which isn't the best when you're trying to eat a meal you've looked forward to after a long hard day.

We also discovered that he likes to pinch things for the fun of it. If he's in a shop, it's like a dare. He'll stuff something in his pocket and try and get away with it. Of course he can afford to buy it but it's like a game to him. He would often boast about what he had nicked. Anyway, after a while, Sandra and I had enough of him taking his false teeth in and out of his mouth, so we decided to finish our meal, pay up and drive home. We offered to give Gazza a lift. While I was driving, Gazza was sat in the back of the car and began pulling out from under his jumper the pancake holder for the crispy duck, the chopstick holder, plus the chopsticks themselves. I'm thinking, 'why the hell has he done that?'

I carried on driving him to the hotel where he was staying. As we got out of the car we noticed there had been a concert on at the Bournemouth International Centre. There had been some big star on, it might have been Rita Ora, someone like that. Anyway it's a fairly young audience making their way from the venue. I'm trying to get Gazza out of the back of the car while the concert-goers are passing by in their droves. Finally, when I managed to get him out, he suddenly fell and at the same time he knocked me over, and there were people walking by seeing both of us on the ground. It looked like I was as drunk as him. I couldn't get him off me. It needed the porter from the hotel to rescue me. People must have thought I was pissed but I hadn't had a single drink.

But what a talent as a footballer, the way he would run with the ball, beat people and do special things. He was a great player. The word 'great' is quite often overused but that doesn't apply to Gazza. For me he's right up there. I love players who can do something special. George Best was a great player. Like George, Gazza had the ability to get people off their seats, running with the ball and then suddenly producing a piece of magic.

Would I have liked to have managed him? Well, it would have been difficult, I'm sure. I believe he had the right man in charge for much of his career in Terry Venables. If I'd had the chance I would have followed Terry in allowing Gazza some slack. If you tell him you're not doing this, you're not doing that, then he wouldn't be the same player. You had to have a laugh with him, have a sense of humour. If you wanted to be a sergeant major with him you wouldn't have lasted five minutes. He wouldn't have had it. He would have rebelled. You knew he could win football matches for you on a Saturday and so you couldn't be on top of him all the time.

I actually could have managed him just recently if everything had gone to plan. I wanted him to be in the second series of Harry's Heroes (in which he attempts to get a team of former England footballers back into shape for a game against a team of German legends), which we filmed a few months back. I don't honestly know what happened in the end. There might have been problems with the medical people connected to the show, something like that. I thought it would have been fantastic if he had been part of it but I don't know whether his body could have taken it. He didn't last that long in that fund-raising game at Tottenham not so long ago. It would have made for interesting television, though, even if he had been involved in some other capacity.

I know ITV have tried to get him on 'I'm A Celebrity' which of course I know all about. To be honest, I think sticking him out there in the jungle for three months would have been a bit too much for him. I'd never seen the show before, I didn't have a clue what it was about, but it was a good laugh. It had nice people in it when I was out there. There was no one in there you could have an argument with if you tried.

As a football manager I would have loved to have built a team around Gazza. You would just let him play. You would give him the ball, let him go and he would win games for you.

Richard Pelham

Richard Pelham is the award-winning sports photographer for The Sun, responsible for many of the distinctive pictures of Gazza from his Spurs days, England games and life in Rome with Lazio. The pair forged a close friendship and one of complete trust. Many of Gazza's favourite pictures which he has kept to this day were courtesy of Dickie's ever-ready camera.

One day my wife Sue, who was working in the area, popped into a fish and chip shop in Aveley village to get our supper. It's around 20 minutes or so from where we live.

By an amazing coincidence that visit was going to change my life as a national newspaper photographer. Because there buying fish and chips at the same time was Gazza. My missus asked him what he was doing there and he revealed he was trout fishing in the lakes nearby which had a big reputation for anglers.

She told him that she would have to tell her husband because I was a photographer for *The Sun* and, of course, would already know him professionally. Gazza panicked and begged her not to say anything. But luckily for me she couldn't resist and neither could I. As soon as she told me, I went looking for him.

Eventually I found him, happily fishing all by himself. He asked me not to photograph him or tell anyone what he was up to. During his playing days it was all about trust so, of course, I abided by his request. I could have stitched him up, as they say in the trade, but I didn't and never dreamed of doing that.

I think that helped me for the many years ahead because he always remembered that I'd kept my promise despite working for a national newspaper which would have been desperate for the pictures of him fishing. We got on well right from the start. I was working with the big players of the time like David Platt, Ian Wright and Teddy Sheringham, and Gazza quickly joined that illustrious group.

What was even better for me was that with Gazza's fame beginning to spread when he was at Spurs, *The Sun* signed him up for exclusive stories and pictures and I was assigned to supply the images.

One of the first jobs was to photograph him in a hospital bed when he was recovering from a double hernia operation. Spurs were trying desperately to get him fit for the forthcoming FA Cup semi-final against Arsenal at Wembley.

Even by then he had earned a reputation for getting up to no good or having the odd drink too many. He was also in demand on the news pages as well as the sports pages, which is always a bit awkward for the likes of myself and the football report-ers close to him because you want to try and maintain a good relationship and not give the news side any ammunition which could harm him. With the hernia pictures I had Neil Wallis, one of the main guys on the news side of the paper, question-ing me all the time about what he was up to in the hospital. Was he messing about? Was he drinking? But thankfully there was none of that. Gazza was on a mission to defy the odds and get fit for the FA Cup semi-final.

He did make it and he scored that wonder goal, the amazing long-range free-kick. After scoring the goal he ran to the bench and all you could hear him say to the manager Terry Venables was: "Did you see that silly bastard Seaman? He tried to save it!" As we all know, David Seaman couldn't have got anywhere near it – it's still one of the best goals ever seen at Wembley.

We then bought up Gazza exclusively for the FA Cup final against Nottingham Forest. By then I was starting to build up quite a good rapport with him, taking photos in the build-up to the game. Sadly he got badly injured in the match and I was then getting calls from the office to be ready to do photos of him from wherever he had been taken to after being stretchered off at Wembley. The trouble was Mel Stein, his agent, didn't have a mobile phone on him because – being Jewish and the day being Saturday – he wasn't able to work. No one knew what was going on.

He had been taken to The Princess Grace Hospital and that's where the management, players and staff took off to after the game with the FA Cup trophy itself. It was the club who took all the photos of them around Gazza's bed. After that, though, I was a regular visitor as Gazza began his rehabilitation.

My favourite game before I had really got to know him was when Spurs played Luton Town at White Hart Lane. Spurs came back from going 1-0 down to win 2-1 despite being reduced to nine men. The reason for that was Gazza, who ran Luton absolutely ragged. He was unbelievable, not that I thought that at the time when he messed up my camera. There was a hold-up in play for an injury while Gazza was preparing to take a corner. I'm sat nearby ready to take pictures of the action which is about to ensue. All of a sudden, the motor drive on my camera is going crazy. He's got his finger on the motor drive button and the camera is taking picture after picture, creating havoc!

After his FA Cup final injury I was then assigned by *The Sun* to cover every stage of his recuperation because he was still supposed to be joining Lazio. There was always a battle with other newspapers to get the best pictures. Luckily for me, I managed to capture the first pictures of him kicking a ball at the Tottenham training ground which in those days was at Mill Hill. There was a further blow when he was beaten up in a Newcastle nightclub, which put his rehabilitation back a few months and didn't exactly please Lazio, who were monitoring his progress, desperate to have him playing for them.

Later on, Spurs arranged a game behind closed doors to test his fitness. We got to hear about it but the club didn't want anyone to report or photograph it, in case things went wrong with Gazza. But *The Sun* deployed myself and a reporter Pat Sheehan to smuggle ourselves into the training ground and cover Gazza's comeback. Thankfully, there were some bushes near the pitch where we could hide. I remember the heavens opened and the rain was torrential. We heard that Spurs didn't want the game played but Lazio were insistent it went ahead because they could then bring him over to Italy for an official signing ceremony.

There were puddles everywhere on the pitch. Gazza was struggling in the conditions until he took control of the ball and waltzed through the defence to score a brilliant individual goal and followed that up by jumping headlong into this massive puddle. The spray went everywhere and I managed to take the picture – it was a fantastic shot and it's a photograph I've kept.

After going back to the office I was later hauled in to see the editor Kelvin Mackenzie. I thought I was in for a right rollicking because that's what usually happened when you were summoned to meet Kelvin. Instead, he wanted to congratulate me. It was going on the front page the next day. In newspaper terms that's known as the splash, which was ironical considering the actual picture was of another splash! I also gave the picture to Gazza, who loved it. He was always begging for pictures right from his Newcastle United days when he used to ask *The Sun's* North East photographer Keith Perry for any action photos of him. He could never have enough.

After proving his fitness in the behind-closed-doors friendly game, Gazza was whisked to Rome to officially sign for Lazio. I went out there to photograph the occasion and when I returned with Gazza and his entourage to Heathrow Airport, he grabbed me just as we were about to pass a group of photographers who were there to record his return to London. He had me around the neck and, of course, this was a nightmare for the snappers because the last thing they needed in their photos was the sight of a *Sun* photographer next to Gazza. Somehow, later on, he managed to get a picture of the pair of us and passed it on to me. He knew he had wrecked the photos but couldn't care less.

Before he was about to start playing for Lazio there was another trip to Rome and we took Gazza and his then fiancée Sheryl to a picturesque spot overlooking the city for some lovey-dovey shots. Gazza suddenly flipped out because he heard the sound of a camera, hidden away, taking pictures of the pair of them. We had obviously been followed by some members of the Italian paparazzi and our exclusive pictures were in danger of not being exclusive.

There was no messing with Gazza. He discovered the hidden photographer and started grappling with him trying to snatch the camera. The next thing I know, there's another snapper taking pictures of the confrontation. I thought I had to do something, so I ran towards him and ripped the film out of the back of his camera.

By now, the police had been called and we knew through Gazza's Italian minder that we had to get away quickly to escape being arrested. None of this seemed to faze him. In fact, he seemed to enjoy it, but he also knew how important it was for my newspaper to collect the exclusive shots.

With that in mind and the fact that our filming had been cut short, Gazza volunteered to do some photos elsewhere to make the trip worthwhile. "Would you dress up as a gladiator?" I asked him. His eyes lit up and he told me to turn up at the training ground the next day at 9.30am with a gladiator's outfit and he would put it on. He went into the dressing room with it and came out as a Roman gladiator, much to the amusement of his team-mates.

After finally getting a few games under his belt he got injured again during training. It meant more time on the sidelines and, where Gazza is concerned, that's always dangerous because he gets bored easily. He would raid the rooms at the hotel he was staying in for chocolate. Any door that was open he would nip in and take the bars of chocolate from the minibars. If the club had known they would have gone berserk but he had too much time on his hands and he was never into eating what he should have been eating.

One day we joined him in watching a behind-closed-doors friendly. He was under orders not to do a thing because he was still recovering. He had been ordered to sit and watch the game. But, Gazza being Gazza, he couldn't sit still. He left his seat and started kicking balls around. The Lazio management went ballistic. Little did they know that later on he insisted we went ten-pin bowling. He wasn't happy, though, when I managed to beat him. He liked to win at everything so I know he was well and truly brassed off – but not as much as the Lazio management would have been if they had found out.

When Graham Taylor was manager of England he decided to take Gazza away with the squad to Spain, even though at the time he was recovering from an injury. One evening, Gazza was lurking around the hotel foyer and he noticed that myself and a group of my photographic colleagues were getting ready to go out for a meal and a few drinks. He asked us where were we going and could he come out with us? Graham's assistant, Lawrie McMenemy, came down the stairs and was informed of what was going on. "Yes, lads, you can take Gazza out with you," he said. "You must be joking Lawrie, there's no way he's coming with us, we want a quiet night," we replied. So poor

Gazza ended up staying in and he wasn't very happy about it.

He soon got his own back. Before an England friendly at Wembley, the players were warming up in one of the goalmouths near where all the photographers were preparing to cover the game. As I'm sorting out my gear, someone raced behind me and placed their hands across my eyes so I can't see a thing. It's Gazza. He asked me if I had anything to eat because he was starving. As it happened I still had a hotel lunch box with me. Inside it was a jam doughnut and Gazza promptly removed it and started eating it while he continued to warm up, much to the amazement of his team-mates. What a sight that must have been, Gazza going back into the dressing room with bits of jam down his cheeks.

During another England game, Nicky Barmby went through on goal and just had the keeper to beat.

All the photographers were scattered around the pitch in different areas with the agreement being that, on this occasion, the photos would be shared. John Dawes, a fellow national news-paper snapper, is the one behind the goal Barmby is aiming at. Just as he's about to score and Dawesy is preparing to take a picture of it, all of a sudden he can't see a thing. Gazza, who was a substitute and was warming up behind the goal, decided to place both hands over Dawesy's eyes. He missed Barmby's goal completely.

At half-time the rest of us asked when he could send us the pictures of the Barmby goal and celebrations. He told us the bad news and at first we thought he was joking. No, it was true. None of us were getting a picture of the goal – and neither would the national newspapers. In the tunnel before the second half kicked off, there was Gazza laughing his head off at what had gone on. Honestly, Gazza was at times a photographer's nightmare, especially if he wasn't starting a game.

When he was at Rangers, I was sent up to Scotland to do some pictures of Gazza, who was staying in a lovely hotel on the banks of Loch Lomond. When we went out for something to eat, we bumped into one of the locals who got talking to Gazza and offered to take us out in his boat. He didn't expect Gazza to say he wanted to go straight after dinner.

So off he went while we followed and, true to his word, it was a fantastic boat moored on Loch Lomond. It was now midnight but Gazza insisted he wanted to go out on the boat. His big mate Jimmy 'Five Bellies' was with us. Just a few minutes into our ride on Loch Lomond, Gazza turned to Jimmy and said: "Jimmy, you've always said you love me." "Aye," replied Jimmy, "you know I do." I couldn't believe it when Gazza then said: "Well, if you love me, jump into the water." It was pitch black and the water was freezing but the stupid so-and-so did what Gazza asked. He could have drowned. Anyway, we eventually hauled him back on board and tried to dry him. He was given some spare clothes which the boat owner had kept in his cabin.

As we headed back to where he kept the boat anchored, Gazza told Jimmy to jump into the water again. Unbelievably, he did. When we arrived back at the jetty, there was Jimmy in some borrowed clothes which clearly didn't fit, shivering and slowly making his way to the bank. But before he got there, Gazza ran alongside him and pushed him into the water. So three times he experienced at first hand the delights of Loch Lomond – not that Jimmy appreciated it at the time.

We photographers didn't appreciate it either when Gazza soaked us with orange juice when he was playing for Lazio in a pre-season friendly against Spurs which had been arranged as part of his transfer to the Serie A club. It was in Rome and Gazza was substituted. After coming off he grabbed this great big drinks dispenser full of orange and aimed it at some of the snappers who were sitting close by. It saturated some of them and when your equipment is running with orange juice it's not ideal. At least Gazza, chortling away to himself, thought it was funny.

The last time I saw him was when it was arranged for Gazza to be reunited with Vinnie Jones to re-enact the famous picture of Vinnie grabbing hold of Gazza's crown jewels in a game between Newcastle United and Wimbledon. Gazza was on good form and gave me a huge hug, which was fantastic.

Even though at times we had suffered through some of his crazy pranks, there was always a good rapport between the photographers and Gazza. He seemed to get on better with the snappers than the reporters. Part of that was his love of pictures. He never tired of asking for them. Safe to say it was never dull with Gazza around. It certainly enriched my career.

Mel Stein

Mel Stein became Gazza's agent and, together with his business partner Len Lazarus, handled his day-to-day business. Mel was at his side throughout Gazza-mania and became a father figure as he tried to keep the often errant superstar on the straight and narrow.

I had originally come into contact with Gazza at Newcastle United, where I was a fan, despite living in London. I got to know a few people at the club. I was introduced to Chris Waddle and at first became his lawyer before taking over as his agent. That led me to eventually represent his Newcastle team-mate Gazza.

I was introduced to him for the first time by his then-agent Alastair Garvie in the Newcastle players' lounge after a League Cup game against Barnsley. "You're Waddler's (Chris Waddle's) lawyer aren't you?" he enquired. I made some polite comments about his performance. "Nah, I was crap," he answered. "Anyway if you're good enough for Waddler, you're good enough for me. Will you be my lawyer?"

His profile, fame and reputation were beginning to spread, not just in the North East but around the country. Newcastle had a hot property but he was troublesome.

Even at the age of 20 he had his cult following on Tyneside and the manager Willie McFaul wanted Paul to sign a new five-year contract. Alastair arranged a confidential meeting with some Newcastle officials at a hotel in Durham. I came along with my friend and business partner Len Lazarus. When Paul was offered something to eat, he patted his stomach, muttered about a diet and said he wasn't hungry. After a moment's reflection he said he might have a steak and then added he would have some chips and a beer to go with it. He then saw an unfinished plate of canapés and polished them off as well. Len, who was meeting Paul for the first time, couldn't believe what he had seen.

I asked Paul if it was the right offer – did he want to stay at Newcastle? "I'd like to stay but they've got to pay me what I'm worth," he replied. I don't think Newcastle were prepared for our proposals. Russell Cushing, the Newcastle secretary, piped up: "Haven't you forgotten to ask for the Tyne Bridge?!" After a couple of hours' negotiations, Newcastle improved substantially on their first offer but nowhere near enough. At that moment, if they had been generous, there was every possibility Paul would have committed his long-term future to the club. But they weren't and, from then on, Paul knew that sooner or later he would be plying his trade away from the North East.

Before he left, he became great friends with a Brazilian player Newcastle signed called Mirandinha. Mira couldn't handle the English winter, although that wasn't helped by Gazza cutting a leg off the tights he wore in training to keep warm or cutting fingers off Mira's gloves!

Mira invited the whole squad around to his house to partake of some Brazilian culinary delights. When they approached his house they were greeted by a terrible smell drifting out of the windows. There was Mira stirring a giant metal dustbin in which lay his food. He then heaped generous spoonfuls of its contents onto Gazza's plate. Paul would normally eat anything but now he was looking around in desperation. He spotted a Springer Spaniel christened 'Gazza' which he had bought for Mira's boys. He managed to coax the dog outside and emptied his food into the dog's bowl. But Gazza couldn't believe it when the dog even turned his nose up at the offering and walked away.

With other clubs now looking at him seriously, it seemed inevitable he would leave Newcastle. Paul had always said that if he ever left Newcastle it would be to go to Liverpool. Paul didn't want to go south. At the time he had an inherent suspicion, even dislike, of anything or anybody born south of Gateshead!

Manchester United were keen and I received a telephone call from Maurice Watkins (director and club solicitor) saying that Alex Ferguson was interested in Paul. Alex was prepared to agree with Newcastle an exchange deal with any player except Bryan Robson. There was an informal meeting in my house and Alex and Paul talked in my office. With hindsight, it's clear that Ferguson went away thinking he had got his man.

Afterwards, with Gazza wanting to eat, a group of us went to a smart local restaurant called La Fondue. Paul asked what was good and was told to try the fondue speciality. The waiter duly brought the fondue flames and prongs followed by the uncooked meat. Gazza looked at it with horror. "It's raw," he said. "It's meant to be," somebody gently explained to him. "What's the fire for?" he asked. "To cook it," was the reply. "Blimey, I thought that was what you paid the restaurant for," he said.

Paul was still not keen on moving to London and at first had not even wanted to talk to the Spurs manager, Terry Venables. Eventually he was persuaded to meet him. And the two of them got on incredibly well. Paul had made his mind up to join Spurs but his obsession with Liverpool refused to disappear. Kenny Dalglish, the Liverpool manager, had wanted him but he couldn't do anything until the following season. He had to sell before he could buy.

It was agreed to suggest a clause in the contract whereby if Liverpool made an offer for him equal to the cost of his acquisition by Spurs during his first season with them, then the London club would be obliged to sell Gazza if he still wanted to go. Irving Scholar, the Tottenham chairman, wasn't happy with the condition but felt sufficiently confident that Paul would be so committed to Spurs once he'd joined that he wouldn't want to leave. However, when he signed the contract, Paul wanted the clause removed. "I've changed my mind, I'm happy just to sign for Spurs," he said.

Sir Alex still blames me for Gazza not signing for Manchester United – he apparently said that if he saw me walking in the road when he was driving, he would hit the accelerator pedal rather than the brake.

My two sons used to tell me that I loved Gazza more than them in the early days. He became part of the family and I became part of his. I went to his sister's wedding. He came to one of my son's mitzvahs. I remember him sitting beside the rabbi's wife in the synagogue. He loved it.

Gazza was like a third son to me. We had some incredibly good times together and I still love him to this day. Sadly at times he has struggled with addictions that he simply couldn't control but nothing can erase the memory of the good times.

Who can forget the events of the World Cup in 1990? That was mind-blowing for Gazza and the people around him. The interest and hype which followed was just incredible. The only player who has come close to the same level of hype and celebrity status since then has been David Beckham. Everyone after Italia 90 wanted a piece of Gazza. The sponsors were queuing up while merchandising went off the scale.

In Sardinia, where England were based for the group games, Chris Waddle had the short straw of rooming with him. Gazza would be up before 8am, off to the swimming pool, having a game of table tennis, taking a sauna and then be raring to go for training. When that was finished he'd be down to the beach for a pedalo race or dragging somebody out of bed to play tennis with him. He couldn't sit still for a minute.

He made friends with everybody, the security guards, the soldiers, the children who couldn't get enough of the England team. He gave away so much kit – and it wasn't just his own –

that he had to be restrained. Otherwise, the England side could have been forced to play their first game in their underwear!

After Italia 90 was all over, Gazza-mania really took off. I imagine it was like trying to look after The Beatles. I remember the day I realised it was all going to turn into something bigger than football. It was my birthday on July 13, 1990, a couple of weeks after Gazza's tears. Gazza was in a hotel room with Chris Waddle. He turned to Chris and said: "How long do you think this will last? How long will people be interested in me?" Chris answered: "This is it mate. This is going to last for the rest of your life."

That year was manic. Crazy. Gazza was asked to turn on the Christmas lights on London's Regent Street and when he came out onto the balcony and started unbuttoning his shirt the girls started screaming. It was also the year of his hit single 'Fog On The Tyne', the Lindisfarne favourite. It reached number two in the pop charts. I wrote the follow-up, 'Geordie Boys'. He was huge.

According to the press I was his 'svengali', his 'guru'. But there was nothing I could do when he was stopped from meeting Princess Di. He was due to be introduced to her but because he'd previously kissed Margaret Thatcher at an event, Di's advisors were worried about what might happen. He was hurt by that. I remember him falling onto his hotel bed and crying.

You could see the problems even in the early days. It just wasn't the drink – he had deep psychological problems. He didn't enjoy being away from his family, for instance. Sometimes he became lonely. He was also obsessive to the point of being neurotic. His house was extraordinarily tidy. One day when he was at Spurs I got a phone call from Terry Venables. "Can you come down, we've got a problem with Gazza," he told me. I found out that the problem was a plumber hadn't fitted Gazza's bath properly and he was so worried that he couldn't concentrate on his training.

Even in the transfer negotiations which would take him from Spurs to Lazio there was a comedy element. Lazio had asked Paul whether there was anything in particular that he wanted included in the deal. He said he was happy to leave the financial arrangements to them but he'd like a house with some private fishing facilities. There was no trout fishing in Rome! Okay, they would have to create some. Paul's house had to be in grounds sufficiently large for him to install a trout farm where he could fish to his heart's content and be sure of a catch. Sure enough, the trout farm was to be an item in the Lazio contract.

Before he joined Lazio and was recovering from injuring his knee again in a Newcastle nightclub incident, he was invited by his sister Anna to a Pet Shop Boys end-of-tour party. Anna had appeared in one of their videos. Paul was sitting on the lawn with a drink in his hand when up came Janet Street-Porter.

"Allo, Gazza, Janet Street-Porter," she said in a broad cockney accent. "Well you can just bugger off," Gazza replied, hardly bothering to lift his head. "Well, I'm just . . ." She couldn't finish her sentence before Gazza uttered: "Fuck off, I'm trying to enjoy my drink." He was asked why he had done that. "She just breezed up to me and said she was a reporter," he revealed. "No Paul, it was *Street-Porter*!"

Paul eventually moved into a large villa in Rome. It had a large snooker table in the basement which had previously belonged to the king of Italy. But the problems were never-ending. The security gates regularly jammed and Lazio would have been horrified to see £5 million worth of investment scaling the walls and then leaping down some six feet just to get entry to his own property!

Eventually he managed to find his own way to the training ground. One day, though, his car refused to start. The owner of the villa he was renting had left behind an old motorbike which Paul had got going. He took off to the training ground like a TT rider minus a crash hat and no insurance.

What Gazza needed more than anything was to grow up a little bit. But everything came so quickly for him. He never had much of a childhood so he never got all that fun you have when you are growing up out of his system.

Eventually, I couldn't control him anymore. Nobody could. He was unpredictable, wild. But that was all part of the charm.

One day he woke up and decided he wanted to be his own man. I wasn't fired, I just received a letter saying that any inquiries should be directed to a lawyer in Scotland. I was hurt, but not angry because that wasn't the real Gazza.

Sir Alex Ferguson

Sir Alex Ferguson is said to have had two main regrets during his all-conquering spell as Manchester United manager – failing to sign Paul Gascoigne and Alan Shearer. He insists that life would have been a lot different if Gazza had followed up on his agreement to sign for the Red Devils.

We played Newcastle United at St. James' Park and they were battling against relegation and Gazza had been injured but had been back for a couple of games. Our three central midfield players that day were Bryan Robson, Norman Whiteside and Remi Moses – three very competitive footballers, three great footballers. He absolutely tore them apart. At one stage he nut-megged Remi right in front of me in the dugout and, after he had done it, patted Remi on the head.

After the game I said to my chairman Martin Edwards to get on to the Newcastle chairman because we've got to get this boy. I told Martin he was the best I'd seen for years and years.

We were given the chance to speak to him and so were Tottenham. I spoke to him the night before I was due to go on holiday. Afterwards he told me: "Mr Ferguson, you go on holiday and enjoy yourself, I'll be signing for Manchester United." I thought 'great'.

I went on holiday and when I was sitting by the side of the swimming pool there was a tannoy announcement for Mr. Ferguson to go to reception.

It was Martin Edwards on the phone. He said that he had bad news, Paul Gascoigne had just signed for Tottenham. I said: "God almighty how can that be?" He said that apparently Tottenham had bought his mother and father a house in the North East and that had swung it.

I think that was a bad mistake and Paul admits that to this day because as a 19-year-old lad going down to London it can be very hard. We could have taken London out of the road for him. At the club we had Bobby Charlton, a Geordie. We had Bryan Robson, a Geordie. We had a structure of players who would have given him some discipline.

During my time at Manchester United I wished I had signed Alan Shearer but for me the biggest disappointment was not signing Paul Gascoigne. He was the best player of his era. He was a breath of fresh air because he also played with a smile on his face.

Ian Ridley

Ian Ridley is a much-respected sports journalist who has written for a number of national newspapers. The author of several football books, he helped Tony Adams and Paul Merson pen their much-acclaimed autobiographies and has also experienced stints as chairman at Weymouth and St Albans City.

I had got to know Paul quite well going back to his days with England – more of that later. I also became aware of many of his antics while I was helping Paul Merson with his autobiography when the pair were together at Middlesbrough.

I went up to the training ground one day. Merse and I were having lunch when Gazza came over. Merse was winding Gazza up, saying he was going to rip into him in the book and that sitting here was his ghost writer. I was wearing glasses at the time and Gazza leant over and said: "Don't worry, I will remember your face, specky, if you do!"

The pair shared a house and, according to Merse, Gazza would smoke 20 cigarettes a day and was a complete nightmare. He was also drinking heavily and one day he was found very drunk on a platform inside Stevenage station after a trip to see his wife, Sheryl, which had appeared to have gone all wrong. I wrote a profile of where Gazza was in his life for my newspaper, helped by much inside knowledge from Merse.

There were some things I didn't use because they were too horrific, like the time Gazza came across some darts and started firing them at Jimmy 'Five Bellies' while chasing his big mate through the house. One of them landed in Jimmy's back and stuck in there because he was so overweight. Gazza and Merse refused to pull it out because they were doubled up with laughter. Jimmy couldn't get it out because it was right in the middle of his back and he couldn't reach it. Instead, Jimmy walked to the pub in the village where they were living to ask someone to pull it out.

That was the sort of mad household it was. No wonder Merse eventually moved to Aston Villa, to get away from Gazza. He thought if he had stayed he would have started drinking again and would have gone nuts. Tony Adams, who I also helped with his autobiography, had also mentioned that Gazza was prone to drinking binges. I revealed the problems he had on the Sky Sports programme Hold The Back Page, which went out on a Friday night and was the forerunner to The Sunday Supplement. I'd also written it for that Sunday's newspaper. Regretfully, nobody seemed to understand the seriousness of what was happening to him at the time. The general attitude was, 'Oh, that's just Gazza.' I was arguing that this was damaging him, that he was self-destructing.

A little later, I was working for the *Observer* newspaper. Everton had a Ghana international player called Alex Nyarko. He suddenly disappeared back to France, where he was living before he joined Everton, after a row with manager Walter Smith. No one could find him. I received a tip via an old sports editor, Brian Oliver, that he was living in Lille with his brother. It had been a big tabloid story for the previous couple of weeks – where was Alex Nyarko?

I tracked him down and went out to see him. While his brother cooked us a meal I conducted a big interview with him about how he felt that Walter had been treating him badly and why he didn't want to return to Everton. It was a big interview for the paper, a real exclusive. The next day, Monday, Walter rang me and questioned me about the piece I had done and how I had managed it. He wasn't angry, he just wanted to know how I had been able to find him while the football club had failed miserably.

Around six or so months later, Walter and I were chatting again when he mentioned that he believed I knew Tony Adams. He told me they were sending Paul Gascoigne, who had joined the club, to Arizona for treatment for an alcohol issue. I asked him whereabouts in Arizona and he replied Cottonwood. I told him I'd spent a month there with my own problems. He then promised me the first interview with Gazza when he returned to England. It would still be a few months down the line but, true to his word, I was eventually allowed to interview him.

I met Gazza at the training ground. We did the chat and during it he would nip outside to smoke one of my cigarettes. When we finished he said he had read Tony Adams' book and really enjoyed it, and discovered that I had helped Tony with it. He asked me to help him write his autobiography which he was planning. I'd heard that his agent, Mel Stein, was doing it. Gazza revealed that Mel and him had been involved in putting it together for the past two years but Gazza wasn't happy with how it was going, suggesting rightly or wrongly that he wasn't getting a big enough share of the money. He asked me to try and get him a new deal with another publisher.

I went to HarperCollins, who had published the Tony Adams book, and they were prepared to offer a lot of money. I spoke to Gazza a couple of times but in the meantime I heard that he was drinking heavily again and I didn't want to get involved. I heard eventually that Hunter Davies, a well-known writer, had been brought in to rescue the book. Of course I would have loved to have helped him, utilising some of my experience after being around Tony Adams and Paul Merson, who also both had problems. I felt at one stage he would have gone sober and working on his autobiography together could have helped him, I'm sure. I reviewed the book that came out for *The Observer* and I felt it could have been better. I don't think Hunter Davies quite grasped what was happening to him at the time.

It was never, for instance, just alcohol with Gazza. He was also a binge eater, a bulimic. When Graham Taylor, the former England manager, famously came out with the stuff about Gazza 'refuelling' I think much of it went over people's heads. There wasn't then the same understanding that there is now about addictions.

The build-up to France 98 was incredible surrounding Gazza. The England squad and the media went to La Manga in Spain as preparation for the tournament. Glenn Hoddle, the Three Lions manager, had to reduce his 28-man squad to the 22 who would take part in the World Cup. It was a Sunday and my work had been done for the week on the *Independent On Sunday*. It was the same for Joe Melling of the *Mail On Sunday*. Joe asked if I wanted to join him in a game of golf, so he booked the tee-off time for 5pm.

Making your way to the first tee, you had to go past the swimming pool where you would often find the players sun-bathing and relaxing. As Joe and I were passing, Paul Merson leant over a hedge after spotting me, saying: "Ian, Ian come over here." A security guard tried to stop me but Merse said it was okay for me to join him and Tony Adams at the side of the pool. Merse said: "He's not going." I replied: "Who's not going?" He said: "Gazza isn't going." I told him not to be so daft, of course Gazza would be in the final squad. Merse said no, that wouldn't be the case. Gazza had been pissed for the whole of the previous day and some of the players had tried to sober him up, taking him to the pool and giving him coffee. Glenn, though, had seen enough and had told him he wouldn't be going to France. Merse and Tony then revealed that Gazza had trashed Glenn's hotel room after being told the bad news.

I walked back to join Joe at the first tee and said he would never have guessed what had just happened. It was one of the biggest football stories ever and, as Sunday newspaper journalists, we were stuffed. The story wasn't going to keep until the next Sunday. It wasn't going to last an hour, never mind a week. We had to just get on with the golf. After that, all I could do was ring my office and say I knew what had gone on with Gazza but it was a day too late for our paper. A few hours later, the FA's head of communications, David Davies, was briefing the daily paper England correspondents that Gazza wasn't going to France 98.

The last time I saw Gazza was two years ago. I know the head of a place in Bournemouth called the Providence Project, where Gazza went to try to get sober again. It's a treatment centre and it's why Gazza lived in Bournemouth for a time. They did everything they could for him.

I rang the head, a guy called Stephen Spiegel, who is a big Spurs fan. I asked whether I could do a piece with Gazza once his treatment was over. Stephen said Gazza needed money. I had just left the *Mail On Sunday* and I was doing some freelance work for the *Daily Express*. I told the sports editor I thought I could get to Gazza with a big exclusive and asked whether he would pay. He said yes and so I managed to have two or three hours with Gazza.

I also used part of the interview for a book I did about 20 years of the Premier League. He had been the constant through the Premier League era. He was the man. He popularised English football through Italia 90 and helped the Premier League get off the ground with the TV contracts and so on. In many ways, he did for football what Tiger Woods has done for golf in the modern era. I also managed to come away with about three days' worth of back page stories for the *Express* plus inside page interviews. For that we handed over £5,000 and Gazza gave £1,000 of it to the treatment centre.

Sadly, he went back to drinking and had some awful publicist in the area who would take pictures of him coming out of an off-licence and sell them to the tabloids. He and Gazza would then split the money.

Anyway, a couple of years ago I read that he had a new agent, was off the drink and was living in Leicester. I got hold of the agent and said that if Gazza was truly sober then why not do a book together about his recent years? At the time I was also involved in a stage production which was going around the country with John Barnes, Neil 'Razor' Ruddock and Jan Molby. I was the question master. It was good fun. We were due to do a gig at Peterborough and, with Gazza living in Leicester, I drove to meet him. I spoke to him about the possibility of putting together a new book but he couldn't settle. Every 10 minutes he would have to dash out for a cigarette. It was impossible to have a real conversation with him. I thought then there was no way we could get a book off the ground.

That was the last time I saw him.

Hunter Davies

Hunter Davies is a brilliant journalist and writer who ghosted Paul Gascoigne's official autobiography 'Gazza: My Story' and penned the authorised biography of The Beatles. He has also helped Wayne Rooney and Dwight Yorke with their autobiographies and in 2014 was awarded the OBE for services to literature.

Remembering Gazza! On a plane during the World Cup in Italy in 1990 he persuaded the pilot to let him into the cockpit. He was not supposed to touch anything but Gazza managed to grab a lever and the plane went into an immediate dive.

Another time, in the team hotel during a meal, Terry Butcher and Chris Woods were sitting wearing their clothes back to front, egged on by Gazza.

They then proceeded to eat their meal in reverse: starting with coffee and ice cream, they moved onto the main course before finishing with soup. They drank huge amounts from wine bottles filled with water just to wind up the manager Bobby Robson. When they stood up, the rest of the team noticed they had no trousers, just jock straps. They walked backwards out of the dining room with the whole squad cheering.

One jape did end badly. According to Gazza, he managed to sneak out of the hotel with some other players and spent the evening drinking and arm wrestling with some Italian fans in a local bar.

When he got back to the hotel half cut, he fell into bed. Bryan Robson, the captain, was furious and tried to tip Gazza out of his bed. The bed fell on Bryan's toes. There was blood everywhere, his toe smashed. They tried to pretend it was a pure accident, that he had done it in the bidet when he was washing his feet. Robson was out of the World Cup. It was officially announced as achilles tendon trouble.

Despite all these capers, England got to the semi-finals only to lose to West Germany on penalties, of course. It was the game when Gazza was seen by the nation to cry after his second yellow card of the tournament, knowing he could not play in the final.

After I had finished ghosting Gazza's memoirs back in 2004 I had to go up to Newcastle to let him read the manuscript. He was staying in a flat in Gateshead with Jimmy 'Five Bellies', a surprisingly chic flat with white carpets, white walls. They had a massive fridge, filled to capacity. All it contained was cans of Red Bull.

I gave the manuscript to Gazza to read, walking around the flat, thinking he would just skim read it. Five hours later I must have walked the length and breadth of Gateshead waiting for him to finish.

He read every word, corrected mistakes, spelling, punctuation. Gazza was hyperactive, the modern term being bipolar. He was not a true alcoholic like George Best, only turning to drink when he was depressed. He was clearly intelligent, good at chess.

On the train back to King's Cross I had quite a lot to drink, celebrating the book finally being finished.

I got a taxi home and went straight to bed. After half an hour there was an awful banging at the front door. It was the taxi driver holding the corrected manuscript in his hand, the only existing copy.

I had left it in his taxi!

Vinnie Jones

Vinnie Jones can claim to have come closer than anyone to Gazza through that infamous grab at his crown jewels during a game against Newcastle. Vinnie went on to win the FA Cup with Wimbledon and play for Wales before later becoming a Hollywood actor, appearing in a variety of films including Lock, Stock And Two Smoking Barrels, Gone In Sixty Seconds and The Condemned.

I had missed Wimbledon's earlier league game at Newcastle through suspension but the rest of the players had come back with stories of how good this kid Paul Gascoigne was. They said forget about Georgie Best and all that, this lad had the potential to be even better. They were really ramping him up and looking at me because they knew it would be my job to try to sort him out the next time we played Newcastle.

When the match finally came around, it was a real circus. He'd even had roses thrown at him by some of the girls who had come to watch the game.

We'd had a special practice match in training looking at ways to deal with him. Andy Clement, who was our reserve right-back, was told to assume the Gazza role by going all over the pitch. Andy, despite normally playing for the reserves, ran rings around me. It ended with me walking off, getting a shower and clearing off.

Our coach, Don Howe, rang me up and asked whether I remembered Claudio Gentile from the World Cup. The Italian defender was a real hard nut. If I was to stop Gazza I would have to play like Gentile. I had just been embarrassed by the

Wimbledon reserve right-back, don't forget, so what was Gazza going to do to me?

By the time I got on the pitch at Plough Lane to finally face Gazza, I was really wound up. I could already see him in the warm-up flicking the ball and playing tricks, so I knew I had to be really at it if I was going to make any impression on him. The first thing I told him when I got near him was that I wouldn't be playing any football and neither would he. I then left him, adding: "Hey, fatty, I'll be back for you in a minute."

Monte Fresco, the newspaper photographer, who eventually took *THE* picture of me and Gazza, heard that and decided to just concentrate on the pair of us. It was a gamble which paid off.

As a Newcastle free-kick was being taken, I didn't want Gazza to move forward towards the ball. As we're jostling, he suddenly said to me: "You're earning your £100 today." It was meant as an insult, so I just grabbed him by the you-know-whats and it was spot-on. There was no messing. It was straight on the button and I didn't let go.

Some people thought for quite a while that it was a set-up. In the end I got sick of denying it. A look at Gazza's face told you how real the incident was.

I didn't know that it had been captured by Monte's camera. The next day I went up to the pub for a drink and to look at the Sunday papers. One of the old boys in the pub shouted across to me: "Vinnie, you've really done it this time." I wondered what he was on about. He then added: "You're not just on every back page, you're all over the front pages as well." And in the centre pages there were six different shots of me grabbing Gazza's luncheon box.

The match ended up 0-0 so I suppose everyone was glad the grab happened because there wasn't much else to talk about. In the dressing room after the game, the lads were telling me what a great job I'd done on Gazza.

Then the door opened and one of the ground staff came in with a red rose, telling me that Gazza had sent it. I told him to hold on a minute while I ran into the toilet area and got the bog brush, and then asked him to go back to the Newcastle dressing room and hand it over to Gazza. I was pleased how the game had gone because we all knew that Gazza could have destroyed us. He'd done us up in the North East and no one wanted any repeat of that. He had to be stopped. He was the best young player around and on his way to becoming one of the greatest ever players this country has ever known. I didn't want to be embarrassed by him, nutmegging me and things like that. I followed him everywhere and I think in the end I ground him down, helped by that little squeeze.

I don't think a week goes by, even when I've been living in America, when someone doesn't mention it. But after that we had great respect for one another and became big friends.

We became so close that I would get a strange feeling sometimes and that would often be when Gazza wasn't well, when he was suffering from his problems. I'd have to check on him and see if there was anything I could do to help. It genuinely affected me. It's like having a twin brother. It's helped me understand what he must have been going through.

Too many people can dismiss problems surrounding alcohol, for instance, because they don't understand. Often it's been a case of, 'Oh it's Gazza again. What's he done now? Why doesn't he give it up?' But it's what it is. Some people need educating. It's hard when you retire as a player, as Gazza knows. You're used to training with the lads every day. The banter is flying, it's great fun and all of a sudden one day it stops. I was lucky enough to go on to something else.

I think that picture defined me as the hardman of football. But the manager, Bobby Gould, and Don Howe praised me to the newspapers for the job I'd done on Gazza. I was probably more hyped up after this game than I was a few months later when Wimbledon shocked Liverpool at Wembley to win the FA Cup.

Gazza came around to my house shortly after he had moved from Newcastle to Spurs. He came over to join me in a bit of clay pigeon shooting. It turned out to be like an episode of Only Fools And Horses.

He took a shot and turned around with his double-barrelled shotgun in mine and some mates' direction and said: "Do ya think I'm doing alreet like?" We fell to the floor with me yelling: "Point the gun the other way you stupid prat." Back came the reply: "Why don't you try and grab my bollocks now?!"

Chris Waddle

Chris Waddle has played a large part in Gazza's journey. Both played for Newcastle United, Tottenham and England, and shared some never-to-be forgotten experiences. Chris is now one of Radio Five Live's main pundits covering the big occasions, including World Cups and European Championships.

I remember the first time I saw him. He was still at school and must have been around 14 or 15 years of age. Gazza would come in during the school holidays to train with the apprentices. The only thing I really noticed about him at first was he couldn't run! He looked a bit podgy and when they were doing shuttle runs he was miles behind.

I think that became a big thing of what was going to happen to him. Was he going to be taken on? I know they were really worried about his lack of pace. Most people at the club were aware of his skills but they weren't much use if he couldn't move around the football pitch. He was so slow it was like he was wearing divers' boots. So it was a case of would he have the legs to compete at a higher level?

He was also eating all the wrong stuff, mounds of chocolate, biscuits, Mars bars – everything the modern player would avoid. There were no club dieticians around then so you had to look after yourself, and if someone said you looked a bit fat you had to do something about it.

No one encouraged you to eat salads or pasta, chicken, things like that. I remember at Tottenham, when we stayed at hotels for away games we were able to select anything off an a la carte menu. You could have any starter followed by a curry if you wished. You could have anything, whatever. And all finished off with a large piece of gateau with cream!

At least in his younger years Gazza wasn't a drinker. He loved his junk food but he didn't aggravate it by drinking loads of alcohol. I don't think he discovered drinking until he got into the England squad many years later.

He first began to impress in the Newcastle United youth side – one which went on to win the FA Youth Cup. He stood out with the likes of Joe Allon and Paul Stephenson. People at the club believed these three had a chance of making it.

The one thing Gazza has always had – and I don't know, maybe because of his outlook on life and the way he is as a person

– he doesn't give a shit. When you watched Gazza play it was probably like going back in time and seeing him as a 12-year-old or 13-year-old in the school playground. He wouldn't listen to coaches and was always getting rollickings and being told he was crap when he did something wrong.

But in his own mind he didn't give a toss because, deep down, he believed in what he was doing. He knew what he was good at and just wanted the ball fed to him because he felt he could make things happen. He could score goals. He knew he wasn't the best tackler, although he wouldn't bottle making one. Even from a young age, he caused himself some injuries from bad tackles. Basically, he was an off-the-cuff footballer who, when people told him things, he let it go out through one ear to the other without taking a blind bit of notice.

Gazza was scared of most managers he played under, though, starting with Jack Charlton at Newcastle. He was scared of Arthur Cox when he was at St. James' Park. He was even scared of Terry Venables at Spurs, even though Terry wasn't that type of guy. If someone told him Terry was on his way he would suddenly look worried – for the life of me, I don't know why. I think it was the fact he didn't want to let them down or upset them in any way. They were his gaffer and carried the power.

It was the same with Bobby Robson when he was manager of England. He would shout to everyone "the gaffer's coming" and look petrified while if it was anybody else he wasn't bothered and wouldn't move a muscle.

Yet you couldn't meet a more laid-back guy than Terry Venables. For me he was anything but a bully. He had a great sense of humour and you felt you could talk about anything with him, but strangely Gazza would worry and fear Terry was about to lose his rag and have a go at him. Even when Gazza was out of order with some daft prank or piece of stupidity, I can never recall Terry shouting at him. Terry would always try hard to get into Gazza's mindset because although he had the ability and was, by then, an outstanding player, you didn't know what he had been up to the night before or what he was thinking as the game approached.

At Spurs, Gazza always had his entourage around him, including his big mate Jimmy 'Five Bellies'. At times there would be a dozen of his pals from Dunston (Tyneside) staying with him. In this respect he always reminded me of Elvis Presley. Elvis always had a big group around him but, like Elvis, Gazza would be very much alone in his own head, not entirely happy with his life. He once won a load of money on a big horse racing bet and went out and bought them all Harley Davidson bikes. Can you imagine it? Gazza turning up and paying cash for a load of top-of-the-range motorbikes?

I know most of them quickly sold them and used the cash, although Jimmy actually kept his. He might still have it. You used to read about Elvis doing things like that – lashing out on expensive gifts for his entourage. I know that Gazza was an Elvis fan and he might have been influenced by him.

He was into his music. I used to brainwash him a bit with Phil Collins because I was always playing his music in the car. The younger guys at the club would be into rap so he would get into that as well. I think he killed his music with that rendition of Lindisfarne's big hit 'Fog On The Tyne'.

I had one year with Gazza at Tottenham and that was long enough! But I was instrumental in him signing for Spurs. It had looked like he was going to join Manchester United from

Newcastle. I met him on Tyneside for a pint on a Sunday lunch time. As usual, he had a gang with him. Anyway, I asked him what he was doing because Newcastle were prepared to sell him and he told me he was ready to sign for United.

I just told him that Terry Venables would love to speak to him but if he had set his mind on joining United, fair enough. He asked me what Terry was like. I told him he was a good manager. Anyway, we left and just after that he was walking up the road and he shouted back: "Waddler, see you at White Hart Lane on Monday."

I thought the drink had got to him and he was just having a laugh. Sure enough he turned up at Tottenham. That was it – he ended up joining Spurs.

A lot of people have often said it was the wrong choice – that he should have gone to Manchester United because Alex Ferguson would have sorted him out. But it wouldn't have made any difference, whoever was managing Gazza. Alright, he might do daft things around the training ground, but when he's out on the pitch that's where he is at his happiest and it would have been the same for whoever he was playing for.

Lots of people have said if he had gone to Old Trafford he would have been better looked after. But at the time there were personalities like Bryan Robson, Paul McGrath, Norman Whiteside and Viv Anderson. Did they not like a drink? What would have happened to Gazza there?! Honestly, it doesn't matter who was in charge of him. Nothing would have changed. The Queen could have been in charge and that wouldn't have altered things one jot.

I know that in his first year at Spurs he found it hard to settle. It didn't help that he was in a hotel for a year. Most players were just given three months maximum. At times he was a bit lonely because he loves company and that isn't always possible. He wants the lights on all the time because he is scared of the dark.

When he was at the hotel he would often come around on a Friday night to my house, where the missus would cook him a Bolognese. He would always bring a bottle of Prosecco or whatever. Actually, I think it was Asti Spumante because it was so sweet. He would stay until around 10pm watching the telly or whatever and then go back to his hotel.

The football in his first season was a bit hit and miss, we weren't pulling up any trees. In fact, we were nearer a relegation place than fighting for the title.

It was the 1989-90 campaign in which he started to blossom and become the main man, scoring spectacular goals. He was enjoying himself and then, of course, came the horrific injury in the 1991 FA Cup final against Nottingham Forest when he did his cruciate knee ligaments.

Gazza hadn't done himself any favours in his first season at White Hart Lane. He would sometimes go home to the North East after a game on a Saturday and return for training on Monday – which meant leaving Dunston at 5am. I told him that his body couldn't take that on a regular basis. It kills your system.

At times he would tell me he wanted to go back to Newcastle. I said: "Forget that." The club wouldn't be able to afford him and it would send his career backwards. Eventually he got into a routine and settled, although I know it was a blow to him when I joined Marseille a year later. He had no one to cook him his Bolognese! Of course he followed suit later and joined Lazio.

By then he had damaged his knee in the FA Cup final – a game

I watched at home in France. It was just crazy. I saw the first manic tackle on Garry Parker. He should have been booked for that. Maybe if he had received a yellow card then it might have settled him down. I know it was early in the game and you sometimes get away with things but he should definitely have been booked.

The next challenge on Gary Charles was just horrendous – absolutely stupid. Suddenly the house phone starts ringing and I'm expecting someone to go on about the tackle and it's Gazza himself on the other end of a mobile phone. He's on a stretcher having been taken into an ambulance, ringing me.

He's distraught and bellowing down the line: "I'm done, I'm history." I said: "No you're not. Everyone comes back from this sort of injury nowadays. You'll be alright." I insisted he wasn't finished, not with all the modern technology available to surgeons. I was trying to calm him down.

Later, he rang me again and was in better spirits because he had been assured everything would be alright.

I knew the worst part for him was the rehabilitation. I knew for him it would be a nightmare. He gets bored watching people train and so having to do all the remedial work would send him bonkers. I know he used to pay the physios extra so they could get in at 6am, put him through his paces and allow him to get away before the rest of the squad came in for training. He couldn't bear the thought of not being with them. Then he would pay them again to come back in the evening when everyone else had disappeared.

Until that injury the progress he had made had been startling, with Italia 90 the crescendo. Going into the World Cup finals he was on fire, unstoppable. He had no fear. It wouldn't have mattered if it was a meaningless League Cup game or the World Cup final itself, it was just a game of football.

He wasn't one to listen to advice on how to handle opposition players. He would just mumble that he had a better trick than anyone he was facing. "Who is he anyway?" he would blurt out. I remember Bobby Robson telling Gazza before the semi-final against Germany that he would be picking Lothar Matthäus up.

Afterwards, as we were heading back to our rooms, he asked me: "Who have I got to pick up?"

I told him it was Matthäus. He then asked me who was he?! I knew he wasn't joking so I replied that he was just an average German player. You never wanted to build up anything because he might have self-destructed like he did the next year in the FA Cup final – unable to handle the hype. You always had to calm him down.

I joined up with England a week or 10 days later than the rest of the players because I was involved in the French Cup final. He had been on his own because I was down to room with him. He had a real buzz about him, saying how great it was being in the hotel in Sardinia with all the England players. He was getting hyped up. He was either going to have a brilliant World Cup or he would collect a red card in his first game. He had absolutely worked his nuts off and was in prime physical condition. He was in the best shape he had ever been in.

Life was obviously going to change for him. He would rapidly become front page news as well as back page. It was something which would stay with him through his life, something that he hasn't ever got to grips with. He thought he would remain in the spotlight for a short time and then everyone would move on to someone else.

I tried to tell him that whenever he stepped out of line or did something wrong he would attract the wrong headlines. Whenever I could see him getting into something stupid I would try and stop him and shout "front pages".

He would ask me what was that all about. "No, that's not going to happen," he argued.

The next day, there he is plastered all over the front pages. I would ring him up, telling him I had warned him. But he would insist that he had done nothing wrong. He could never get the fact that he sells newspapers with his numerous misdeeds. He was naïve wanting the headlines when things were good but not when they turned nasty. I would tell him they would write nice things but nine times out of 10 they wanted to hit him hard. That's why he had to think twice over pranks. He didn't realise how big he was in the media's eyes. At one stage he was the number one personality.

If he didn't turn up at a charity event it would attract a bad headline. There was negative headline after negative headline. That's the way it works, I told him until I was blue in the face. I said you can't blame them and you can't have a go at them. He could never understand why there would be stories about him sitting in a bar having a few drinks.

This has continued right up until the present day. Some days everything is fine and then he will have a dip and he's in the newspapers again for the wrong reasons.

Sadly, I think for Gazza something that upsets him offers him an excuse to turn to the drink. I know that he has gone on silly benders after something has gone wrong. But should that be the case? Can he not think of another way to satisfy his frustrations?

I often think it's an excuse for him to ask people to leave him alone and hit the booze. It appears to be his way of releasing his tensions. I can't see that changing. I can never see him completely free of the demons which seem to haunt him from time to time. I can't see stories of Gazza going 20 years without a drink. I honestly can't, which is so sad.

I would love to see him settle down but he doesn't trust anyone. He needs to be loved. He looks at people who are happily married with kids and thinks, 'why can't I have a slice of that?' It's something quite simple but he can't find it.

I would love to see him back in football but everyone has tried to help him. A number of us have sat down with him and offered advice. He always agrees. "You're spot on," he will say. "Unfortunately, I can't do it." So you know then you are banging your head against a brick wall. I know there will always be photos of him looking desperate.

People do care for him and like him but no one can change him. The Professional Footballers' Association has helped him out on numerous occasions. God knows how much they have spent on him. I know some people who have questioned that, saying the money has been wasted and could have gone to better causes.

I can see both sides of the argument because he does need help. It's up to him as he gets older to admit that he is fucking up. He seems to be able to do it for a period but can't get rid of the problems long term. I know he loves fishing and for a time he can escape from his personal woes by the side of a river or stream. He still loves his football but no one is going to trust him with a job.

I know he does these gigs nationwide talking about his life but that's not going to last for ever. He always seems to be drifting. There is no clarity of direction on what he wants to achieve. So you can see him going back on the drink, off the drink and back on it for the rest of his years. That has been the formula of his life for the last 20 years or so.

We have to be thankful that he is still with us. I always used to joke to him that I would outlast him, that I would live longer. I always said that if he got to the age of 50 the way he was going he would have done well. But he does love proving people wrong, so he's done that with me. He's had his 50th birthday.

As a player, if you wound him up saying he couldn't do this, couldn't do that, he would be seething inside, ready to show us all. So that's what he should do with his life now, prove us all wrong.

I would love to see him in football again. Just be involved in some way. It doesn't have to be at the top level. Be with a club where he can join in things. Too many times, after people have given him a chance, he has turned up stinking of alcohol. He's got to put all that behind him.

Everyone has to have a goal in life, some direction. After playing I've gone into the media. I've got something to focus on. What is Gazza's goal now? Only he can answer that. I don't think he enjoys the talk-ins and dinners he attends. It's not him. It's just good for his bank balance.

He has blown too many opportunities.

He was given a high-profile media chance coming on with me during the 2018 World Cup finals to talk to Robbie Savage. Sav asked him how he was and back came the reply: "Why don't you just shut the fuck up." I thought, 'Oh by God.' Then he nearly said the C word.

Luckily, the BBC had heeded my advice not to have him on live but to record it, but there was no way the Beeb were going to entertain him again – so another chance went begging. Who can trust him?

It's sad because the fact that he is one of the greatest players we have produced for years has, in many ways, gone by the wayside.

Acknowledgements

Thanks to all who have contributed to
'Our Gazza: The Untold Tales'.

Copyright permissions:
Mel Stein: 'Gazza' The Authorised Biography
of Paul Gascoigne' (Bantam)
John Greig: 'My Story' (Headline Publishing)
Andy Goram: 'My Life' (Virgin Books)
Paul Ferris: 'The Boy On The Shed' (Hodder and Stoughton)
Paul Stewart: 'Damaged' (Reach Sport)
Paul Merson: 'How Not To Be A
Professional Footballer' (HarperCollins)
Roy Reyland: 'Shirts, Shorts And Spurs'
(John Blake Publishing)
John Gibson: 'The Gibbo Files' (Reach Sport)

John Richardson